A Natural History
of Empty Lots

A Natural History of Empty Lots

FIELD NOTES *from* URBAN EDGELANDS, BACK ALLEYS, *and* OTHER WILD PLACES

Christopher Brown

Timber Press
Portland, Oregon

Timber Press
Workman Publishing
Hachette Book Group, Inc.
1290 Avenue of the Americas
New York, New York 10104
timberpress.com

Timber Press is an imprint of Workman Publishing, a division of Hachette
Book Group, Inc. The Timber Press name and logo are registered trademarks of
Hachette Book Group, Inc.

Printed in the United States on responsibly sourced paper
Text design by Sara Isasi
Cover design by Hillary Caudle

The publisher is not responsible for websites (or their content)
that are not owned by the publisher.

The Hachette Speakers Bureau provides a wide range of authors for speaking
events. To find out more, go to hachettespeakersbureau.com or email
hachettespeakers@hbgusa.com.

ISBN 978-1-64326-336-6
A catalog record for this book is available from the Library of Congress.

For William Brown

(1936–2022)

CONTENTS

Part Three: Rewilding the Future   255

Part One

Finding the Wild City

1

Empty Lots, Mesquites, and Parakeets

The only animals that come around to eat the sweet seed pods of the mesquite trees that grow around our house now are, like my wife, immigrants from Argentina. You could call them an invasive species, but so are we, and in the case of the monk parakeets, you can't blame their arrival for the extinction of the Pleistocene megafauna. The legend of the parakeets who build their massive multifamily stick nests in the power poles of Austin and other American cities is that they descended from birds who were imported for the exotic pet trade, broke free from a crate on the tarmac of JFK in 1967, and proceeded to colonize their way down the Eastern Seaboard, all the way to Texas and points beyond. The ones who drop by on hot summer days to picnic on our lot live in places like the cell tower behind the 7-Eleven, the transformer pole behind the abandoned elementary school, and the old AM radio antenna across the street, which transmitted soft rock at 1490 kHz under the call sign KNOW until its final sign-off in 1989.

You can always hear the parakeets before you see them. They are loud little chatterboxes, communicating in short, high-pitched squawks that seem weirdly well suited to our postindustrial streetscape, even as they also bring the sound of the South American jungle. Their leprechaun color makes them easy to spot, as does the tropical profile of their wings in flight and that characteristic parrot beak when they are at rest. When they alight on the branches of the mesquites clustered near the chain-link fences at this double dead end at the edge of town, they pull the pods from the thorny branches, crack them open, devour the seeds, and toss the husks to the ground, the same way the after-hours partiers around the corner toss their empty beer cans to the curb. The adaptation of these magical animals to this weird, run-down place seems perfect, but not quite in balance, as there are not enough birds to eat more than a small portion of the pods the trees produce, and none of the other critters seem to touch them, other than a few beetles.

The people who inhabited this region of the continent before Europeans arrived figured out you could make a sweet flour from mesquite pods. They say the best flavor comes from pods that have dried on the tree, an insight that provides a clue to

the secret history of the plant: Before humans arrived in North America, mesquite pods were eaten by the megafauna that once roamed this landscape. Long-tusked American mastodons, sloths the size of bears, armadillos the size of Volkswagens. In their absence, the mesquites have acquired a mixed reputation among the contemporary human occupants of this land. They are gnarly, hard-wooded trees with thorns that can puncture tires, whose desert-ready toughness, slowly running their roots deep into the earth to find water, makes them well suited to survive in blighted landscapes—both the ones nature makes and the ones we make. Trees that bring life to polluted empty lots in the land of long, hot summers, like the one in the edgelands of East Austin where we made our home.

The mesquite at the front of our lot reveals the damaged past of the place in the weird grace of its form: trunk bent at abrupt angles as it rises, branches canopying out where they can to soak up the sun on fronds of tiny leaves, and big scars where older branches were lost to weather and human abuse. Seventy years old, according to the wizardly master arborist who came to help us care for it after we finally grew to appreciate its wonders. It may be only a tenth as old as some of the live oaks you can find in the hidden sanctuaries near here that the city has not yet devoured, but it's probably the oldest living witness to what happened on this lot before we got here.

I barely noticed the mesquite when I first visited this property with a pair of real estate brokers in April 2009, looking for a new place to live at the onset of middle age and the peak of the financial crisis. I'm not even sure I could identify a mesquite tree by sight back then, even though I had been living in Texas for more than a decade. I have no training in the natural sciences other than the unofficial one my life has given me, learning what's what at the same time its importance to my world becomes evident to me, and a wariness of our tendency to put the naming of each object in nature before the unmediated experience of it. The call of the wild amid the manufactured unreality of contemporary life is what had me walking that empty lot, along with my weird idea that a sensible place to look for natural beauty was in the fenced-off zones behind the industrial parks.

Once you opened the padlock and stepped through the ugly chain-link gate at the front, in the peak of springtime, the place looked pleasant but unremarkable. Texas pastoral, with a clearing of tall grasses and wildflowers ringed by a grove of big hackberry trees. Next door was a quaint green cottage with a picket fence—a very old house, the listing agent explained, that the property owners had moved there when it was marked for demolition at its original location. As we followed the dirt path toward the back of the lot—a path that was just like a trail you would find in the woods—butterflies and songbirds fluttered around us. Then we started to notice the signs of ruin.

All over the back side of the lot, under the shade of the tall trees, were huge slabs of concrete. Fragments of demolished buildings, giant chunks of curb cut, even sections of cement staircases. Some more than half-buried in the earth, others still lying on top of it, with weedy plants growing up around and on top of them, intertwined with gnarls of exposed rebar. There were old tires, too, sticking up out of the dirt, one housing a colony of killer

- - - -

bees making rich honey in its cavity. You could see other trash all along the face of the rough hill that graded down to the floodplain of the urban river: the metal frame of an old car seat, bits of colored wire, fragments of porcelain from a busted-up toilet, looped threads of orange-and-yellow shag carpet poking out of the dirt where there should have been spiderwort. At the very bottom of the hill was the wreck of a mid-'60s Ford pickup, sticking up out of the ground at the same angle as those old El Dorados at the Cadillac Ranch, its front end aimed at the Moon.

Two-thirds of the way back was a more enigmatic object: a 6'-by-6' steel box embedded in the ground, in the middle of which was a big wheel like you would find on the hatch of a ship. It looked like one of those portals into some secret underground facility the stranded passengers found on the mysterious island of *Lost*, a TV show my then-middle-school-aged son and I watched together on DVD. The way in, or maybe the way out. To where, at least officially, only became clear from the white metal sign sticking out of the ground nearby, with a notice in bright red text:

WARNING

PETROLEUM PIPELINE
BEFORE EXCAVATION OR
IN EMERGENCY CALL COLLECT
713-222-XXXX
THE TEXAS PIPELINE CO.

The sign was so old that the text had faded over the years, and parts of its message were obscured by rust, but you could fill in the blanks—even if you couldn't get all the numbers for that collect call.

The pipeline, the listing agent assured me with the characteristically positive spin of his trade, was no longer in use, and the current landowners had commissioned environmental studies to confirm the land appeared free of contamination. He showed me a model site plan on which some architect had sketched a possible homesite that worked around the maze of industrial easements that carved up the lot. But you could be sure it was not a property your typical future homeowner would zero in on, especially in an economy reeling from the collapse of the real estate markets. There's always a reason the empty lots are empty.

Building a house from the ground up was the last thing I needed to add to my plate, as a half-time single dad already loaded up with financial obligations and two busy careers. I had gone there to look at an existing house for sale next door by the same owners, hoping to trade my monthly rent for a mortgage. But the house was too big and expensive, whereas the price of the land was in my range—just barely—and it was the only acre of undeveloped land I could afford. Behind the lot was a pocket of urban woods that abutted the river, a zone whose existence I had discovered years earlier and the reason I had asked my downtown condo-broker neighbor if he could help me look for a place in this part of town. I was a lawyer, with plenty of experience dealing with big companies and a reflexive confidence that the global petrochemical giant that owned the pipeline would be happy to have me pay them to remove their environmental liability from my property. I was also

- - - -

a science fiction writer, with a particular interest in the aesthetics of ruin and rewilding, the kind of orientation that makes you think nothing would be cooler than to live in an overgrown concrete bunker that looks like the last outpost after the end of the world. And I had come to believe that places like that, where the worst of our industrial abuses of the Earth collide with wild nature, were where the essence of real life and the possibility of a better future could be found. A refuge, but also a place where, by working to harmonize the radically conflicting energies of the place, I might do the same to the conflicts in my own life.

The journey did not begin that day—in a way, I had been on it most of my life—but that gate with the barbed wire on top opened a portal. It was a different sort of portal than the valve box opened, and a dirtier one than those found in the secret worlds of magic and make-believe down the rabbit hole or through the closet that I had gravitated toward as a child. This portal told the truth, even if you had to blaze your own trail to find it.

It took me a long time to really begin to understand its lessons. Finding a beat-up piece of land like this, making it your home, trying to bring back the biodiverse life it is capable of sustaining, and integrating daily wanders into the urban wild as part of your life, you start to see things more clearly. You learn to banish from your mind the illusory fantasy that there is some precious, intact wilderness still out there, beyond the horizon, where wildlife can eke out a healthy existence outside the realm of our dominion. You come to see how the other species we share this planet with occupy the marginal spaces we leave for them—usually those we can't figure out how to more directly occupy or exploit, like the floodplain of the river behind the factories; or places we have already trashed, like landfills and the pathways of abandoned petroleum pipelines. The beauty of nature is still there. In a way, it is more beautiful when it manifests in these fallen places, because of the resilience it reveals. But it is also deeply damaged and scarred, evidence of the way we have remade the world into some butchered cyborg. The deeper lesson that accretes as you learn to really see these places is that the damage we see in the natural world around us is a mirror, a reflection of the damage we feel inside ourselves, even on the days when we feel healthy. We, as a collective, are the ones causing the horror show of everyday life that we live in with our eyes averted. We cause it by our sometimes willing, sometimes hoodwinked, sometimes coerced participation in a system of subjugation, extraction, and accumulation that makes the Earth and each of us its slaves, training us to see ourselves as apart from nature in the same way it alienates us from each other and from ourselves. While the path out of here is a long one that will take generations to map, rewilding projects—which can be as small as my friend Matt's guerrilla planting of native wildflowers on a patch of dirt beneath the M train in Queens or as big as the multi-acre restorations undertaken by communities all over the world, from the Fresh Kills Landfill in Staten Island to the brown-fields of Ballona Creek in West L.A., from Cheonggyecheon in the heart of Seoul to the Isar River in old downtown Munich—provide us the agency to start working our way there, learning to see the native life ready to burst through the pavement, doing the work to help hasten its emergence, and beginning to heal ourselves in the process. It can be as simple as learning to really see the damaged

----

old tree in your yard, the lost birds that feed on its fruit, and the ghosts of the creatures who used to. Seeing the tree, seeing the way it mirrors you and the way it feeds the world and feeds from it, in a simultaneously hyperlocal and global system of exchange of which we are each a part. A system we have the power to make more reciprocal, as we work to make our own society more just.

THE BIRD BOOKS SAY monk parakeets can mimic human speech. I have not yet heard them speak our language, but they still teach me things. Things about adaptation, making home, building community, and making the best of the world you find yourself in. They are charismatic creatures, one of the first natural wonders I connected with after we moved to Texas and found them living in the light towers of the intramural fields behind the garage apartment we rented. Queer, kooky birds that didn't belong here any more than we did, and yet made it richer, as they made you smile.

Two decades later, the parakeets taught me to pay attention to that beat-up old tree under which I parked the Airstream trailer I made into my home office. They did so rather noisily at first, making me think it was raining strange objects as they tossed their empties onto the aluminum hull over my head. When I went outside into the heat and light of the Texas summer, the parakeets helped me see that the crooked mesquite in our yard, and its nearby cousins of younger vintage, provided food that could help sustain life. They drew my attention to the way the tree grew and changed over the seasons, and to the way new mesquites came up out of the ground no matter how brutal the weather got, trunks from the same plant emerging at different spots, more under than above, the sun-seeking tendrils of ancient organisms that were all about the roots. Trees like icebergs whose visible wonders are just a small part of the story. These revelations from the observed world were supplemented by things found in books that compile our accumulated knowledge about the world around us. I learned that the name "mesquite" is not really Spanish, but Nahuatl, from *mizquitl,* a name used by the Aztecs and perhaps other Indigenous tribal groups whose cultural memories and knowledge of the world are not as completely erased as we might think. I learned that the fruit of the tree was one of many in our landscape that had evolved to be eaten by the giant mammals who disappeared from this continent not long after humans showed up, one of those factual nuggets that punctuate a truth about the deep history of the Anthropocene in ways reading alone cannot.

I have not yet put to use the knowledge that the prodigious pods of this big, busted-up tree, which barely looks alive itself, can provide food for us. I write this in the middle of the hottest summer since measurements started to be recorded, a summer of wildfires and floods and coastal waters hotter than the baths we run for our daughter, of refugees desperately moving across a destabilized and shrinking world only to run up against militarized borders and a dehumanizing suspension of charity. As relentless development capital continues our sprawl over the green spaces of a world that has lost 69 percent of its wildlife population since my sixth birthday, and as I worry about what we will do when the power runs out again and the air-conditioning goes with it, I get some reassurance when I walk out to my office and see the pods laying there on the ground beneath my feet and look up to see

- - - -

many more still hanging from the branches. Reassurance about the resilience of nature, about its capacity to help us get through each season and teach us things we once knew but have forgotten, and about our capacity to be the loving stewards of planetary life our sacred books instruct us to be, instead of the self-absorbed creatures of insatiable appetite we have become. That, and a looming sense that we will soon need to learn not to take for granted things like the wild food that goes uneaten due to the absence of the animals whose extinction our dominion coincided with.

I wonder what kind of cake we will make, if we have to make it from the fruit of the old tree that grew up in the brownfield. A tree that can make you bleed. There's a chance it will be better, and a certainty it will be more real.

2

A Wilderness of Edges

Fences, Foxes, and Buteos

From the street, the lot where we made our home is not a place where you would think nature is close by: a paved corner where two roads terminate at the edge of an industrial zone. Every side is fenced with chain link, some of it topped with barbed wire. Behind the fences stand shipping containers repurposed as storage sheds, stenciled with the records of their years at sea and their origins in faraway places where even the alphabets are sometimes different. There are three wide gates at the corner. One opens to the loading dock of a commercial door factory, another to our little driveway, and the third to an empty lot. It's a spot where infrastructure intersects, some public and some corporate. There are manholes in the street that access huge storm sewers, a fire hydrant that gets frequently tested in case there is an explosion at one of the factories, and a tall pipe sticking up out of the ground behind the sidewalk, bent like a big check mark, with chipped and faded yellow paint to mark the location of the buried pipeline. Most of the trees you see are dead ones: the telephone poles that line the streets, carrying power lines and the transmission cables of four different telecommunications service providers. There are live trees, too, growing next to the busted-up and rarely used sidewalk, but you probably wouldn't notice them if you drove by. They have been rendered invisible by their subservience to the cables hanging from those poles, pruned back over decades to create a strange vision when you look straight down the lane: a blocks-long symmetrical line of trees trained into Vs as their limbs yield to the telephone poles and their ethereal cargo, locked in a dance without touching, branches of networks that occupy the same space but never really interact.

At night the corner becomes a black hole, the only signs of life the occasional semitrucks that idle in the darkness while their drivers wait to make their deliveries in the morning or the lovers who take advantage of the darkness for their private intimacies. Sometimes the next afternoon you will find a used condom on the pavement, slowly melting under the Texas sun, or spent nitrous canisters left over from last night's euphoric whippets. Just a few hundred feet from a major thoroughfare, so close the stoplight casts its ambient red pulse into the darkness, the corner is a strangely secluded spot when the factories close at night or on the weekends. It gets quieter as the traffic becomes sparse and the internal combustion cacophony of the city dials down. Step out in an especially quiet moment and you might hear the eerie call of an owl. And when the quiet is interrupted by a police siren screaming down the boulevard, the urban coyotes will answer back from the darkness beyond the fences with an unearthly chorus of banshee yips and howls. Despite its industrial brutality—and maybe even because of it—our corner is one of those spots where the wildness sneaks back into our world.

The first season we lived here, renting the little cottage next door to our lot while we tried to figure out how to build a house of our own in this unlikely zone, we had one of our first real experiences of the everyday wonders of the feral city. Agustina and I were coming back from a movie on a Saturday night, driving down our long block, which is the length of three regular blocks. It's the sort of street that is darker and creepier at night than other streets, with two asphalt lanes divided by double yellow lines and dimly lit in a way that might make you think the engineer who laid out the streetlights had a love of film noir. As we rolled toward home, we saw motion at the curb, behind the diner. Animal as apparition. Canine trot. But not a dog. Something wilder, not much bigger than a house cat, with a big bushy tail and flashes of red and gray fur in the intermittent bits of light.

A fox.

It was the first one either of us had seen in our lives, but we knew immediately what it was, in that weird way we are trained from an early age to identify animals we will never likely see outside of a zoo. The name we were taught to give that animal, and its name in many other European languages, derives from older words that describe that distinctive tail, for reasons you can only appreciate when you see one in person—even if it is flashing that tail in your headlights behind the truck tarp installation shop instead of above the tall grass at the edge of the woods. Not the rarest or most exotic animal one could see, and yet also totally remarkable. To spend decades outside only to finally see one not in a national park, but on a gritty urban street. The immediate wonder we felt was intense and validating, confirming our counterintuitive instincts about where to find signs of real life beyond the city's mirrored veneer.

We followed the fox the length of the block as it trotted casu-
ally along the curb, phasing in and out of the incandescent cones
of the tired old streetlights. It continued at that pace, fast but not
urgent, all the way to the very end of the street. And then it suddenly disappeared, through an almost imperceptible gap at the
base of the chain-link gate where the road ended, like one of those
imaginary beings in comic books who can render themselves
intangible and walk through walls.

The fences at the end of the street were a barrier, but also a portal. They mostly worked to keep people out, but in doing so, they
created a sanctuary for animal life in the empty lots behind the
factories.

Years later, I put a trailcam at that gate and saw how often the
foxes came and went—almost every night, even on the night of our
city-crippling blizzard in 2021. Hunting as we slept, taking advantage of the unique opportunities the city afforded—probably cap-
turing the rodents that gather around our dumpsters at night, and
maybe even dumpster diving themselves. Foxes—especially red
foxes, but also gray foxes like the one we saw that night—thrive in
ecotones: areas that straddle two very different types of habitats.
And the foxes around here have figured out that the zone between
overgrown empty lot and industrial streetscape creates similar
opportunities for predation as the border between grassland and
forest or prairie and wetland.

They are not the only ones. In the warm months, the fence at our
corner is overgrown with vegetation. Four different species of vines
climb the chain link and poles, exploding at summer's end with
flowers that look like hot pink popcorn and dark, gamey grapes from

- - - -

24

which you can make outlaw wine. Poison ivy and skin-puncturing agaves grow thick in the right-of-way, swallowing the accumulated litter in vegetation so aggressive it disappears the sidewalk. At night, it sometimes swallows entire cars, when the corner becomes so dark that people who miss their turn for the on-ramp on their way home from the bars find themselves accelerating into the void. One recent morning I walked out to find a late-model Honda caught in the net of our front fence, silent and empty, the eerie eyes of the LED headlights shining like some crashed UFO, its driver as vanished as if they had been abducted in one.

There is one big, old tree right at the corner where the fences meet, its branches just far enough from the Google Fiber lines to be left alone by the chainsaws, the base of its trunk pushing up against the pavement that surrounds it. It's a sycamore, mature enough to have mostly shed its outer bark, unveiling a ghostly whiteness that manifests most potently in the cold light of our short winters. I never really noticed it, my eyes drawn instead to the door factory loading dock sign in its shade, until one afternoon when I saw how its bleached-out high branches catch the last sun of the day. As I looked up to admire that druid-worthy descendant of the native woods that must have once covered the street, I noticed how the line of telephone poles continued beyond the gate, the thick cables draped diagonally above the intersection to their anchor on another pole whose top you can see poking up against a background of trees further back. And I learned that on a nice afternoon, there's a good chance you will see a lone hawk sitting atop that pole, just above the porcelain insulators that tether the high-tension wire to the wood of what is probably a southern pine embalmed in pentachlorophenol and diesel oil. Raptors love the surveillance posts dead trees provide, including those we use to line our streets and carry the power we have harvested from the Earth.

The red-shouldered hawk, *Buteo lineatus*, is smaller than some of its cousins, almost stout. When you see one sitting there atop a pole, it might even look a little pudgy and cute. On the wing, it is an amazing avian interceptor, a forest hawk especially well adapted to flying at insanely high speeds through the branched maze of the woodland canopy, deftly threading the line between treetop and ground-crawling prey. You usually hear them before you see them, and that piercing *skree*, which is a lot like the better-known clarion of the red-tailed hawk, always gets your attention. They are often hard to spot when perched on a branch, but if you can observe them up close or with field glasses, you see they are not pudgy but stocky, wearing their wings over their broad shoulders like the furry capes of ancient warriors, washes of autumnal brown and rusty orange collared with black and white ermine. They are wary of us, with good reason. But they have also learned to adapt to the hunting opportunities our encroachment on their habitat has created. Like that empty lot behind the factory, where the right-of-way for those telephone poles—the path of an old road, abandoned and allowed to go back to wild—creates an open zone foxes and smaller creatures of the field must cross on their own forages. Sometimes the hawks come out even further into our domain, like on quiet Sunday mornings when you might find one surveying the mowed zone of the highway feeder from its perch on a tall post.

Hawks were rare things to see when I was a kid, even in the country. Their populations had been decimated by DDT and other pesticides. By the time I was in college in the 1980s, they had started to become more common—especially red-tailed hawks, who learned to take advantage of the interstate highways. On some stretches when we drive between here and my parents' home in Iowa, we see one every couple of miles, especially in Kansas and Oklahoma. When I started seeing hawks in the city, I didn't really know the differences between the species, their different habitats and adaptations. But once you start paying closer attention, they teach you revelatory things about your own habitat.

When you see or hear a red-shouldered hawk in the city, it is a sign that a pocket of urban woods must be close by. Finding those

woods is harder, because they are almost as hidden as the wildlife they harbor, in the wilderness embedded in the city's edges.

Roads, Rivers, and Time Travel

The secret wilderness I found here twenty-five years ago is disappearing now. Not completely gone, but you can feel it slipping away, day by day. Because this is one of those zones where wild nature infiltrates the city, when you live in it you learn to see, in the fabric of your everyday life, how the wildness is bleeding from the world. We don't tend to notice those changes that slowly manifest in the other life around us. The city has a way of keeping us focused on feeding it, and the faces we see in its ubiquitous mirrors. Sometimes the waking dreams of our popular culture give us peripheral glimpses of the truth about how we relate to our world, but vampires can't see their own reflections.

It's strange to me, thinking back to when it first happened, that I found this place not on a wander, not at the end of a hidden trail, but through the window of a moving car driving down the highway. It was 1999, a year after we moved to Austin, the year they opened the fancy new airport on what had been the site of an air force base. A place whose very existence was a product of the End of History, in a moment when Austin was one of the epicenters of the Long Boom the forecasters promised would never end. I had come here to be a part of that, as a young lawyer who had left government service to help a friend start an Internet company, and I soon found myself living the life of one of those corporate mercenaries of cyberspace I had read imagined versions of in the '80s. Even then, dispatched to Dallas, D.C., or NYC for the day to

- - - -

negotiate a new level in the virtual world we were building, the real world beckoned. Even if you could only see it in flashes so brief you might have imagined it.

It helped that I had to slow down a little when I got on the bridge to get to the airport. It was an old bridge, a camelback truss of curved and bolted steel built in the Great Depression. One of those bridges whose lanes were designed for a time before half the cars on the road were spawned from monster trucks, its safety features seemed inadequate for the more dangerous world we now live in, built at a scale that brought you closer to the world around you. The route to get to the bridge went through East Austin, past industrial neighborhoods and run-down commercial strips I paid little attention to back then. But the view from that bridge, from the very first time I crossed it, was like a window into another world. The world that once was, and could be again.

You could only see it from the right lane—and unless the traffic came to a stop, you could only glance at it without crashing your car. Through the window, beneath the bridge, a stretch of wild shallow river meandered through a thick, green landscape devoid of any signs of human occupation. It was hazy and mysterious, atemporal and confounding, like a scene from a Romantic painting somehow inserted into the brutal landscape of the late-twentieth-century city. But there it was, so ordinary and obviously real that your conscious mind didn't even take that much notice of it, focused instead on the workday at hand, a day of travel itineraries and life billed out in six-minute increments.

I drove on, not really thinking about it. But over time, that momentary glance stuck with me, implanted in my mind like a dream you can't forget. Maybe it was the way it looked like the series of riverine landscape paintings my brother had done early in his career, one of which hung on my wall—more Gerhard Richter than Caspar David Friedrich, paintings like the covers of imaginary compilations of ambient music. Maybe it was the innate surreality of it in that context. Or the absolute reality of it, in contrast to the dammed up and domesticated version of the river I could see from the window of my office just a couple miles away. Lady Bird Johnson and her rich friends hadn't touched this.

I can see now, after half a life looking for it with greater intention, that it had the same power over me as the fleeting glances I sometimes had of wild animals, animals whose names we learned as children but almost never saw in real life and who disappeared from our view almost instantly when we did. Or the experience life sometimes affords of great trees, trees that have somehow survived the sprawling of the human city around them but only rarely display their majesty, their near-immortality, in a way you can really see. The river I saw was the river as it was meant to be—or as close as we would let it get to that. And in that moment, I saw it the way I was supposed to.

I tried to find it. I would run toward it on long lunch breaks, away from the manicured and densely peopled central trail of downtown. Past the dam, I found unofficial footpaths through the woods that grew around the river but few fresh vantages of the river itself. I would see that same atemporal album-cover vista again every time I went to the airport. But it was only when my young son helped me see the world through his eyes that I was able to read the signs nature manifested in the landscape of the city—invitations to step off the pavement and into real life.

Hugo had an innate affinity for the outdoors, with a sensitivity to other life I lacked at that age. My son was not an adventurer, the sort to take physical risks for fun. He was a tactile empath, who intuitively understood how to more richly see and experience things that were right there, without damaging them. Like the creatures in the front yard of our little rental house that my mother had taught me to call potato bugs when I was his age, which the Texans called pill bugs or roly-polies. In the months leading up to his fourth birthday, Hugo became fascinated with them, so much so that I read up on them, learning they are not insects but terrestrial crustaceans. He learned how the life in the yard responded to his gentle touch, expressing the same gifts that would make him the middle-school tinkerer who could get broken old watches, cameras, and phonographs working with a few minor adjustments and cleanings, then a gifted painter, sculptor, and woodworker who feels and expresses the life of the material in his hands. He became a fisherman at a precocious age, the sort who could, through that interspecies empathy, lure the savviest flounder at the end of the lighted dock onto the plastic tackle and then release it back into the water. I was a crummy fisherman but a natural born wanderer, with an innate sense of direction and an urge to find my own shortcuts to nowhere. We started to go out into the world together to see what we could find, and we discovered a richer realm than I had ever seen before.

The places we lived were always near a creek, as are most homes anywhere. We followed their meandering routes as a way

- - - -

to break out of the prescribed paths of our new city and see where we ended up. That took us into the backyard of a mysteriously wooded private estate behind our house, through a long meadow at the end of a dead end that we later learned was an intramural archery range, and into the expansive empty lot that secreted the old cemetery of the state psychiatric hospital, its half-hidden grave markers nameless and numbered. We found our first tadpoles swimming in a pool behind the obstacle course where state troopers would train, saw our first feral parakeets nesting in the light towers of the playing fields behind our garage apartment, and picked our way through beds of exposed limestone littered with fossilized remains of Cretaceous marine life you could pocket and take home. For a second-grade science project, we searched for the source of one of those creeks using the location marked on a local street map and a web-crawled copy of some geology professor's field notes from the 1960s, until we found ourselves staring at a gabion well in an office park behind the strip mall.

In second grade, Hugo joined his school's scout troop. We started going on weekend campouts, almost always at one of the Highland Lakes upriver from Austin, made from the series of dams that trapped the natural flows of the Colorado for flood control and power generation. The troop was chill—no uniforms, no badges, all family members and genders welcome, no real rules except regarding fire—and the trips were fun. We made huge campfires, told stories, played music, caught fish, and had a lot of laughs. On one trip, we borrowed another dad's canoe and I rediscovered how much I loved to paddle. It was something I had learned to do when I was not much older than Hugo, sent off

----

to a summer camp at the edge of Minnesota's Boundary Waters, where we were trained by Jeremiah Johnson–looking 1970s Outward Bound alums. I had spent much of my youth exploring the woods—I even considered going to an outdoor leadership school after high school but got diverted to more urbane pursuits until fatherhood helped me rediscover the balance outdoor exploration afforded. We got our own canoe and started looking for interesting places to take it. In the beginning we spent a lot of time honing our skills on the tame and tranquil waters of Town Lake, which you could access from ramps right along the main hike and bike trail. But as conventionally pretty as it was, it was weirdly lifeless, at least if you were looking for nonhuman life, so we pushed further. We paddled up from downtown toward the

----

massive dam that holds in Lake Austin and explored the thickly wooded side channels just off the spillway, where the bird life was vital. One Saturday morning we spotted a pileated woodpecker in that Anthropocene delta, which felt like finding a creature of legend, then pulled our canoe up on the far side of an island and explored the woods around a suburban water facility. There we found a powerful totem—a deer skull next to an empty can of Budweiser—that captured the essence of the wild city we were learning to find.

It took me a while, probably a year or two, to get the idea to use our canoe to more closely investigate that mystical-looking stretch of urban river I had seen at the eastern edge of town. One Saturday morning Hugo and I put the boat on the car, navigated labyrinthine loop roads, and found a run-down zone under the bridge where we could put in—a place I had never found before, even as I ran right over it. It was the kind of place where people park and party at the edge of town, where folks who never got real swimming lessons wade into the water to cool off on hot summer days, and where at nighttime anything goes, because the zone under the highway is within the jurisdiction of the state transportation department and therefore mostly ignored by the local police. As I carried the boat to the water, I looked back and saw my curious Cub Scout holding a used hypodermic needle he had picked up off the ground. I wondered what unlikely merit badges remain to be invented for the postindustrial landscape our children get to explore.

Even there, under the shadows of elevated highways and the drone of tires on pavement, signs of more authentic life were

----

all around—starting with the hundreds of cliff swallows coming and going from the mud nests they had built on the beams of the bridges. The nests looked like brown pustules growing right out of the steel, as if its ferrous rigidity spawned organic tissue. The sense that the bridge had come alive was enhanced by the intense energy of the birds darting zigzags over the access road, stealing insects from the river-fed air to feed their babies and themselves, revealing a riparian ecology that had figured out how to incorporate and even take advantage of our engineered interventions.

We headed in the direction I had seen from my drive-bys—upriver, against the current, but seemingly navigable as the channel was not fast. As soon as Hugo and I got on the water and began to paddle away from the put-in, it was like we had pushed through some invisible dimensional boundary. We found ourselves on a stretch of river that seemed so wild that we immediately felt transported to a different time, even as we could still hear the sounds of the city in the distance. The trees were tall and lush on both sides, hiding the nearby buildings and roads from view, the river clear and bright as it flowed over mussel shoals and cut deep channels around unexplored islands. We hadn't been in the water more than ten minutes when a hawk grabbed a duck from midair just above our bow, sending feathers floating into our boat—the duck somehow wriggling its way free before our eyes. We spent two more hours paddling until we could see the signs of the city, stopping to explore secret beaches along the way. It wasn't a big area, really—probably just a mile from bridge to dam—but the seemingly undisturbed ferality of it made it feel bigger than its linear dimensions, a hidden wilderness that had somehow been

----

allowed to exist in the middle of the city. An accidental refuge, paradoxically protected by industrial land uses that were oblivious to their ecological imprint but kept most of the human activity out of the riparian corridor hidden behind them.

We returned there many times over the years, sometimes paddling further downriver, where we found hidden lagoons full of turtles the size of tennis rackets tucked behind aggregate pits, and baby turtles out in the main channel for their first swim. We made tentative explorations on foot of some of the zones along the banks—mysterious ranches and expansive industrial sites at the edge of town, always watched over by raptors and vultures. For Hugo's fifth-grade science project, we went out with a copy of Fred Alsop's *Birds of Texas* and compared the multitude of species below the dam with the much smaller selection above. We encountered a trio of hippies on one of those secret beaches who warned us not to tell anyone else about this place we had found.

The warning would prove prescient.

Town and Country

We set out for Texas on a spring day in 1998, not long after Hugo's third birthday, in a red 1993 Volkswagen van we had bought used. We didn't have to carry all of our possessions with us—the moving company handled that—and we didn't have to worry much about the dangers we might encounter on the trail, which was an interstate highway that got us all but the first and last mile there. We were following the all-American life strategy of trying to find happiness and prosperity by moving to a new place, traveling on pathways widened by our forebears after they took the land from its prior inhabitants. We had looked all over—even in other countries—but settled on Austin, a place we did not know or even have a single friend in but had convinced ourselves was just what we wanted: a laid-back college town where one could make as good a living as in a much bigger city, but without all the hassle. A town with two indigenous chains of natural grocers, great bookstores, a vibrant literary community, an economy riding the tech boom, and a beautiful ecology that somehow traversed pastoral, tropical, and western desert. We also thought by moving away from extended family we might save our marriage and build a happy home life for our son. Only when the wreckage is complete and the irremediable design flaws fully evident do you learn there are smarter ways to try to fix those kinds of problems, and some work in our emotional lives can only be done outside of the relationship. Or outside, period.

We were also, I realize now, repeating patterns deeply embedded in the histories of our families, histories that blended fact and dinner-table legend over patterns of colonial settlement. My dad's family, per the research my grandmother did to establish herself as worthy of that small-town white lady elite known as the Daughters of the American Revolution, had been doing it since the 1750s, when the first of her line had come over from County Cork—purportedly escaping Catholic persecution of Protestants—and settled in Maryland. His descendants would colonize Ohio, and theirs would emigrate to Iowa as it became a state in the 1840s, establishing a family tradition of editing and publishing small-town newspapers that often saw the sons moving to a new town to start or buy their own weekly or daily. The tradition was broken only when my dad decided to become a dentist instead. My mother and her family were more recent immigrants, having come here from Germany after the end of World War II in circumstances that made them an unusual kind of refugee household. My son had other stories in his lineage, of Catholic immigrants from famine-era Ireland and Japanese immigrants of the Meiji era who arrived via the Pacific instead of the Atlantic. The little sister he would have twenty years later would carry the secret histories of Jews who left Spain for the fruitless reaches of southern Patagonia, where they built car dealerships and theaters, and Italians who emigrated to the foothills of the Andes and planted vineyards, only to have their great-granddaughters grow up in Houston after their parents left Argentina seeking political and economic stability when many of their college friends disappeared during the Dirty War. And down each of those streams flowed deep histories of migrations that, if the geneticists are to be believed, can be mapped through the codes we carry in our cells, back to essentially the same ultimate origin. A reminder, when the maps come in the mail or appear when you log in after sending your spit to the lab, that we are all nomads in our bones, always ready to pack up and move on if we need to. That the recent history of the planet we live on is the history of its colonization and recolonization by human beings, propelled by the back-to-back bargains with Prometheus and Demeter that enabled us to enslave the world.

EVEN BEFORE WE LEFT Des Moines, I had found myself walking away, looking for ways out, paths into the real. Sometimes I explored the opportunities for time travel my slow-growth hometown harbored in its well-preserved but boring streetscapes—in used bookstores and antique malls, the lunch counters of old diners, and even the hidden corners of malls, like the one built on the site of an old monastery that had, tucked away in a back corner, a little shop whose red neon letters over the door promised **THE SECRET**. But the most fulfilling and authentic secrets were outside.

Nature is not as easy a thing to find as it should be, growing up in a state like Iowa. It takes a while to put it together, to explain to yourself the incongruence between where your instincts tell you to go and what you find when you get there. It should be a beautiful place—the rolling hills between two epic rivers, the Missouri and the Mississippi, interlaced with the tributaries of both, with the wonders of all four seasons but little in the way of extremes. And it is beautiful on good days: distinctly pleasant in the way the paintings of Grant Wood showed, a place that once conjured a Norman Rockwell variation on the Shire. But when you leave the city for the country on a beautiful summer day, seeking the wild that should be there, you find a place where everything is green but nothing seems really alive. A place where the beautifully rich soil made by glacier and prairie has been brought entirely under the plow, the marshlands have been filled, and the forests have mostly been cut. All in service of endless rows of crops that, come harvest time, will fill the silos next to each barn and the massive grain elevators at the edge of every little town, much of it destined for processing into fuel for machines. A place where there is water everywhere, in rivers and creeks that branch across the land like the tree of life but are almost totally dead, poisoned with the chemicals used to artificially stimulate the soil and kill insects

- - - -

that eat the crops. As recently as when my dad was a boy in the 1940s, the fields were flush with pheasant. The alluvial marshlands along the Missouri where he grew up southeast of Omaha would fill in spring with flocks of migratory waterfowl so huge that they darkened the sky. The last truly epic migration event was in 1947, when cold weather to the north impeded the birds from continuing on, accumulating a population so loud my dad remembered it keeping him up at night. But even then, the marshlands were no longer the habitat they had once been. The ducks stopped to pig out on waste grain left in the fields over the winter, in zones that a century earlier had been verdant wetlands where their ancestors would summer. Now they had to fly further north to find suitable habitat in which to breed, in Canada or the Dakotas.

The Midwestern city, ironically, was the best place to find wild nature in that region. Pockets of woodland could still be found, especially along the rivers. Our little city was located at the confluence of two such rivers, the Raccoon and the Des Moines, the latter of which feeds into the Mississippi, where the French explorers Joliet and Marquette were taught the name by the Peoria Indians. The name of the town was always explained as a mystery when I was growing up. People theorized it was a reference to the middle river, as in *moyen*; a reference to a monastery from the French word for "monk"; or a French variation of the Indian place name *Moingona*. Turns out the latter is right, but only recently did a clever anthropologist and linguist of the region figure out that Moingona was the Peorias' way of teaching Joliet and Marquette to call their neighbors on the Iowa side "the shit-faces." A joke that has lasted 500 years and will probably last 500 more, even as the Indigenous Peoples who once cared for these lands are as gone as the mammoths. You can find woods along the Des Moines and the Raccoon as they pass through town, and we explored them, including the ones right behind our house—sometimes with BB guns or .22s—but they are mostly populated by ghosts.

A couple miles above the confluence, down behind the bottom lands where my brother played Little League, there was a place in the woods that the stoners a little older than us named "the Lost Planet." It was where the municipal waterworks would dump the lime used in its treatment process, creating an unearthly landscape: a dead zone that would glow like a cratered alien plain in the moonlight, providing a perfect place to drop acid or make a home movie about other worlds. My earliest memory of the woods is of crossing the street where we lived when I was very young—aptly named Pleasant Street—and watching the bulldozers clear the trees to make room for the city's first freeway, right where our neighbors' backyards ended.

When we first moved back to Des Moines from D.C., a few months after my thirtieth birthday and right before Hugo was born, we lived in suburbia, just a few miles upriver from the Lost Planet and the neighborhood I had grown up in. Our dog gave me a good excuse to wander off seeking pockets of wild space hidden in that manufactured landscape, where the auto-centric regulation of one's movement through space compelled small acts of resistance, like stepping off the designated walkways. We found our way into a creek bed at the end of the subdivision, where strangely rounded stumps were all that was left of many of the young trees. Every day there would be new stumps, and it took me weeks before I figured out they had been cut by beavers. I never found the animals, probably because I never thought to look and they knew how to avoid me. Not long after, a summer guide at Aspen's Maroon Bells told me that the North American beaver only became nocturnal after French and English trappers showed up. I don't know if that's true, but it tells several different truths about the American landscape and what it hides. It made me wonder what else was there that I hadn't learned to see.

As the first winter settled in, our warm-weather hound and I found our way back into the floodplain of the Raccoon, this time at the edge of town, and discovered a riparian woodland that could only be accessed when the river was iced over. In those days I often tried to read a paperback as I walked, roaming some Cimmerian snowscape or noir alley until my dog ran off after a deer and circumstances compelled me to put the book away and learn to track. I read Bernd Heinrich's amazing book *Ravens in Winter*, about a biologist holed up in a frozen shack in Vermont watching birds interact with the bait he had hauled up. But Iowa had no ravens; only crows, whose song—if you can call it that—I had learned to associate with the otherwise lifeless aftereffects of factory farming.

When we finally got our own place in an older part of town, near the university, we couldn't afford a second car. I became a reverse commuter, riding the bus to my job at the outermost edge of suburbia. I remember reading Samuel R. Delany's *Dhalgren* on that bus in the summer of 1995, a transgressive text that follows a mysterious kid trying to find his way through a ruined city whose systems of control have mostly failed. Outside the bus window was a city whose systems of control worked perfectly, despite the absence of any overt coercion. A place where compliant worker-consumers, many of them raised in smaller towns, occupied a world of endless work, inadequate pay, and unremitting boredom, in a landscape of cookie-cutter homes, office buildings, malls, and freeways built where a few decades earlier had been farms—and a hundred years before that, beautiful prairies that stretched from the Mississippi to the Missouri. My transgression was modest: to violate that order by walking in a zone that did not really contemplate, or even tolerate, the idea of a pedestrian. When I got to my stop, there were no sidewalks to follow for more than a few steps, so I intuited my own routes, cutting through the surreal lawns of corporate estates and the interstitial woods that grew between them, testing the bounds of what sort of trespassing you could get away with without bringing out the guards. I applied the same instincts I had developed as a boy, finding shortcuts to school through the green space beyond the cul-de-sacs. The wild was hard to find except in the cold of winter, when you could see signs in the snow from creatures that occupied the slivers of time and space we left for them. When you walk where the land tells you to go, right through the often-invisible boundaries we erect to partition it, you can almost feel what it would be like to truly be free, even if you might also be hungry.

In the sky overhead, there were always contrails—pollution scratched across the air like linear clouds. In the evening rush hour, as the sky was dimming down, they would come into greatest relief, marking out machine geometries and cryptic glyphs slowly dissolving into atmospheric flow. You could almost imagine that,

----

if you watched them long enough, you could decipher their signs and portents and use them as an oracle to find your way out.

The real signs were there at the edge of town, where the suburbs ultimately collided with some farm field not yet swallowed by the city. There was a connection between that idealized pastoral world of our great-grandparents and the dark malaise lurking behind the artificial smiles of the hardworking people who filled the city's office buildings and staffed its stores. A connection between agriculture, the absence of real nature, and the soulless drudgery of labor and urban life. I could feel it, but I couldn't put my finger on it.

I could start to see how broken the model was out in the countryside. In the '80s, when I was in college, skyrocketing interest rates and plummeting grain prices sparked a crisis, as the huge debt farmers needed to obtain their modern means of high-yield production became unsustainable. Every few weeks, there would be a story in the paper about some farmer driving into town and shooting a banker. The family farm model that was the mythical building block of the American democratic experiment had been broken by the very business models it had spawned. Land prices became cheap. My parents could finally afford to buy a piece of scrappy acreage in one of the poorest counties, land that had never really been farmed because it was ridged timber that wasn't worth the trouble. When I drove down to check it out, instead of the well-kept white-picket towns I remembered from childhood, I found a bombed-out place that looked surprisingly close to the post-apocalyptic fantasies I used to watch on VHS.

Three decades later, in the autumn of 2023, I went back to see those minimalist landscapes of Midwestern suburbia where my search for urban nature had begun. It was on a Monday, the holiday consecrated to Christopher Columbus and the Indigenous peoples who once occupied these lands. The sprawl had overtaken a few more miles, but the zone along the Raccoon River remained wild, a rare American waterway not yet engineered into submission. Behind the long rows of cookie-cutter houses, the industrial land uses persisted—gravel pits and staging yards; the long, wooded path of the freight rail that followed the path of the river; and beyond that, an old grain elevator surrounded by big windowless warehouses at the edge of town. Right off the interstate, just south of the river, was the unmarked data center where Microsoft spawned the large language model artificial intelligence known as ChatGPT. You could see that it was growing, even without researching all the development permits its owner had pending to rededicate the surrounding cornfields to a different kind of production. Overhead were the vultures one always sees near interstate highways on sunny days, and just one hawk, flying away. The connections are hard to trace, but sometimes they manifest in the way the tracks in the field tell you the story of what happened before you got there.

Demeter and Dionysus

The Greek town of Elefsina used to be called Eleusis. It is a ten-mile walk from the heart of Athens on a road still known as the Sacred Way, though you can also take the highway if you are in a hurry or don't have the appetite for driving in the Greek metropolis, where lane markers often seem merely aspirational. The town is on a bay that connects to the sea, and characterized today by heavy industry, a lot like the neighborhood where we live now—petrochemical facilities, concrete factories, steel fabs, and an air force base. But in the ancient period, it was a pilgrimage site where all members of society could travel to experience the ritual known as the Eleusinian Mysteries—so called because we still don't know what secrets they revealed to the acolytes, even though thousands of people attended the festival over the more than 2000 years in which it was conducted. What we do know is that it related to the myth of Persephone, the daughter of Demeter who, while wandering too far into a field chasing butterflies, was abducted by Hades, raped, and kept as his consort. Persephone's mother, after starving the people to show she meant business, cut a deal that let her daughter come home every spring, returning to her husband in the underworld only for the winter. The story is, self-evidently, tied up with the life cycles of plants, their interrelation with the seasons, and human mastery of this process to provide the grain that is the fundamental source of our sustenance.

The cult of Demeter at Eleusis is thought by many to have originated in antiquity, well before the classical era, and some of the archaeological evidence supports that theory. Like many classical religious traditions, we don't really know what came before the things that were written down or rendered in art. We have linguistic evidence, commonalities in names across different cultures that suggest a migration of gods that came with the migration or interaction of peoples. The record is free, in a way, for the intuitive divination of story. By the classical era, we know the basics of what the Mysteries involved: a procession from Athens along the ten-mile route to Eleusis. The participants wore garlands of myrtle and carried bundles over their shoulders at the end of long, thin sticks, not unlike Indian pilgrims today. The priestesses carried the *hiera*, the sacred objects, covered to protect the secret knowledge they contained. Upon their arrival at the site by the edge of the sea, the pilgrims would ritually celebrate Persephone's return to the surface world and the arrival of spring. In the days prior to the ceremonies, they would fast, make sacrifices to the gods, drink a sacred beverage, purify themselves with water, bathe in the river, sing hymns, and enjoy dances. Each initiate would bathe a piglet in the sea, then sacrifice it, spilling its purifying blood. They would pray for rain. Anyone could attend— even foreigners and those who were enslaved—as long as they spoke Greek and had not committed murder.

Inside the chambers, more discrete rituals were conducted, in which the higher initiates were taught the great secrets of the cult through enactments, words, and revelation of the sacred objects. What these rituals and secrets were, no one knows. Some sources claim to have known; others speculate. Many male authorities, unsurprisingly, assert that the magical object revealed must have been a phallus. More cosmically inclined writers, including Robert Graves and Terence McKenna, have argued the sacred drink ingested by the initiates before the ritual must have been a fungal hallucinogen that triggered an entheogenic trip.

Others theorize that the reveals had to do with meditation on grain plants—an exegetic revelation of how their reproduction works, and how we can manipulate it to change the terms of our

----

relationship with the natural world. A deep lesson on the means whereby we make our food sources grow on command—as long as the weather cooperates.

Author Marta Vannucci speculated that Demeter, with a different name, must have been a historical person who came to Attica in the seventh or sixth century BCE from the matriarchal cultures of southern India, carrying with her the secrets of hexaploid wheat, the grain from which bread is made. Vannucci's article appeared in the *Annals of the Bhandarkar Oriental Research Institute*, a journal so obscure that when I found it, I wondered if it might be a Borgesian fiction implanted deep in JSTOR by mischievous scholars. But Vannucci turns out to have been a respected biological oceanographer who developed a sideline in ecological readings of ancient religious texts, and her argument resonates with intuited truth. The secrets of Eleusis, Vannucci contended, were all about the transmission of that knowledge of how to control the reproduction of plants capable of feeding large human populations. The rituals, as Graves also acknowledges, reenacted and legitimized the way that traditionally feminine knowledge of natural processes was appropriated by patriarchal authorities as the foundation of their power. Embodying in practices of sympathetic magic the understanding of how fundamental to human health and civilization such knowledge was—and how tenuous our control over nature through agricultural techniques really is.

What none of these latter-day students of the Eleusinian Mysteries interrogate is whether the bargain with Demeter was a good deal. The basic idea that agriculture was what lifted humanity up from savagery and suffering is taken as a given.

Around the pilgrimage site at Eleusis still stand the remains of ancient grain silos, on what was once the center of an area of agricultural production. The silo, considered properly, was the true temple—the real source of the power on which the Athenian city-state was founded.

I grew up around grain silos. They were all over the Midwestern cities where I lived and all over the landscape you would see driving in the country. They were often monumental—gigantic, windowless forms of concrete that rose up from the plains in spots where railroad tracks and roads converged, usually at the edge of town, where city meets country. Each farm had its own smaller silo, usually with the characteristic phallic shape, sometimes next to an older barn that looked like a primitive imitation of a Giotto cathedral. The silos often had mesh exteriors through which you could see the quantity of corn stacked up inside. As a kid, it was hard to imagine anything more boring to live around. You wondered what it would be like to live instead amid the wonders of the big city, the mountains, or the beach. Around the farm buildings were the endless fields from which the grains came. Everything alive, but somehow lifeless. Something always seemed off about it. Out of balance. But you couldn't put a youthful finger on it. Especially when what your gut was telling you was so contrary to what you were being taught in school: how that bounty of agricultural production was the foundation on which our affluent and wonderful lives were built.

In his 2017 book *Against the Grain: A Deep History of the Earliest States*, Yale political scientist James C. Scott synthesizes recent anthropological research to argue a different theory of the agricultural

----

revolution and what it did for us. The earliest permanent human settlements, he evidences, were around biodiverse wetlands where otherwise nomadic bands of human beings found they could get everything they could want throughout the four seasons. These bands typically numbered no more than 150 persons and had little in the way of leadership hierarchies or occupational specializations. In time, these groups learned to supplement their diets with protein-rich plants they initially gathered from the wild, then learned to cultivate. At the outset, this provided an adaptive and resilient subsistence culture. Relatively quickly, the value of cereal grains became evident—a food source that was easily manipulated, could be stored for long periods of time without spoiling, and could be used to make all sorts of more complex, pleasing, and versatile foods. These qualities also made grains function well as a store of value—the commodity surplus that accumulated in small units, each of which had an intrinsic nutritional and energy value.

With these accumulated surpluses came the need to control and protect them, to manage their accumulation and distribution, and to ensure their continued production and renewal. These needs, Scott cogently argues, led to the formation of the first systems of state power. And with that power came the idea of labor—of the state developing means to compel people to contribute to the production of surplus. The city-states that arose around the first centers of agricultural production were not, he contends, the new wonderlands to which people flocked to be lifted from the miseries of their previously primitive conditions. Rather, they were militarized zones of new economic power that had to enslave their neighbors to provide the labor needed to work the fields, places in which the majority of people were poor and often sick from diseases such concentrations of population incubated. To be a so-called barbarian, Scott argues with anarcho-libertarian flourish, was the only way to be truly free, living a life with no "labor" other than the natural activities of hunting, foraging, and making tools from the world around you. As a theory for freshly understanding the rest of human history, it's intuitively compelling. Especially when you couple this reconsideration of the bargain with Demeter with the deeper understanding Scott provides of the powers we acquired through the gift from Prometheus. How our mastery of fire coupled with our relentless pursuit of surplus—in its elemental cereal form and all the actual and metaphoric forms we have been able to discover or imagine, from hordes of gold to storage lockers full of stuff and infinite digital vaults of virtual currency—has led us to the brink of an overheated climate that may bring our civilization to the point of collapse before this century is out.

As a parent, I appreciate the value of surplus—of having enough food to feed my family, even if a lean spell comes. As a species, the production and accumulation of more than you need is a masterful strategy for survival and advancement. But it has a design flaw. There can never be too much, especially in an age when most of the surplus we accumulate is in the forms of symbols like money, distantly tied to tangible commodity value, if at all, and largely immune to spoilage. The equilibrium that economists would have us believe this system always wants to return to never arrives, because the things the system values omit the value of all other life on the planet, except to the extent it can be converted to our use.

- - - -

This way of living creates systems of power designed to enslave us and the entire world on which we live. The system is founded, at its essence, on control over the reproduction of others: plants, animals, and even people, as our daily debates about reproductive rights show. The only life it really values is that of the people in control.

The planetary crisis we find ourselves in is a result of this system. The natural human instinct for survival, enabled by our technological gifts, has caused the greatest mass extinction of other species since the Cretaceous period and brought our own endangerment into the realm of the plausible. To really alter our path, we need to confront the design flaws of the Neolithic Revolution, evidenced by our addiction to growth and the accumulation of more surplus than we need. That's not to suggest some twenty-first-century nomadology. Even the most imaginative science fiction writers would find it challenging to envision a human society that had developed without agriculture, without the bureaucratic systems it engendered to count the accumulated wealth—the original reason we developed mathematics and written language. But we know that the tiny bands of humans who managed to survive into the nineteenth and twentieth centuries outside that system were—and in a few cases, are—happier than us, even if they do not get to read novels, hear symphonies, or binge-watch a season of a television series after dinner.

Walking in the edgelands of the twenty-first-century city, finding the wild nature they harbor, you can get glimpses of your own true nature as a creature that lives in and from the world, and maybe even a way to be a nomad without leaving your house.

- - - -

Finding such places is easier than you think. Finding your personal connection is harder.

Stress and Satori

On the Saturday before Father's Day in June 2007, six weeks after the judge finalized our divorce, I went out to paddle the urban river at the edge of town solo for the first time. The house I was living in—the first real house we had bought in Austin a few years before—was, ironically, on the neighborhood homes tour, which I joked should have a special "broken homes" edition. My work life that spring and summer was intense, sending me sneaking off for afternoon cigarettes and sometimes losing my patience with my colleagues. Seeking solace and solitude, I strapped my canoe

to the car and checked into a South Austin motel. In the morning I put in at that same spot my son and I had first found under the bridge. The river had flooded that week after an early summer deluge, and the water had only just receded back down within its banks. Paddling against the current was harder than usual, but you could get there, especially if you found the slower shallows closer to the banks.

In the morning mist, as I worked my way upstream, I watched three deer wade across the river ahead of me and quickly got out of my own head. The foliage was thick and green, in that moment before Texas summer becomes too hot to endure without immersing yourself in the water, and the air buzzed with insect and avian life. Canoeing, especially alone, has a meditative quality. I had to tune into the water, into the current, into the air. I felt and followed the flow of the elements around me, moving my body and the vessel that carried it through space, my form propelled by the paddle I stroked along the sides of the boat with learned grace, at the pace of the place, mostly silent. Not unlike the rudimentary meditation practices I had learned in high school from a visiting Zen priestess, I realize now, the activity had a way of emptying the mind of active thought. In zazen, the aim is no more mind than a dim mindfulness of the act of breathing. In a canoe, there's a lot more going on, a way of moving through the natural environment that by its very essence leaves little room for distracted thought— an exorcism of the self that compels you to let the world around you into your consciousness. I literally had to feel my way using all my senses, opening my being up to everything it was interacting with. To do so without leaving the city, finding myself totally alone

----

in a pocket of urban reality filled with bountifully diverse life, was absolutely transcendent.

When I got to the secret beach and stepped out of the boat to soak up the sun, I noticed the normally dry creek was flowing fast through the sand, still draining the rain. Watching the water, I found a young catfish grounded at its edge, gills gasping. I returned it to the main channel, gently massaging it the way you do when releasing a fish you've caught with a hook, and watched it swim off. As I stood there in that spot, wet with river water and sweat, my mind voided of my own worries and fears, I felt a sudden and overpowering sense of connection to all the life around me—trees, bugs, birds, fish, the river itself, the power of the sun. A feeling that the separation I had always felt between me and other life that surrounds us had been dissolved and we were all part of the same thing, like nodes in a network or currents in the river. A momentary but indisputably real sense of ascension beyond the alienated ego, a oneness with what a more religious person would call the divine. It didn't take my inner pain away, but it put it in perspective, connecting it with all the pains and rewards and cycles of life in the world around us. It was a simple reminder that one's own struggles are mirrored everywhere one looks, and of the balancing power of renewed wonder at the infinite richness of the little corner of the universe we inhabit.

You can't teach the love of nature. It has to come from within, through serendipitous discovery of one's own unmediated presence in the world. Most of us have it as children, instinctively, but our anthropocentric society knows how to

----

drum it out of us—first with our own natures, when adolescence distracts us with sexual attraction and the alienated cosplay of adult identity formation, and then with the lifelong treadmill of work and home life. The environment we shape into our own habitat works hard to keep nature at bay, protecting our families and our food from predators and four-legged thieves in ways we rarely notice. We feel the pull of the outside, seeking opportunities for recreation and refuge in parks and public commons, but the experience of nature in those places is often simulated, landscaped, or, upon closer inspection, barren of real wildness, usually as a consequence of heavy human traffic. We see what we believe to be truly wild places through our screens, in Instagram feeds filtered through the romantic gaze and television shows that bring the animal world into sharper relief than any real-life experience could. If we are lucky and have the time and financial resources such activities take, we might get to travel to some of those wild places. A very select few of us might get to live in such places, working as rangers, guides, or hospitality personnel. We tend to ignore the wild nature that lives in the city, right under our noses, integrated into the fabric of our everyday life. Learning to see the nonhuman life that lives in the urban edges—like the coyotes that prowl the Chicago Loop, the raptors that nest on Manhattan skyscrapers, or the bats that fill the summer skies of downtown Austin—can rekindle our dormant connections with our own wild nature. It can also make you see that on a massively urbanized planet all nature is some variant of urban nature, echoing the traumas and evidencing the adaptations of life under human dominion.

Herons and Hotels

Sometimes at rush hour in East Austin, I see a great blue heron flying home for the evening over the congested traffic of the city as I'm driving home. A big bird, almost too big to fly, moving with the motion of a slower world through a different dimension of time, giving the lines of cars lined up at the light a glimpse of natural grace we don't really deserve and mostly don't notice. Some nights I see a flock of egrets, maybe half a dozen, their white feathers rendering them almost spectral at twilight. Or the caracara, a dark-crested raptor that looks like an eagle wearing a toupee, often credited as the cactus-perched bird on the Mexican flag, a symbol of the Aztec founding of Tenochtitlán and a reminder of the deeper human history of this region. Birds who move between planetary hemispheres and sometimes between worlds. As beautiful as they are, they are no longer rare. And in the grind of the human day, it's easy to never wonder where they come from and where they go.

Thanks to the military history of this part of town, the heritage building stock is heavy on machine works and Quonset huts. On our street stands a long row of crappy metal warehouses that would be unlikely to survive a tornado, but have held up just fine since they were tilted up in the '80s. In a concession to the Austin aesthetic, some have been painted pretty colors—pastel pinks and blues, now faded from years under the Texas sun—and the array of businesses they house these days includes hipster chop shops, prop yards for indie films, gourmet caterers, underground music clubs, and a workshop where they make "the Stradivarius of Wind Chimes." At the western end of the street long stood the

----

biggest of those warehouses, one of the last tenants of which was a muffler shop where you could also get your taxes done. When the new owners cleared the building out to tear it down, all the old dead parts cars finally got hauled away, along with the fencepost mosaic of used tires painted in the colors of the Mexican flag. You could walk down and stand in the busted-up parking lot, look over the edge above the decades' worth of trash, and find yourself staring at an unlikely sight: five great blue herons in treetop nests the size of beanbag chairs, primping and socializing with the awkward grace of scaly stick-figure legs, feathered serpent necks, and wings that could wrap a human. If you stood there long enough, you might even see one of their gangly bodies lift awkwardly into the air, expressing its annoyance with the loud *skronk* that earned the birds one of their human nicknames. The blue crankys would mostly tolerate your gaping presence, because they know that even though they seem so close, they occupy a spot no human could ever reach.

For years, that parking lot was fenced in and closed off behind big signs. The warehouse sat atop the edge of a steep bluff along the Colorado, just below the dam that holds in Austin's downtown lake. Called Longhorn Dam, it was once the site of the main low-water crossing of the Chisholm Trail, where cowboys would drive semiferal cattle rounded up from deserted borderlands to be sold at faraway Midwestern railheads. It used to mark the city limits, and for a century this was a place where people would dump trash. The bluff is full of it, maybe even made of it: concrete and brick remains of buildings torn down in the century before, painted sheet metal and rotted upholstery of old cars, and infinite

----

gnarls of rebar, rubber, plastic, and wire. When I stand there looking at those herons, I am standing on that mountain of trash. If I
look down over the edge, that is what I see, even as the hackberries and bamboo manage to find enough footing and nutrients in
that polluted soil to provide a stand of foliage thick enough to hide
the birds come summer.

The long, marshy island on which the herons have made their
home is also thick with trash. If you disregard the "No trespassing" signs and the safety warnings from the code inspectors, sneak
through the fence that now surrounds the empty slab where the
warehouse once stood, and find your way through the ruin to
the treacherous path down, you see the rainbow fragments of
old apothecary glass and soda bottles glistening amid the mussel
shells that litter the side channel separating the island from the
bluff. You see tires being slowly sucked back into the muck, and the
fresher flotsam of plastic trash that comes when the river floods:
empty bottles, damaged toys, shopping bags that hang from the
once-submerged branches like Anthropocene ornaments. And rising up at the eastern point of the island is the tree, a sycamore that
may have spawned from the seed of some landscaper's ornamental planted upriver. But if you try to get any closer to that tree, you
find yourself confounded by a marshy terrain that is not meant
to be trod by creatures who wear shoes. The herons have found
refuge in a sliver of dirty wilderness inadvertently created by the
collision of industrial downzoning and an ancient river.

They are not alone. Against the drone of the city, if you linger
on a clear day, you will hear the whistle of the osprey patrolling
the river with its back against the sun and the film-projector rattle

of the kingfisher as it cruises above the water. On a warm day, the urban hawks take to high altitudes, their trademark calls cutting through the traffic noise. Once in a while I see rarer raptors: a kestrel hawk perched on a streetlamp, a peregrine falcon flying over the terraformed berm between the off-ramp and the dairy plant, the mysterious black profile of a zone-tailed hawk seeking refuge in the woods below the dam.

Sitting right there, hiding in plain sight a few feet from the road, the heron roost is an uncannily beautiful thing to witness, like a green branch of Eden appearing at the edge of the dystopia we made. Wondrous, wild, unexpected. And yet, not actually all that rare. A bit of research reveals reports of heron nests in intensely

urban areas all over the country, from a trashed-out island in Newark Bay to an industrial park in North Portland; along the Susquehanna in Harrisburg and the James River in Richmond; and the exurban sprawl between Dallas and Fort Worth, where the forks of the Trinity River meander north of DFW Airport. Not just great blues, but also yellow-crowned night herons, little blues, and especially cattle egrets, who almost seem to prefer the nastiest sections of America marred by our sprawl. They come back to these places most years to breed, even though they rarely receive any human welcome and more often are subjected to active campaigns of expulsion, mainly to prevent suburban homesteads and car hoods from being quickly caked with the excrement of big birds. They write paeans to them in Portland, but the Dallas suburb of Arlington hands out guides for how to heron-proof the subdivisions by pruning back the tree canopy before the birds come—and hazing them when they do, with air horns, water hoses, owl decoys, and "scare balloons" that look like the shiny mylar eyeballs of some nightmare alien predator. Even the state wildlife department is in the game, with a handy four-minute video that shows all those techniques in action, bookended by a brief natural history ode to the birds and a stern warning that, once there's an egg in the nest, the game is over, and any further interference with the reproductive lives of these living dinosaurs is a crime under federal and state law. Mixed messages that remind one how much more likely we are to see majestic wildlife on television than in real life, and why. The big wild predators that have successfully adapted to live in our domain mostly do so by figuring out how to occupy the

----

marginal parts of our cities that remain almost invisible to their human occupants.

Even with the buildings that once protected them from the street now gone, the herons that nest on our block manage to hide in plain sight, mostly unseen or ignored by human eyes. Every weekend I see folks walking right past them on their way from their cars to the bars. Even if they did look at the tree, they might not notice the birds, the way they gracefully disappear in the shadowed lattice of branches, without any true camouflage. Their persistence in such unlikely conditions is as ephemeral as it is beautiful. While some of the industrial buildings have been remade as affordable maker spaces for artists and artisans, others are further along the path to gentrification, with a machine works that once repaired aircraft motors turned into a gastropub and a Quonset hut that once housed a building contractor remade into a Munich on the Colorado biergarten owned by an actual Bavarian prince. The warehouse that long stood between the heronry and the road was torn down at the end of the pandemic to make room for a boutique hotel. Even if the rookery survives its construction, you can bet the herons won't abide the human stares from the pool deck.

As we wait in slow-motion suspense for the day our backyard pterodactyls fly off and never return, I wonder where they will go from here. When I learn about how many of the continent's herons try to survive in the urbanized world humans have made for them, it makes me wonder whether there might be a way we could better make room for them in our unceasing occupation of the available space on this planet. I thought the discovery of five nests

----

behind the muffler shop was amazing, but if you believe the bird books, in truly wild conditions a heronry can number as many as 500 nests—a statistic that makes one wonder whether the reason herons and egrets seek refuge in the city is because the expansive wetland wilderness that is their true home can no longer be found.

3

Where the Wild Things Are

Train Tracks and Coyotes

In the winter that followed my epiphany on the river, I had my first close encounter with an urban coyote. I'd had glimpses of others around town in the years before, on woodland trails along the greenbelts, but I would always see them only after they were almost gone, usually through the trees, barely long enough or close enough to register a clear picture. I went back to those places hoping for another sighting, not realizing I didn't need to drive to the edge of town to do so.

It was February 2008. The Financial Crisis had conspired with changes in my family life to find me living in a half-empty new apartment building downtown. The apartment was a high-rise on a block that had previously been occupied by old warehouses. A few years earlier, the most likely wildlife sightings would be characters stumbling out of the punk clubs and coffee shops that had since disappeared under the bulldozer blades. The blocks around our building, in the southwestern end of downtown, were still dominated by industrial land uses, most of them already shuttered in anticipation of the massive redevelopment that our building was part of but which had been suspended by the real estate crash. That also meant rents were cheap, especially in a newly constructed building they were eager to lease. I took a second-floor unit with a view of an empty lot getting by as a paid parking lot and a mothballed municipal water-treatment facility awaiting the day of its demolition, beyond which were the smokestacks of a shuttered old power plant and the high-voltage pylons of an electricity substation. Hugo was with me every other weekend from Friday to Wednesday, and we spent a lot of time exploring the entropic zones we found around us, looking for wonder between the hulking relics of twentieth-century industry and monuments to failed futures, like the concrete form of the Intel building that had been standing on a prominent corner nearby since its abandonment after the Long Boom of 1999 crashed into the bust of 2000, followed by the long dark of 9/11 and its aftermath. No wonder the coyotes were out prowling at the edge of downtown.

We were not looking for wildlife that morning. We were looking for breakfast. Hugo was in middle school but still an early riser, so at daybreak Sunday morning we decided to walk to the new all-natural-but-still-greasy café that an enterprising lady had converted from an old lunch counter a mile or so from our apartment. There were many easier and safer ways to get there. We could have gone on the street. We could have gone down along the creek that cuts through the west side of Austin, one of our old fossil-hunting spots. We chose the way you were not supposed to go: along the railroad tracks.

Railroad rights-of-way are weird zones that you can find almost anywhere in the American landscape. Our urban spaces have worked to overwrite them in favor of motor vehicles in the era since World War II; often you can see the traces of tracks from old streetcar lines or intercity routes peeking through the asphalt of a public street. Sometimes the remains persist as actual ruins.

Two blocks from our apartment, an old rail bridge still stood over the deep cut of Shoal Creek, overgrown with vegetation, its spurs probably not sturdy enough to support more than a couple of diminutive wanderers. But if you stepped into its gateway, it put you on a trajectory that connected with an active rail line, where the old Missouri Pacific route comes across the river from the direction of San Antonio and cuts west for a mile or so before turning north toward Waco, DFW, and ultimately Kansas City, St. Louis, and Chicago. The remains of the old passenger station are still there and in use, where Amtrak's transcontinental lines show up on their elusive and unreliable timetables. The stretch of right-of-way between the usually empty station and the turn north was one of those zones where time seemed a little slippery. Especially in the twilight of early Sunday morning, when the machinery of human commerce is paused.

We walked along the tracks, mostly on the line not in active use, where a few rail cars were parked as easy fodder for graffiti artists. To the north were the backsides of auto repair shops, building contractors, and a lot full of old military amphibious vehicles that once put marines on the beach but had since been converted to use as river city tourist buses. Along the south side ran a narrow band of woods that graded down toward the river. In the floodplain, all the buildings that had been erected before the dams and its flood control were gone, except for one weird old wood-frame saloon still serving. It was mostly empty fields used for youth sports on the river side of the woods, as well as a YMCA and an animal shelter. You can always hear the dogs calling out from their cages, over the sound of the passing cars, though

----

even that is quieter on a Sunday morning, the kind of morning that reminds you not all canines have adapted to survive as our servants and intermittently loved companions.

In his book *The Ecology of Stray Dogs*, Alan Beck documented the lives of free-ranging dogs in early 1970s Baltimore. Some abandoned, some escaped, some born free, some solitary, and others in packs. They proved to be crepuscular creatures, on the move at dawn and dusk, mostly traveling through alleys, scavenging trash, and sometimes hunting small rodents or ground birds. They sheltered in abandoned buildings and empty lots, and some of the packs made home in the urban woods. They got their water from puddles, gutters, and in the case of one pair, a persistently leaky air-conditioning unit. In the decades since, urban renewal and enhanced animal control have mostly kept strays off the streets. Their authentically wild cousins have moved in, traveling the same pathways through the negative space of the city, hunting more than scavenging. I had been reading about their colonization of cities like Chicago and the scientific documentation of their adaptation. Seeing one while walking to breakfast, I experienced their mystery in a way statistics and maps cannot convey.

The coyote appeared in our path not far from the station, crossing the tracks, its coat of putty and quicksilver dappled in the first light that had just come up over the office buildings behind us. In the ruins, near the old steelyard full of rusting hulks, close to the spot where a few weeks earlier we had found an empty gumball machine standing in the ballast. The animal stopped right there, framed by the aperture of the right-of-way, and returned our gazes.

It was my second close encounter with a coyote. The first was walking alone in midwinter a few years earlier, in the deep country. I was tracking along the edge of a wetland that had been drained by early farmers and then remade by duck hunters with a dam of bulldozed earth, leaving an expansive marshy plain at the base of a washboard ridge that, on a cold January afternoon, was a wide sheet of ice dusted with snow. A landscape of dull crystal mutedly sparkling against the dim browns and grays of winter woods. What first caught my eye, looking north across the ice and grass as the sun hung low in the western sky, did not look like an animal at all, but a trick of the light. A shimmer, but one that was clearly suspended above the plane of the wetland. And moving, slowly, right toward me. Like a tiny UFO, an object that seemed simultaneously material and ethereal. In my later memories, it reminded me of the spinning objects the last astronaut encounters on his journey through the infinite in Kubrick's *2001: A Space Odyssey*, or mushroom magus Terence McKenna's description of the "self-transforming machine elves" he encountered on his first DMT trip. A mesmerizing, alien apparition leaking through some slipstream rupture in our dimensional reality.

As it got closer, I could see that it was an animal. A canine. And I could clearly see how the silver in its coat produced that shimmer, giving it the ability to baffle the eye in the right light, especially in a winter landscape dusted with snow and ice. I realized it was a coyote. And it kept walking toward me, registering an indisputably determined hunger. It was like the feeling when a loose dog approaches you on the street, and you can't tell whether it is coming to beg or to attack. A primal response quickly ignited deep in my brain—the recognition that it is still possible in this world for you to be some other animal's food. It was an intense feeling.

The coyote we found behind the YMCA was not tracking us, but the feeling was similarly intense as we locked gazes for one of those brief moments of mutual threat assessment that accompanies an unexpected encounter between free canid and naked ape. Time slows when instinct activates like that and you take in every detail, registering each bit of animal motion and what it telegraphs, looking into those alien eyes of lunar yellow and trying to perceive their intention across the mostly impassable gulf of interspecies communication. The possibility of real danger jolted me awake, even as I quickly realized we were more dangerous to the animal than it was to us. A momentary window into mortality, into the wildness lurking around the edges of our carefully curated reality, and behind our deluded sense of self. I felt authentically alive.

The coyote broke the gaze and loped on its way down the alleys behind the warehouses, along the road that leads into downtown. Not to the woods, but back into the shadows of the skyscrapers where it had made its home, navigating not only through the interstitial habitat we have left for our animal neighbors, but through the even more challenging dimension of time.

As children, we learn to identify and name all the major animals, especially the ones big enough or dangerous enough to harm us or serve us and the ones cute enough to amuse us without doing either of those things. But other than the birds and the rodents and the domesticated animals we keep close by, it's rare that we see any big wild animals outside of a zoo. The reality we have created for ourselves is designed to keep them out, for the safety of us, our children, and our food stores. This is one of the reasons why, when we do have a close encounter with a wild animal, it is a source of wonder. One of those rare moments in life when, for an instant, you feel the charge of pure instinct and experience life the way your ancestors did.

I have had many encounters with urban coyotes since then. Enough to have a sense of their diversity, their behavior, even the unique characteristics of some individuals. The variations in their color, from ghostly gray to the browns and reds of a patchwork vintage coat. Big ones and small ones, some with mange, some with permanent injuries. Individuals who stare back at me, packs that trot by in single file. Every encounter makes the next one easier to find my way into. I learn to spot their tracks, read their recency, find the remains of the food they have left behind, maybe even find their dens. I get clues as to how they live in the city, and why. Even then, such encounters are rare, relative to the time I am able to spend outside trying to make serendipity happen. But when they do happen—even if only once—staring into the eyes of another predator opens up the reality of the other world that exists beyond the simultaneously illusory and impenetrable barrier between human space and wild nature. It lets me see the city through their eyes.

Foxes, Waste Lands, and Interstitial Frontiers
The first time I saw a fox on the other side of the magical gate at the end of our street was the day I showed a realtor how to get through it.

It must have been a year or two after we finished building our house, as the real estate business started to recover from the crash and the black Range Rovers and BMWs began to appear in this scruffy neighborhood. You could always tell, not just from the cars, which were meant to signal very particular status cues and professional traits. They revealed what they were up to in the way they drove, slow rolling down our little side street, sizing up every property, often backing up to take a closer look when they saw one with promise. Scanning the landscape a lot like the predators they could not see in those empty lots behind the fences.

The broker I found that day was already out of his car, a black Chevy Tahoe that was parked nearby. You could tell he was a broker. A tall, good-looking white guy with the eat-what-you-kill bearing of a hunter—the kind who sees a huge acreage between the factories and the river on Google's satellite map of the Earth, estimates the price he could sell that for and the commission he would pocket if he could persuade the owner to let him list it, and sets out to do so with all the hungry determination of a Neolithic tracker trying to take down a mammoth.

I walked up, said hello, and offered to show him around, out of curiosity about what was happening next door and a sincere but maybe naive programming for reflexive fellowship with strangers. I led him into our yard, through our back gate, onto the unfenced portion of our yard, and then into the empty lots he had his eye on. As we walked through the tall grass, he told me about the bro-kerage where he was working, looking to land a nice deal. How he had returned to Texas after a few years in Los Angeles trying

----

unsuccessfully to make it as an actor. How he had been looking on the county tax assessor's maps and seen these undeveloped lots.

As we came up the rise onto the old right-of-way, I saw the fox. It was running away from us—probably wisely so—down one of the barely visible tracks of the human path, where the tires of telecom and utility trucks had worn the grass lower. I watched that signature bushy tail as it quickly disappeared into the dense patch of cactus, scrub trees, and mustang vine grown up around the drainage culvert behind the construction supply warehouse. I did not bring the furry orange trickster to the broker's attention, and it was evident he didn't see it. In his defense, it wasn't what he was looking for.

IN TIME, OVER THE course of a decade, I would get to know the foxes who live back in that weird zone better. Sometimes they would interact with our dogs through the fence, and I learned that the vocalization of a fox is like if cats could bark. Eventually they accepted my presence with less wariness, letting me watch them from nearer distances for longer periods, sometimes watching me back but mostly interested in other things. I came to see how the unmowed grasses of the empty lot suited their hunting methods, letting them move through the landscape as stealthily as they chose, while still being able to see right over the top of the cover. From the very beginning, I became invested in their presence, in the idea that they had made a multigenerational home here just like us, and we have a duty to try to protect them from displacement. Even as I knew that was a quixotic undertaking, and a presumptive one.

- - - -

The first case I read in law school, and one of the first cases almost all American law students read, is about how foxes have no rights in the eyes of the law, and no real legal existence until they can be made into the personal property of a human being.

The legal issue in *Pierson v. Post*, decided by the New York Supreme Court in 1805, was who owns the fox: the guy who first saw it and chased after it, or the other guy who intervened and killed it first. The case is used as a lab experiment to program future lawyers to believe in the property rights we acquire by bringing the things we find in nature under our control. Rarely does any student ask about the fox as anything other than an object free for the taking, let alone suggest it could be a being that should qualify for personhood in the eyes of the law. If they do,

chances are the professor will steer them off that through ridicule, Socratic misdirection, or both. A more interesting and important question, for the teacher, is one that is almost as invisible in the written opinions of the court: Who owned the land the fox was chased onto? That it was the public commons, something that was much more plentiful in the early days of this country, is important background to the ruling. But the judges don't call it the commons. They talk about "waste, and uninhabited ground."

The word "waste" is deeply tied up with our conceptions of the land. It's a thousand-year-old word, with much older roots than that. The etymological authorities will tell you it denotes a particular kind of place—desolate, wild, deserted, often vast (a word that comes from the same root). Dig deeper and you will find all sorts of folkloric and mythological representations of the wasteland, from the pre-Christian stories of damaged monarchs and cursed countries that lurked behind the Grail legends and still echo through our culture, to the war-ravaged fields of Flanders conjured by T.S. Eliot's seminal modernist poem "The Waste Land," which riffs on those legends, and on the deep sense of loss in the land—inverting springtime into a horror from which you avert your eyes, and encoding that sense of death, destruction, and their aftermath that is always lurking in the term's evocations. But the real meaning of the term is better revealed by the more contemporary conception of the verb: "to waste," as in to waste an opportunity, or your money, or your time; the idea of squandering, of failing to realize value that could have been gained. The wasteland is the land from which human beings can extract no value to sustain their lives. It is always there in stories, if sometimes only

----

in the negative space of the narrative. It is there in the void on the other side of Genesis and, in a way, in Eden. It dominates our visions of apocalypse, from Irish myths to Australian road warrior movies. It's the desert that must be crossed and the arctic tundra. It's where Frankenstein's monster goes at the end of the story. The wasteland is conceived as remote—out *there*—and expansive. But it has other, closer manifestations, as the judges in *Pierson v. Post* revealed with their dicta about the underutilized property at the edge of town, and our own contemporary language of urban planning encodes. On a planet we have fully occupied, the wastelands—the unconquered wildernesses—become liminal ones.

Early in J.R.R. Tolkien's saga *The Lord of the Rings*, the interspecies Fellowship travels past a mysterious zone where nature seems dead. They are in boats taken from the elf queen, paddling down the great river. On the third day the tree cover disappears on the eastern banks, until they are looking at a vast, formless expanse in which there appears to not even be a blade of grass—just desolate, empty space. The area has a name—the Brown Lands—but not even Aragorn, the ranger, guide, and dispossessed heir who seems to know every corner of the continent, can explain what happened to cause such ecological ruin.

The same term, "brown lands," is sometimes used to describe those parts of the modern urban landscape that have fallen to ruin, at least in the eyes of the planners who measure the city's health based on its contribution to the wealth and growth of the human community. Empty lots, abandoned buildings, trash woods—all the parcels whose former use for industry, residence, agriculture, or other productive purposes has been abandoned, often due to changing economic or technological conditions, and have not yet been replaced by or redeveloped for some more lucrative and vibrant contemporary use. They're zones of economic entropy that become almost invisible due to their removal from the dynamic commercial flows of metropolitan life. Since the postindustrial cleanup era began in the 1970s, the more common official term used to describe such zones is "brownfields," but that has a more specific meaning, describing areas polluted with environmental toxins. Brown lands are more inclusive, encompassing all the properties where human occupation has effectively ceased for many different reasons. We all know such places, even if we tend to give them little attention. And in some cities, they can start to take over—consider the endless blocks of empty lots and gargantuan abandoned prewar factories of Detroit that symbolized the dying Rust Belt in the years around the Motor City's municipal bankruptcy. The term "brown lands" encodes how we tend to think about such places, and it's not a mere coincidence that Tolkien—a linguist turned fantasist—used the same term to describe a very different and yet remarkably similar place on the map of his imagined world. A designation that evokes not just emptiness, absence, and negativity, but also a connection to the Earth. Earth without life. In the modern urban context, often because our own agency and technological instrumentalism has extinguished what life was once there. The term is charged with that sense of loss, but it is also seeded with possibility.

The wastelands, in the emptiness we project onto them— which is not really emptiness, but rather an absence of human dominion—are also the open spaces that beckon the nomad inside us, the explorer, the wanderer. They are the uncharted realms of the European Age of Exploration, and the misty mountains and riparian valleys of the Romantic imagination envisaged by Caspar David Friedrich's 1818 painting *Wanderer above the Sea of Fog,* whose composition recurs in thousands of contemporary book covers and movie posters. They are also the *Blank Spots on the Map* of geographer Trevor Paglen's exploration of military space in the Nevada desert, and the brownfields of the postindustrial city.

That secret longing for the wasteland is deeply embedded in American culture. We just don't use that term, loaded with negative associations, to describe it—unless we are judges whose job it is to promote the privatization of property in service of productivity. We call it the frontier: the zone beyond the line of settlement, where things are still wild and free. A word that was imbued with all sorts of romantic associations over the course of the last 200 years, to turn the idea of the wasteland into a promise instead of a curse.

The idea of the frontier runs so deep in American culture that we internalize the idea that to find nature—*real* nature—you have to get in your car and drive out of town. The illusory myth underlying those pioneer-era stories of Western settlement—the idea that the American continent was an empty wilderness, when it was more like the world's most minimally tended garden—persists in the way we think of the natural areas we have preserved amid our conquest. And while we do have many insanely beautiful parks in this country, most of them are not as immaculate as we like to think. Try finding your way out of the traffic jam that fills California's most gorgeous Pacific refuges on a pretty Saturday afternoon.

- - - -

Real wilderness is still out there, mostly in places where the climate is too extreme for us to fully occupy. I have hiked examples of it in the hemispheric redoubts of Alaska and Patagonia, and in the harshest reaches of West Texas. But there's another, hidden wilderness that most of us walk or drive by every day. It hides in plain sight, in the liminal spaces of the city: behind chain-link fences, along the pathways of infrastructure, around abandoned buildings. In the brown lands and in the topographies we can never really occupy, even as we encroach as closely as we can. Urban creeks and floodplains, empty lots, rights-of-way, industrial parks, storm sewers, traffic islands, medians, brownfields, and the rare pockets of land that have somehow escaped development. Places that, maybe for just the current moment in nature's long now, are mostly undisturbed by human activity even as they are surrounded by it. They are not beautiful in the way of a national park. Many of them feel weirdly apocalyptic, places where nature is in the process of reclaiming spots we trashed, and the romance of the green wild coexists with Anthropocene ruin. You could fairly call them urban wastelands, in both the economic and aesthetic senses of the word. But such places are equally, if not more, wondrous than our greatest wilderness preserves, in part because of the way they show the promise of nature's resilience, its capacity to adapt to and recover from our damaging impact on the planet.

English ecologist Marion Shoard coined the term "edgelands" to describe the brown lands as they exist in the contemporary landscape. It's a good name, lyrically encoding the liminality and romance of such places in a way that has inspired a rich body of writing about them—including poets Paul Farley and Michael

Symmons Roberts' 2011 book *Edgelands: Journeys into England's True Wilderness*, which is where I first encountered the term. Shoard had a very specific kind of place in mind: the exurban zones where the outskirts of twenty-first-century UK cities collide with the countryside that is such a mythical part of the British identity. But the term had a memetic potency that has led to its wider adoption, especially since it gave a name to a new kind of place that had previously been mostly invisible.

The American edgelands are different than the postindustrial peripheries of London, Bristol, and Birmingham, in part because the imprint of production agriculture and big industry on our landscape is so much more recent. When you stop mowing an American lot, there's a good chance some of the plants that were there before we got here will start to come back up. If such conditions are allowed to persist long enough, the insects, birds, reptiles, and mammals of the prairies and woodlands will begin to return, as if out of the ether. They will usually share the freshly feral space with invasive species that came here with us. But even the gnarliest overgrown lots can manifest similar natural beauty as our greatest parks, if their beauty is the kind that comes with scars. In the hidden folds of our cities, they provide habitat for wildlife, space for wild plants and bugs to mature into pocket ecosystems, and zones where the human explorer can experience what it really means to be the descendant of hunters and foragers of faraway savannas.

Such places don't have a widely used name in the vernacular of American nature writing. That may be a good thing. Taxonomy can be the enemy of wonder, and sometimes of survival. To describe such places with human language, or to mark them on the map, is a sure way to endanger them. But learning to see such places in the landscape of our own hometowns enables us to visualize the very different world that could be, if we could learn to value them for their emptiness—which is not really emptiness, but the absence of us. And in our place, space for other life to express. The experience of such spots can help us better understand our own nature, learn to see the ways in which the institutions of our civilization distort that nature and make us its indentured servants, and begin to imagine a future that better balances green life with human control. More simply, we can help realize the promise of edgelands' emptiness, encouraging vacant lots to grow into pocket parks and miniature forests, as is beginning to happen in cities around the world. In a world where hope seems endangered, the kernels of its rekindling can be found in what we have long treated as its most hopeless corners.

Primrose and Pavement
Walking the streets of our neighborhood, outside the ubiquitous fences, signs of life are sometimes hard to see. It's a classic urban dead zone, where light industrial land uses have drifted slowly over the years into obsolescence and decay. Capital dreams of its transformation into a new urbanist wonderland, but those kinds of projects—requiring changes in the base zoning, environmental testing and cleanup, and favorable market conditions—move forward on a slower calendar, if they move forward at all. The absence of investment leads to an absence of care, especially in buildings that have no tenants, which quickly fall into

disrepair. Graffiti, broken or boarded up windows, cracked walls, the corrosive effects of the seasons—the signs of ruin that will eventually come to all things find their way into the edge of the twenty-first-century city, creating the kind of neighborhood that makes urban planners cringe. These derelict blocks are full of life, but it is mostly invisible—especially to tax assessors and those who only experience it through the window of a passing car.

Walking north from our place, the only new building around is a bus depot built on what had been, when we moved here, a deserted traffic island. Long-haul, low-budget travelers gather there for their connections, on rides that can take you across town, into the rural counties to the east, and south across the border into Tamaulipas or Nuevo Leon. The other buildings are all relics of the twentieth century. Some are long abandoned, like the novelty lighting factory that has been empty close to twenty years, its graffiti-covered loading dock an intermittently popular skateboarding spot. In the canopy that covers the old truck bay, the fiberglass roof liner has slowly eroded, leaving perfect little cavities for wild birds to nest in the crevasses of the corrugated ribs, and turning the zone behind the fence into an unlikely and astonishingly vibrant aviary of sparrows and chickadees. Across the street, starlings have colonized the billboards at the base of the on-ramp, nesting behind giant ads for personal injury lawyers and cash-back debit cards.

The long block west of the lighting factory was emptied more recently by industrial business owners who sold their real estate at the top of the market and moved their operations to the city's new edge. The AT&T maintenance depot was abandoned during

----

the pandemic, leaving behind an obstacle course of practice utility poles and light posts that is quickly acquiring the totemic power of some enigmatic edgeland henge. The massive truck leasing center with its acres of pavement and empty mechanics' bays now alternates between use as a television backlot, where they film cop shows and zombie apocalypses, and as an asphalt rodeo where new Amazon drivers are trained. Further on, there are oxygen tank yards and sawmills, mechanics and cabinet makers, and even a few artists' studios. If you follow the trucks carrying flammable tanks of new motor oil to market, you might see the beautiful old art deco factory now filled with used hospital equipment, including cadaver trays you can buy on eBay. And if you were to look down while standing there waiting for one of those trucks to pull out, you might notice the little patch of green space next to the driveway, dotted with a constellation of tiny pink explosions guaranteed to blow your mind.

You'd have to get down on your knees to really see the flowers. Maybe even crouch on all fours, in a way likely to cause some second looks from the passing cars. The flowers are no bigger than one of your fingernails, but if you adjust the aperture of your perception to properly take them in, you'll see little balls of fuschia petals, each of which terminates in a node of bright yellow sunshine. All somehow finding room to grow in a spot that is regularly mowed along the line between two industrial properties at the side of a major road, invisible to all but the most attentive passersby.

This little powderpuff, known to the botanists as *Mimosa microphylla*, is sometimes called "shame vine" for its unusually animated quality: leaves that visibly recoil at your touch. The name my nature nerd son taught me when he first showed me a specimen in the hidden woods near here is sensitive briar. Others call it catclaw. The fernlike leaves that jump back from your finger are so tiny they don't seem much bigger than eyelashes. That could lead you to presume they are correspondingly delicate, but the plants are remarkably hardy, with fine woody stems, a way of spreading out to soak up the sun and rain while hugging the ground and avoiding even the lowest blades of the mowers, and a capacity for sharing the space with other plants, including grasses. They are increasingly rare here, where they once flourished. Maybe not as rare as a unicorn, but almost as wondrous, in the psychedelic possibility they tantalize you with, of a hot pink springtime in the ruins of the future.

They are not alone.

A hundred years ago, this flat terrace of alluvial soil—now more than half covered in concrete, asphalt, and big buildings—was farmland. And a hundred years before that, it was prairie. Blackland prairie, a biodiverse grassland that occupied the transition zone between eastern forests and western hill country, running in a long band from Dallas to the north side of San Antonio. Ninety-nine percent of it has been eradicated since Anglo-American colonization of this region began, scraped from existence by bulldozer or plow. But you can still see the signs in the slivers of liminal space we leave unpaved and unmowed.

Every spring, wildflowers of the prairie come up out of the ground—in culverts and drainage ditches, in the strips between fences and sidewalks, at the side of the road and in the lots where the buildings have been abandoned, awaiting their inevitable

----

redevelopment. The early bloomers come as early as February, especially evening primrose, a delicate pink cup of a flower that is as hard to grow on purpose as it is persistent in edgeland conditions. The primrose is usually the first of the full-sun wildflowers to show its colors, before the big wave comes, with bluebonnets and flowers we mostly know by the sometimes unfortunate and revealing names the Anglo settlers gave them: the orange-and-red fire wheel explosions of Indian blanket; the yellow-and-brown petals and cone-like stamen of Mexican hat; the bright red bracts of Indian paintbrush; the deep maroon unfoldings of winecup; the green-to-white-to-purple cascade of horsemint, whose lemony aroma and sedative secrets earned it the alternate name bee balm; and the astonishing white-to-pink architecture of bee blossom, a native *Gaura* whose adaptation to the feral corners of industrial landscapes is evidenced by the remark in some of the field guides that its "fragrance has sometimes been compared to cat urine."

The dead zones of the city are where real life can be found. That is true in every city, not just here, and not just now. In 1855, Richard Deakin inventoried the *Flora of the Colosseum of Rome*, finding 420 plant species growing in that enduring first-century relic, some of which he speculated had been carried in the fur of African animals imported to fight in the gladiatorial games. In 1883, Richard Jefferies documented the wild nature that existed in the urban peripheries of the English metropolis in *Nature Near London*—an undertaking repeated in a more sensitive way in 1973 by Richard Mabey in his beautiful book *The Unofficial Countryside*. In his book-length essay *On the Natural History of Destruction*, German novelist W. G. Sebald documented the remarkable ways in which the aerial bombardments of German and English cities in World War II effected an unlikely rewilding of the urbanized landscape, as wild plants quickly appeared in the bombed-out quarters of the cities. Plant life, native and naturalized, is always ready to return in the spaces we let it. I've witnessed it not just here, but in places as diverse as a former gravel quarry in Boston, a recovered oil field in Los Angeles, an old farm in Iowa, and a reclaimed landfill in Seoul.

None of the native wildflowers that appear in the drainage ditches and empty lots of our neighborhood grow from seed we spread or from any effort to encourage them. They have persisted despite our efforts, intentional or reckless, to eradicate them. They manage to eke out space amid competition from acres of imported ornamental grasses and invasive weeds that dominate the unpaved spaces outside the fences. And their emergence every spring is a reminder that the erasure of the biodiverse wilderness that was here before American colonization was recent and incomplete. That the prairie could come back to life if we made room for it. Even if it has to adapt to being an interstitial prairie, an archipelago of biodiversity in the sea of our dominion.

Portals and Psychopomps

One Saturday morning at summer's end in 2015, our fifth year living in this American edgeland, I followed the same route the foxes take to travel from the city into the wild, and encountered a strange intervention in a place where signs of other people were rare.

It was down in the woods of the floodplain, along the edge of an ephemeral trail, a place where the most likely things you will see at daybreak are deer out for a browse or a coyote returning home from the prowl. Just off the trail, a damaged hackberry tree had been transformed into a magical portal. In the space where the already bent tree had split, such that one of the main branches drew the third side of a triangle between trunk and forest floor, thick lengths of mustang vine had been elegantly woven into a whirlpool of wood that defined the resulting aperture and created, at its center, a perfect circle. A work of anonymous land art, so sympathetically tuned into that place that it was as if some lost druid was at work down there behind the factories. You didn't need to walk through it to get to the other place, because by finding it, you were already there.

We went through anyway.

PORTAL FANTASIES WERE EVERYWHERE when I was a kid. Stories promising that if you looked in the right place, you could find a way out of here and into a more magical world. Through the looking glass, down the rabbit hole, out the back of the closet, to Narnia, Oz, or a habitable Mars. I started to make my own such stories, imagining portals hidden in the storm sewer, the basement of the mall, the woods behind our house. Sometimes those glimpses would recur in adolescence, when we would park our cars and walk into the wild green spaces where you could party far from adult surveillance. But when it came time to leave home for good, most of us found the more interesting world we were looking for in the cultural wonders of bigger cities. Cities where

- - - -

suburban kids who spent their teenage years in cars had to learn to walk again.

I explored a lot of great cities in my late teens and twenties, and lived in or had extended stays in several of them. Boston, New York, D.C., New Orleans, Chicago, London, Munich. I never liked underground trains and I didn't have the money to take cabs, so I mostly walked, distances and routes that my friends who had grown up in those cities thought were crazy. There was always a destination, but you had to reckon your own route with whatever primitive map was available and the wayfinding means all cities provide. That would take you through neighborhoods and blocks you would not otherwise see, let you experience more of the totality of the city and reveal all kinds of otherwise hidden curiosities

and patterns. Sometimes it would take you into blocks that felt unsafe, in an era when most American cities had much higher street crime than they do now, and you would have to alter the route and dial up your alert level. Other times it would take you into detours that were hard to return from, like the times I found myself in the subterranean levels of downtown Chicago, the weird infrastructure zones New Orleans hides in its margins, and the strange corners of the federal city of Washington that you can gain admission to with an intern's hall pass. I learned to get a little bit lost on purpose. The more lost I got, the more it could turn scary. At the same time that was when I learned the most, and had the most fun. And in time, I started to look for ways to go deeper—walking where I was not supposed to walk.

Seeking fresh ideas in bookstores and conversations, I started to discover some of the rich literature urban culture in the modern era has produced about the ways walking in the city—especially the sort of walking that is more about the walk than the destination—can generate fresh wonder and understanding. Walking as aid to thinking. Walking as meditation, a practice that lets you think with the insight of the dreaming mind and lets you see things normally hidden in plain sight. A practice that also helps you exercise your own true nature as the descendant of apes who learned to come down from the trees and walk the Earth on two feet with senses tuned forward.

The sources were a diverse melange, from medieval and Renaissance narratives of exploration to literary noirs and J. G. Ballard's 1970s novels that explored the same kinds of landscapes I had started to gravitate toward—exurban frontage roads, concrete

----

islands, and inner-city empty lots—reframing them through a science-fictional prism, with the ingenious conceit that "Earth is the alien planet." Looking for new ways to understand the semiotic traps of the city, I sampled bits of theory like Guy Debord's *Society of the Spectacle,* a manifesto about the way consumer marketing in the age of mass media insinuates itself into our heads so effectively, replacing our authentic experience of real life and social relations with transactional exchanges. That led to the discovery of Debord's earlier investigations of the way we experience the city.

"Psychogeography" is one of those theory-drunk monikers that seems designed to exclude those who don't already know what it's about. Maybe it lost something in translation from the original French, but the jargon of Debord and his fellow Situationists encoded a simple and universal idea worth wrestling with: how the physical places we go in our lives make us feel. Looking for fresh means to resist the ways the mercantile city wants to regulate your movement to serve its appetites, they tapped into the tradition of earlier French movements devoted to walking as loafing, a proto-beatnik scene that practiced window-shopping in the first urban malls of nineteenth-century Paris as a sort of cultural surfing. As practiced by the Situationists in the 1950s and '60s—as well as the English writers and artists who later picked up those ideas and took them further, all the way into the territory of time travel—psychogeography provides a tool kit for hacking how you move through the city and experience the ways in which it communicates with you. It typically involves randomizing your route, whether by literally drawing a random line on a map, picking some deeper route thought to have been erased, or tracking the way between two otherwise disconnected points. Along the way, you collect information about what you see by whatever your preferred means may be—text, image, sound, maybe even touch or taste. Then you reassemble the experience in your preferred mode of self-expression, most typically through a written journal of some sort. The resulting reassemblage of reality should yield fresh vantages, insights, revelations—deeper meaning found through the occult means of diverting yourself from the routes the city is designed to keep you on. Getting you out of your car, off the route you take to work every day, out of the consumerist simulations of pleasure and leisure the culture has duped you into to make you think you are happy. These methods may not liberate you from work, but they liberate your mind to see where you really are, to step outside of it long enough to feel authentically free.

There's a deeper, left-handed maneuver the psychogeographers explored less often, if at all: stepping off the sidewalk, going through the fence, to see how the city also hides the natural world it works so hard to erase. If you can find your way there, you can gain more than a window into a world beyond work. You can find a way free from the prison of the self, and feel your place as part of an interconnected network of life. Or at least of the wonder that exists beyond human self-absorption. And you don't need any French theory to get there. You can just follow your natural human instincts.

Sous les pavés, la plage. Beneath the pavement, the beach. That slogan was spray-painted on walls by French student protestors of 1968, weaned on Situationist ideas, who barricaded the streets in their moment of believing they might remake the world into one

- - - -

they would actually want to live in. When they ripped out the paving stones to throw at the police, they found sand, an observation they riffed into a metaphor about the other realities the city hides beneath its surfaces and signs. It encodes a powerful truth. But what's really beneath the pavement and behind the fence is not the beach, but the grassland, and the forest. And it's not so much beneath the pavement as when you step off it. The city contains green frontiers that are very real, but the line that defines them is often a "No trespassing" sign.

The psychogeographers understood a truth we rarely acknowledge: that the city is a machine designed to make you believe you are free, when its real aim is to control you. We are trained to think we can walk out the door or get in the car and go wherever we want, when in fact the urbanized space we inhabit is a labyrinth of enclosure that regulates our movement through it with almost infinite layers of access control. We stick to the sidewalks with occasional transgressions onto desire paths, stay in our traffic lanes while daydreaming of off-road adventures, experience nature mostly through simulations and screens. We see doorways and windows everywhere, but only a small number are actually open to us. We think we are autonomous agents who have chosen our paths in life, as we circulate through the city in much the way blood cells move through the body, each performing assigned tasks that keep the machine of the collective running. The landscapes we move through are manufactured ones, shaped by us, even when they are green. Maybe because the city knows that if we encountered an authentically wild and natural space, we might try to disappear into it.

Car Dealers and Animal Trackers

One of the weird ways that our dreams of the frontier persist in the collective American imagination is through the visions automotive manufacturers try to seduce us with: advertisements that show the latest model of rugged four-wheeler or sexy sedan cruising through some otherwise depopulated landscape. The car will often be named after some place or terrain to be found in that landscape—Yukon, Denali, Silverado, Tundra, Tacoma, Malibu—in the same way our military combat helicopters are named after the Indigenous peoples the US government and white settlers forcibly evicted from those lands when the air cavalry units were still horse brigades: Blackhawk, Apache, Chinook, Cheyenne, Lakota. That our cars are one of the main engines of the destruction of that wilderness is an irony we rarely note, because the idea of procuring the means of autonomous transportation into the untamed frontier aligns so perfectly with the people we have been raised to be, unconsciously echoing the Americans who came before us. Every household ready to pack up their stuff and hit the overland trail. As a young dad looking for ways to make parenting a different kind of adventure, I went all in on that game, a sucker for cars that came with built-in compasses and emergency weather radios, for maps to places we would never really go, for outdoors magazines that were really just gear catalogs selling Walter Mitty fantasy. I didn't have a clear idea of where I really wanted to go, but it was somewhere on the other side of that screen.

It must have been a year or so after 9/11 that a fish tank on the desk of a Subaru salesman opened a different sort of portal for me, into the hidden world of urban wildlife. Buying a car is something most of us hate to do, not only because of the certainty that those guys are ripping you off, but also because we know deep down how against nature that activity is—bad for us and bad for the planet. Imagine how good it would feel to take a check for the car you are trading in and then enjoy the long walk home. That I was buying what was branded as the car of planet-conscious outdoor adventurers, named after my astro-nerd inner child's favorite star cluster, the Pleiades, only mitigated the squirm. But as I waited there on a Saturday afternoon, the aquarium pulled me in.

It was just a little fish tank, but somehow more than that. An entire ecosystem in a watery glass box, with a diversity of fresh-water marine life that looked local rather than exotic. You could believe that it required no fish food to be shaken out of a plastic

can over the surface of the water, no cleaning of the accumulated pond scum, no netting of the dead fish I remembered from our own childhood efforts at such projects. As I waited for my price quote, I found myself staring into the tiny marine scene the way Superman can sometimes be found looking at the bottled remnant of his home planet he keeps in the Fortress of Solitude, with unmistakable melancholy and a bit of survivor's guilt. You could sense what the aquarium was—a little desktop recreation of the biodiverse pockets of wonder that once could be found scattered all over the landscape of Central Texas, but now were incredibly rare, or at least hard to find. An alluring thing to find in a car dealership across from the dying mall, just off the frontage road of the jammed-up interstate highway that connects Mexico to Canada. It was a living relic, like the inlaid box of seashells and dried seahorse that my grandmother kept on her dresser as all she had left of her youth in Barcelona.

The salesman's name, serendipitously, was Chance. And when I remarked on his amazing aquarium, he explained that he had made it entirely of fish, plants, bugs and even water found in local environments. When he could see how much this convinced me he was some kind of a magician, he let me in on a secret.

"I'm really a tracker," he said. Which was better than saying he was a wizard. At least when speaking to a guy who had been fascinated since boyhood by the idea of being able to see signs in the land, entranced by tales of frontier scouts and Dúnedain rangers.

When I asked him to elaborate, he explained that he was a student of Tom Brown Jr. I may have been the first customer in his nook who knew of Brown, the Castaneda of the Pine

----

Barrens. Brown wrote a series of books about the secrets of the contemporary American wilderness, and how they were taught to him growing up in the feral edges of New Jersey by a wise Apache elder—one of those archetypes whose real-world existence you cannot help but doubt even as the truths he imparts are indisputable. At the time I had not read Brown's best-selling first book, *The Tracker*, but I had several of his paperback guides to urban wildlife. Chance told me he had gone to Brown's school to learn the ways of the tracker, hiding in a nature blind of his own making, exploring barefoot, mastering the narrative art of reading the land. He told me how Brown is not like you would imagine—among other things, he smoked a lot of cigarettes—but an even more amazing teacher than you would believe. Chance explained that he and a friend who had also studied with Brown were working on an inventory of wildlife along the urban edges of the Balcones Escarpment, especially interested in sandy landscapes where the tracks are well-preserved. I asked him if he had any interest in teaching some of his techniques to our Cub Scout den. He liked the idea, especially if he could bring his own kids.

He met up with our little troop of third graders on a cool Saturday morning. The spot he told us to meet him at was an unlikely one: the right-of-way under the north-south highway that runs down the west side of Central Austin, just south of the river. Such an implausible spot for a nature hike that we drove by it a couple of times before we realized we had arrived. Chance was already there, with his younger son and even younger daughter. It was raining when we pulled up;

----

when I asked Chance, whose long, curly hair was already wet, if he needed a raincoat, he pointed to his plaid overshirt and said, "Wool is better."

As we stood there under the overpass, listening to the cars rumble and whine, Chance explained to the kids what the place was. How such a seemingly blighted spot as the empty strip of land underneath the expressway bridge was in fact teeming with life. The area around us was an overgrown right-of-way, thick with a mix of native and invasive grasses. Bringing us down into the grass, he showed how that mat of tangled green growth harbored a secret city of its own, tunneled through with the labyrinthine passageways of voles, tiny mammals of the field. He showed the kids how to follow the tunnels with their arms. Then he told how he had gotten good enough, with patient practice, to be able to track and catch a vole by hand.

He led us down past the right-of-way into a small municipal preserve maintained around the dry channel of a creek that occasionally would carry stormwater into the river. The sort of hidden urban park, he warned the dads, where you stand a good chance of being propositioned by strangers for a different kind of encounter in the woods if you come down alone on a normal day. Chance taught the kids a few basic secrets and tricks that provided them the fundamentals of a lifetime of tracking on their own. The understanding that most of the animals in the urban forest (or any forest) will see or hear you ten seconds or so before you would have a chance of seeing them—knowledge that, once you have it, lets you devise strategies to outwit them. Like the basic rule Chance imparted for how to see more clearly in the woods, by always scanning an imaginary horizon line around you as you move through the landscape, because that is the distance at which most animals will let you see them. Beyond the noise of the nearby traffic, he showed the kids how to listen to the sound of the birds singing about them, signaling their presence to others. He taught us how to walk like a tracker, avoiding the locomotive flashing of your human hands as you walk, which he said is one of the main signs animals use as their signal to scatter. Then he showed the kids how to find and read animal tracks in the dust, dirt, and mud. The toe prints of the deer and the way their depth, width, and distance apart revealed the size of the animal and what it was doing. The little hands of the raccoon and how easy they were to follow out of the creek bed. The pads of the coyote and how you could tell them apart from the pads of a dog.

I don't know how well any of the kids remember those basic lessons, but they stuck with me and helped me open up a world I had long been looking for. They taught more than was evident at first, helping me see the myriad other ways you can read the stories the world around you tells. The way of the tracker requires no special training. It just requires open, patient, and curious attention to the signs in the land, big and small, from the majesty of big birds soaring in the sky above you to the sideshow of tiny metamorphs you can find when you look under a leaf. Time helps, and the wisdom of others and knowledge recorded in books are accelerants, but all you really need is a subtle adjustment in the way you let your senses experience the world around you. Combined with the urban hacking techniques of the psychogeographers, thinking like a tracker helped me see the way the city not only secrets nature within it, but is, in fact, nature itself. The real portal you need to step through, the fence you need to jump, is one in your head.

Edgelands, Involuntary Parks, and Uninsurable Zones
Our reflexive conception of the city as human habitat and the country as the place where we go to find nature is no longer true, if it ever was. The rural landscape is not as "wild" as we would like to think, especially in the vast expanses of ecological exhaustion trampled by decades of livestock production and corporate agriculture. The very idea of "wildness," of a boundary between humanity and the natural world, is a cultural construction that came over with European settlers, providing the philosophical framework for the destruction of the American wilderness and the dispossession of the Indigenous communities who had maintained a relationship with their environment devoid of any such separation. Four hundred years after the first chartered colony in what became New England, the possibility of a change in that fundamental thinking is becoming apparent in the way we live. While there are still large areas of the continental United States that remain sparsely populated with humans, our continued expansion across the land has obliterated the boundary between urban space and wild space, bringing more city into the wild and more wild into the city. The evidence is there in the restoration of tree cover: 250 million acres of forest were cleared over the first 250 years of European settlement of the Eastern United States, but by the 1950s, depending on the region, more than two-thirds of the landscape was reforested. In the subsequent decades, states in the Northeast and Midwest added more than 11 million acres of

woodland. And there's a good chance you live in that woodland—or at least a short walk from it. The boundary between human space and wild space is permeable—and mostly illusory—on a planet of sprawl. But taxonomies can be useful as a way of learning to see that, by first defining the ways in which the wilderness of edges manifests most distinctly.

One-third of Americans make their homes in an area that is half covered with wild foliage, or within a short walk from an area that is more than 75 percent wild foliage. We live in a weird realm where forest and prairie intermix with the urbanized world. Our continental habitat expresses an ecological paradox—it has been almost completely reshaped by our dominion, but our colonization is so recent that the native wildness was never fully extinguished, and pops back up whenever and wherever we let it. This urbanized wilderness is all around us, but we rarely acknowledge it, so steeped are we in the mythology of our more epic wild spaces.

The American edgelands are mostly unobserved by everyone from nature writers to urban planners, who persistently reinforce the illusion that nature exists in officially designated parklands. Pockets of wild urban space don't fit easily into the registries by which our societies are ordered. Most of the lands that make up these zones are of limited economic value, like the "waste lands" of the early republic, if they even exist as separate parcels of private property. The trees may be counted in municipal censuses and assigned official numbers, but they do not have a price. The wild creatures who inhabit such spaces have almost no existence in the eyes of the state, unless they are blocking traffic or construction. These zones have acquired an official name in recent decades, the Wildland-Urban Interface, but the term is rarely used outside of the invisible literature of fire prevention. The "WUI" (usually pronounced "woo-ee") is where the wildfires working to make the western states uninsurable occur. That association with property damage may be why the acronym carries a clinical taint of Orwellian negativity—so successfully avoiding any evocation of the uncanny wonder wild urban places produce that you might reasonably suspect it was designed to name them as an essential predicate to their eradication.

The pockets of wild space that exist within the city do so because they are largely unseen and unnamed. They are not the official natural areas maintained by the parks and recreation department, though sometimes they contribute—especially the spaces set aside as wildlife preserves. The interstitial wilderness that exists in every city is unmarked. It is not formally designated as wild space or described as such on any sign or map, and it is often actively hidden by enclosure and cartological obfuscation. It is mostly comprised of zones set aside for some other kind of land use that serves human need but excludes active human presence: places designed, by and large, to keep people out. Or just not designed to invite people in. Places you need to learn to see, even if your aim is not to enter them, but just to appreciate their existence.

The path of the watershed is the most ubiquitous and reliable natural space to find in any city. Creeks and rivers are the one natural element we are generally unable to erase through our sprawl, though we may impoverish their ecological richness, treating them as sewers as we have for most of modern history. We sometimes pave our creeks in our efforts to control them, like the one that runs through my neighborhood and is equally enjoyed by egrets and graffiti taggers. We sometimes even pave entire rivers, as in Los Angeles, or bury them under the pavement, as in Hartford. But we can't really control water, no matter how hard we try, and we can't prevent other species of planetary life from gravitating toward sources of water. Creeks and river channels are the most reliable places to find wild vegetation in the city—whether weedy brush or more substantial tree cover—and to find wild animals, some of whom may live in the habitat the water provides, and others who may just go there to drink and wash, or to hunt. Ponds, lakes, and wetlands have a harder time surviving in the city, as the absence of flow and flood makes them easier to turn into buildable land. The idea that draining the swamp is progress has a long history, from Charles II's seventeenth-century redevelopment of the Great Fens to the march of production agriculture and urban expansion across the American continent.

Mirroring the watershed are networks of urban space designed to carry different kinds of flow: the rights-of-way we set aside for the varieties of movement and interchange that sustain urban life. These include roadways and railways, which, unless they are very old, usually preserve some wide zone on either side of the path they define. They also include the rights-of-way set aside for the movement of things other than people and cargo, such as electrical power, petrochemicals, and telecommunications. Many of our rights-of-way follow older and often more natural pathways. Broadway in Manhattan was once the Wickquasgeck trail that connected the Indigenous settlements of the island. Highways commonly follow the routes of old pioneer trails that were formerly trails of Indigenous Peoples and often have deeper origins as animal trails, like the old highway between Detroit and Chicago that was once the migratory trackway of mastodons. The main trunks most Internet traffic in the United States travels on are cables buried along old rail lines, which themselves follow some of the most ancient routeways cut into the landscape of the continent by eons of geological development and wild nature's adaptation to it. Rights-of-way are sometimes public, sometimes private, but almost never designed as places for you to walk. They are not designed for animals either, as evidenced by the abundant roadkill our roads produce, providing the main experience most of us have of wild animals in the city. But roadkill also reveals how much wildness is out there, finding its way through the world we've made. And in springtime, the green spaces along the edges of the road reveal how many wild and native plants are still there in the seedbed, ready to retake the landscape when we and our mowers abandon it. The corridors of land we set aside for our own transportation, energy, utility, and communications networks inadvertently provide networks also used by wildlife to circulate through urban space.

The city also harbors huge swaths of land zoned off from pedestrian and other public access. These zones of enclosure are often behind tall fences or even manned checkpoints that limit access for safety and security. These include industrial facilities, government complexes (including the gigantic chunks of the American landscape set aside for exclusively military use), and corporate and commercial zones. Wild plants and animals do not observe most of the boundaries we create, and often thrive in these spaces

----

from which the city excludes its human inhabitants. This is especially true at the margins of such places, in liminal zones where access is often less intensely policed. Walk around any such fence, especially in its farthest corner, and you stand a good chance of finding a gap made or at least exploited by animals, some of whom may have made homes inside the fence, where their predators are less likely to roam.

Liminal zones are often the richest, and the easiest to find wherever you are—the wilderness of edges made from the untended borders between different land uses. Zones where trees and tall plants are allowed to grow in areas otherwise cleared for human use. Walk along such edges and look for animal trails on the ground, and you will be surprised how many mammals can turn just a few feet of cover into a safe and secure burrow. Urban foxes seem particularly adept at exploiting such fringe habitat, perhaps because of their small size and their adaptation to hunting small rodents that thrive in the trash we leave outside.

Sometimes the liminal spaces are defined not only by space, but by time. The places we call "empty lots" are usually temporary, in the middle of the transition from one land use to another. Often land that was once used for agriculture, resource extraction, or industry awaiting its redevelopment. Places momentarily empty of human presence but full of the natural activity that quickly reasserts itself in our absence. The places we have stopped paying attention to are the ones where wild nature most quickly thrives. If the plants are allowed to grow without mowing, as is often the case when the economics don't justify the cost of maintenance, the owner doesn't care, or there isn't even a true owner, the change can be rapid and dramatic, as the negative space of the city turns into a successional ecosystem.

Sometimes human land use is so abusive that it renders the land unusable. Lands we have polluted, made too dangerous to inhabit, or too hazardous to build on. Science fiction writer Bruce Sterling, who has been pioneering foresight about our climate future since the 1990s, dubbed such places "involuntary parks": previously inhabited areas that have "lost their value for technological instrumentalism." You already know famous examples of such places, like the radiated zone around Chernobyl, the Superfund sites of industrial America, and the currently and formerly militarized borders between and sometimes within nations, like the Iron Curtain that divided Europe, the fortified portions of Israel, the US-Mexico border. You may be less familiar with a more emergent category of involuntary park—the zones that have become uninsurable, mostly due to climate change. Consider the coast of Florida, inhabited by more than 20 million people—close to 10 percent of the US population—where increasingly frequent and damaging weather events have driven most of the major property and casualty insurers to stop underwriting coverage. The private and public insurance funds that have allowed building to continue are almost all at the brink of insolvency. Where property can no longer be insured, new development and real estate transactions cannot proceed, at least not if they require traditional mortgage financing. In these expanding swaths of our increasingly uninsurable world, nature will find all sorts of ways to reclaim the space it has liberated through its reactions to the damage we have caused.

- - - -

That nature has begun to figure out how to break the complex economic systems that underlie our real-property regime may be the most promising sign of change to come. Hopefully it's not too late.

Rain Lilies and Catclaws

When it rains, which doesn't happen here as often as it used to, the rain lilies appear at the base of the on-ramp. Not immediately, but almost. I often see them coming up from the patch of median where the berm flattens out next to the roadway, right past the pedestrian walkway that none of those cars zooming off the over- pass pay any attention to, even if you are pushing a stroller.

Often, a couple mornings after a good rain, the sun will greet the blue-green shoots coming up out of that sandy, bulldozed dirt. Within a few days, they will open up their creamy white trumpets overnight, beautiful fragrant flowers that last a couple more days before they turn to pink, wither, darken, and eventually disappear, as transitory as the evening star after which pioneers named the plant. Having watched them terraform that area when they trans- formed the old highway into a wide, high-speed tollway, I know how new that dirt is. When the rain lilies first appeared there, I wondered where they came from—whether their seeds were already in the soil, waiting to be turned close enough to the water and the sun, or whether they found their way to that spot once the earthmovers stopped moving. But then I started to notice how ubiquitous the rain lilies are, all over town, in traffic islands and empty lots and dirty medians, reminders of the ways in which the flora and fauna natively adapted to this place—to any place—are always there, even if we don't notice them, because we are never taught to and because they are pushed so far to the edges of our perception. Thousands of tiny miracles hiding in plain sight that give us windows into what the world we live in once was, and could be again, if in a different and compromised way. When I learned how many seeds each one of those flowers produces, I realized that, as common as they are, they are not as common as they should be, holding out despite our near-obliteration of the habitat in which they evolved. And when I learned that they only respond to actual rain, not water from a sprinkler or hose, I had to wonder: How do they know?

The capacity of the indigenous life we have displaced to endure the brutality of our way of occupying this land often seems uncertain. The native wildflowers that come up at the side of the road, the bushy bluestem grass that grows on the riverine island of trash at the end of our block, and the inland sea oats that flourish on the bulldozed grade behind the dairy plant are ephemeral resurrections—most seasons it seems like, as wondrous as their existence in this blighted landscape is, they are mostly losing. There are occasional windows, though, where other possibilities emerge. Like when the canopy of the urban forest becomes complete enough that the aggressively invasive johnsongrass can no longer get the sun it needs to choke other life from the soil.

In the summer of 2023, as July turned to August, the temperature blew past 100° Fahrenheit for more consecutive days than had ever been recorded, a deep drought settled in, and the landscape of the industrial lots around us gave truth to the idea of the brown lands. The weather was so relentless that even the ornamentals and invasives that dominate the slivers of open land couldn't hack it. As I walked across the field in front of the abandoned lighting factory one Saturday morning, I saw just how dead it was as the browned-out Bermuda grass crunched under my feet. And then I noticed something new: The sprawling briar of the catclaw had begun to take over the field, expanding from the narrow strip it had held out on at the edge of an industrial driveway. You could see its deep-green fronds in sharp relief against the burn. The pink of the flowers was not as bright, suggesting the absence of water, but many were still there. Many others had turned to seed—some already spread, others still attached in their hairy little pods. I took some, helped them spread some more, and wondered what

weird permutations of mutant prairie would emerge if we just let it all go.

When I first started learning how to experience wild nature's persistence in the margins of the city, I felt an almost childlike joy at the beauty of it. Each encounter with a wild creature and each discovery of a plant I had never really noticed produced an intense emotional kick, a feeling that everything is right in the world, or could be with a little help. That sense of wonder never goes away, but over time it becomes tempered with realism. I've learned to see more clearly how outmatched the wild things are by our 10,000-year experiment in terraforming the Earth into a machine to feed us, like invading aliens from some sci-fi B-movie. The wildflowers in the right-of-way and the coyotes in the alley remind us that wild nature is always ready to come back, to adapt to the opportunities we give it, to reclaim the territory we destroy. But they also remind us how much biodiversity we have erased from the world.

That recognition tempers the joy of each encounter with sadness—a recognition of the accumulated loss the rareness of such encounters evidences, and an anticipatory grief at what's to come, as the bill for the things we have taken from the Earth comes due.

In that balanced understanding comes the path to redemption: a compromised redemption that starts with acknowledging the failures of our stewardship, and recognizing that the prairies and forests humans have killed can never really come back. Edgeland nature shows us that a healthier, ecologically balanced future is still possible, but it will be one that grows from the scars we have left, and blurs taxonomic boundaries in ways we cannot yet imagine.

- - - -

The path to emancipation—nature's and our own—starts in our heads, by breaking down the boundaries between ourselves and the world.

4

Transecologies

Chupacabras and Coywolves

At first light, strange creatures are on the move in the margins of the city. Sometimes, if you see them, you could be forgiven for thinking they are ghosts, even though they may be nothing more unusual than dogs. These creatures move through liminal spaces. Slivers of territory that provide some measure of wild cover, yet are so tenuous as to be almost invisible. Pockets of woodland or wild foliage that, if cleared, would seem small, even tiny. Too small to provide a secret passageway. And yet sometimes I see a creature sneaking through them, usually too fast for me to see them clearly.

There's one such space on the other side of an unmarked gate at the end of our dead-end street, down a path where the road used to continue but which is now mainly used by the foxes who come and go under the gate. When we see the foxes running through the empty lot, that's usually where they disappear, where they hide their dens.

It's not really a vortex. It's a weird, wild ravine that has grown up around a drainage culvert behind the construction supply ware-house, where the old roadway intersects with ten acres of empty field behind the milk factory and the woods of the floodplain below. They mined gravel there fifty years ago, but you wouldn't know that walking it today. The fences have been up since the '80s, and the land behind the industrial park has been allowed to go back to forest. Up top, an impassable bramble of vegetation has developed where the road used to punch through, with a mix of tall grass, spiny trees, prickly pear, invasive cane, vines that grab your ankles, and other vines that grab your arms, all intertwined. You can see the paths through it made by the creatures of the field, at the same time as you can see why they hide back in there. As a human, usually the only way through is to get down and crawl on all fours.

I have done just that, an undertaking that some might say is unbecoming of a respectable business lawyer, especially in the sweaty heat of a Texas summer day. I wonder if the guys who move the loads from the outdoor shelves to the flatbeds, and sometimes look up to see a fox or a deer moving through, have ever spotted

me crawling through the periphery of their reality like some kind of man-vole.

Sometimes the deer bed down nearby, on a brushy plateau the size of a living room that once was a dirt road trucks would follow down to the river. One morning we found a baby fawn nestled there in a wild bassinet of trampled grass, so young it likely could not even stand on its own, its mother probably watching nearby.

Cottonwoods thrive in the ravines behind the industrial park, where the drainage pipes empty the effluent of the city. They are prodigious trees, each producing as many as 40 million seeds and growing as much as fifteen feet a year. The drainpipes' delivery of occasional bursts of huge amounts of water lets them rise above the valley to the height of the buildings above, 100 feet or more, where their twin-toned leaves can dapple the light and quiet the world with even the mildest breeze. Mustang vine thrives there, too, finding its way up to the high branches, growing thick and woody—sometimes thicker than your arm—and providing a tangle in the understory that amps up the Gothic feeling of the interstitial forest, a tangle that produces bitter fruit at summer's end. And if you look down into the ditch the water cuts, you will find relics: fragments of glass bottles stenciled with the logos of extinct brands of soda pop, huge truck tires slowly getting sucked back into the Earth, the remains of a cathode-ray television embedded in the rocky nook of the ephemeral waterfall.

As if through some weird magic of its residual ability to generate pictures from the ether, that TV, which also happens to be nestled at the best spot to cross the creek, marks a vantage from which I often observe the movement of other life through that space. Standing there, I can see through the thicket to the edge of the tall grass plain behind the dairy plant, along which wildlife often travels. But sometimes wildness is as ambiguous and shape-shifting as the land that hosts it.

Walking regularly in woods like that, scanning the imaginary horizon line like the mystical Subaru salesman recommended, I've experienced how our senses are highly evolved to do things we rarely do. To sense animal motion around us, mostly with our eyes and ears, though sometimes our nose also helps. To be ever alert to predatory opportunity, and to the possibility that we could be prey. A physiology designed to let us see fast-moving, thickly muscled herbivores at a distance where we can kill them with a spear, arrow, or gun and turn their muscles into meat, stealing their fur to keep our mostly hairless bodies warm. And to let us evade the stealthy stalk of the big cats who were the nemeses of our ancestors in the warm savannas of Africa, leopards who could climb trees and carry a hominid back to their lair. Those senses are atrophied by the comforts of urban life, of life sustained by agriculture and markets, but they can be exercised—or at least experienced—by leaving the safety of the pavement and stepping into the zone the feral cats slink into when the sun goes down.

I had a dream once about a mountain lion crossing the U-turn lane where the north-south highway passes the dying mall. When I mentioned it to Chance, he said there probably is one there that no one has seen, hiding in the creek bed. I have had close encounters with mountain lions in the Rocky Mountain winter and with puma in the Patagonian foothills, but the wild cats I have seen in the urban woods have been other varieties, usually passing

through while I am asleep. Burly bobcats sometimes prowl con-
fidently through here, moving more like lone wolves. And in the
deep of the night the ringtail cats come out—not cats at all, but
procyonids, diminutive relatives of raccoons that also have feline
and vulpine characteristics. The first time I saw one of those
climbing over a fence, I learned what a marvelous experience it is
to see a thing that is alive and within the reach of your senses and
not know what it is. All the more marvelous when you reckon with
how it has adapted to the city.

The taxonomy of real life is not as ordered as the books we
are raised on would have us believe. Especially when the creatures move through the margins of your perception, half-hidden,
glimpsed just as they move out of the frame, in and out of shadow,
a flash of color in motion that may leave a lingering wild odor or
tracks in the dirt.

Among the most spectral creatures I have seen move through
that space are wild dogs, animals one might consider very ordinary until you experience the way they have learned to turn
almost invisible. Sometimes the feral dogs will pack up—not long
after we built our house, an aggressive trio tried to get under our
front gate as I went to get the newspapers, rampaging through
the quiet of a Sunday morning, expressing a capacity for sense-
less violence they must have learned from us. But more often dogs
without human homes seem to be solitary, and among the most
wary and elusive varieties of urban wildlife. Maybe because they
come from our domain, are adapted to live in it as our servants,
and therefore know how to move through it instinctively, but also
know how dangerous it is. It gives them special powers. And when

you encounter them, they help you see how illusory our concept of the boundary of wildness is. Even of the boundaries between species.

Back in those woods behind the dairy factory, I met what may have been a coywolf. My dad used to tell me about the hybrid of coyote and wolf people sometimes claimed to have seen in the rewilded corner of southern Iowa that he and my mom retired to, a creature whose romance came in part from the likelihood that it was a modern myth, a species of urban legend. I went on a Bigfoot search once, partly for laughs and partly for what the family member who recruited me for the adventure called "back-packing with benefits"; it was quickly apparent that the desire to believe in such a creature had more to do with other things missing from the lives of its searchers than any credible evidence that it was real. And maybe the way the woods provide more mystery than I expected, especially when I learned how to open myself up to experiencing it. The way they present us with encounters that do not fit into the taxonomy we've been taught. You can see a bird when it is young—a bald eagle, a heron, a summer tana-ger, the proverbial ugly duckling—and learn it looks nothing like the field guide model it will mature into. You can find animals that have transgressed the interspecies boundaries we impose on them. Especially with members of the genus *Canis*, all of which have seventy-eight chromosomes and the potential to interbreed.

Almost a decade after I went on the Bigfoot watch, I had a close encounter with a chupacabra. It was May 2015, on the Sunday night before Memorial Day. We were in Marfa, Texas, where we had taken our visiting friends, Henry Wessells and Mary Jo Duffy,

----

native Philadelphians who lived in New Jersey and worked in New York. After dinner on our last night, we headed east on Highway 90 to check out the Marfa Lights. It was around 9 p.m. The radio was tuned to the local public radio station, which was playing its "Space Music" show—ambient instrumentals that suited the mood. About two-thirds into the nine-mile drive, a ghostly creature crossed our path, walking right across the road, rather slowly. Slow enough that we got a long look as it passed through the beams of our headlights. Four-legged, definitely not a deer, a figure of ethereal white. Bigger than a dog, different than a coyote—even though that's probably what it was. They say most chupacabra sightings are really just coyotes with mange. We all saw it, were similarly baffled, and agreed that it was both something that had a rational explanation that the brevity and circumstances of our sighting would not let us figure out, and that we also had just experienced an encounter that had an authentically paranormal frisson. It was definitely a chupacabra, we understood, as we also understood that a chupacabra is simply a creature you encounter that does not follow the taxonomic indicators of its species, looking so strange, in the moment you see it, as to provide you an experience of the alien and a welcome excuse to make up your own legend.

More remarkable is when you see a wild animal in conditions where its appearance is very clear—clear enough you can get a good photo of it with no more than the phone in your pocket—but you still can't tell for certain what species it is. Not because it is a juvenile in that awkward phase of development, but because it has matured into some more majestic variant.

It was early morning when I saw this particular specter—around 7:45 on a Wednesday, well into the first hour of light. I was coming down the grade where the plain behind the industrial park descends into the forest along the river, just before the overpass bridge, a hill thick with retama, cane, and cactus. The canid was coming down the same hill as well, but in a more wooded section just east of us. Walking slowly, almost lackadaisically, the way urban coyotes I have encountered sometimes seem in the early morning, perhaps engorged with whatever they killed in the night or just exhausted from the hunt. It stepped into the open, where an old truck road cuts through the woods. And then it stopped and looked at us—me and our two dogs, who were likely barking their brains out, as dogs tend to do in such situations, especially when leashed. But in my memory I hear no barks, because I was so captivated by the inner stillness of the animal, who seemed entirely unimpressed by our presence. It had the characteristic silver, gray, and brown coloring of the coyote, the pointy ears cupped forward, and that trot. But it was burlier than any coyote I had seen, bigger and fuller at the shoulders. And more confident, the confidence that seems like it comes from strength. It was the size of the wolves I had seen in Alaska. It stopped to look back at us, first as it crossed the well-trod path, and then again after it had sauntered on into the bamboo that grows thick above the secret wetland. As we stared at each other, it presented a different rostrum than a coyote, who returns your attention with wily eyes over a pointy snout. This creature had a blockier face, with a more squared-off nose, the fur around and under its eyes and mouth a wizardly white. The energy it projected was aloof and unintimidated. When it finally broke my gaze and moved on, we followed it along the edge of the swamp, trying to track it, but it was as disappeared as the rusted-out muscle car that had once sat there, coming and going with the floodwaters.

There was once a species of wolf native to Texas. The red wolf (*Canis rufus*) is an animal whose precise taxonomic status has never really settled, as scientists debate whether it is a subspecies of the gray wolf or a well-established coywolf. Or was—it is endangered now, and considered by zoological authorities to be extinct in the wild. Most states have long allowed wild canines to be killed without limit year-round, and aggressive campaigns of extermination targeting these threats to the money locked up in the bodies of livestock—followed by the destruction of biodiverse wild habitat for farms, pastures, and cities—removed the red wolf from our reality. Or so it was thought until recently, when a community of coywolves was discovered living in the edgelands of Galveston, lurking around run-down apartment buildings near the beachfront dunes, one-third of their genetic material that of the red wolf. A survival strategy that has worked, even if it shows how marginal and tenuous their existence is. The wild things are still there in the edges of the city but they defy our rules of who they are, holding out in tiny bands of survivors whose way of living tells the story of how colonization works from a different vantage than we often witness.

The animal I saw that Wednesday morning in the woods behind the dairy factory could have been a red wolf. If you look at the grainy photos I took on my phone and compare them to the side-by-sides one can find that show the differences between red

----

wolves and coyotes, the possibility seems very strong. It might have been a hybrid, more wolf than coyote. Or it might have been just another dog gone wild—I seem to see one every few months down in those woods, sometimes as a specter through the trees, occasionally as a distant figure crossing the river. I don't know exactly what it was. And while I wish I could see it again, it is probably a good thing that I do not. Sometimes our very gaze has a way of banishing the wildness from our world.

Because capital does not perceive wild animals, it does not count them. When I took the bar exam, one of the things we were tested on was our knowledge of all the different ways a lender can perfect a security interest in a domesticated animal, a crop, or a piece of land. Wild animals were outside the ambit of the law that mattered for the operation of the society in which we live, even though the first case we read was about how a wild fox can become the property of a man. There are people whose jobs it is to count wildlife—biologists, ecologists, game wardens, park rangers, managers of preserves—but they are outnumbered, and most of what they do is guesswork based on the fragments the natural world allows even the most experienced scientists and trackers to see. We don't really know what's out there. We just know that it is disappearing rapidly in the never-ending onslaught of our consumption, making every encounter with the free-roaming predators that have persisted all the more remarkable.

When you see a feral dog moving across the abandoned cityscape at dawn, sneaking through the window of time when no one is likely to see it—a creature that is both very ordinary and yet magical, in the way it has transformed itself into an apparition, a cryptid—you can understand, in that unexpected mix of resilience and fragility, cunning and failure, strength and coolness, the tenuous boundary and lasting connection between us and our own wild nature, even as it seems ever more impassable to cross.

Waxwings and Wax Seals

I was studying the legal history of early medieval England when I first saw the birds. A subject that probably sounds excruciatingly boring, but fascinated me. It helped that the teacher was cool: an outsider to the faculty who had a law degree, a Ph.D. in history, and graying Valkyrie braids that looked more Renata Adler than Renaissance Faire. It also helped that it was the end of the last semester of a three-year degree program, the semester when most students already had jobs waiting for them in the fall and one's grades no longer really mattered. They still mattered to me, because I had turned down a law firm's offer to take the gamble on finding a job in public service.

My place in Iowa City was a little one-bedroom house that had been built before the Civil War on the highway north to Solon. Someone had remodeled the interior in the 1970s, opening up the ceilings and replacing the walls with unfinished wood siding. I put my high-mileage futon on the floor in the loft space—sometimes waking to find a squirrel staring at me from one of the bare rafters as it enjoyed my shelter from the winter cold—and made the bedroom into my office and library, furnished with a mix of thrift-store finds and hand-me-downs. The lot was small, with a little gravel driveway off the alley big enough for one car and the tiniest margin of yard around the house. But the vegetation was intense, and more work to manage than you would expect. The outer perimeter was thick with evergreen bushes and trees that provided some measure of privacy from the truck traffic that rolled by all day and night, the party houses on every side, and the police officer who lived across the alley. Having been raised as a lawn boy, I spent chunks of my weekends maintaining the tiny yard with an old-school push-reel mower, a rake, and leaf bags. It was a good way to clear one's head of torts and civil procedure, and for the first time in my life I really started paying close attention to the way your immediate outdoor environment can teach you about the seasons and the life they bring.

The plants on that little plot, I realize now, told a kind of secret history of the people who had lived there before me. The tulips that came up with the first spring thaw. The crab apple tree, with its bitter fruits that would drop to the lawn and get stuck in the mower—one of those trees that were popular as ornamentals in the Midwest, and which I would only much later learn had a deep connection to pagan English culture, the "sour-apple-of-the-wood" that appears in the 1000-year-old invocation to Wotan known as the Nine Herbs Charm. Older flowers would sometimes appear around the front porch next to the big ornamental bushes that grew on either side, hidden from the street by the evergreens that had been planted along the sidewalk, each bloom and new branch carrying with it the memory of prior occupants and forgotten seasons of settlement in that spot. All of it untended for years, or at least untrimmed—a quasi-ferality I did little to correct, mostly because I didn't know what I was doing.

My desk had a view out the front window. The glass was old, with those beautiful imperfections that have a way of obfuscating the now. Through the foliage you could see the traffic and hear the sounds of trucks downshifting to stop at the light, whose quietly clicking color changes were the constant ambience in that house situated at the beginning of a long grade up from the valley of the Iowa River. The immediate view was the sort of boring vignette one rarely notices: a bush, probably planted fifty years earlier or more, in the morning light of a sunny day after the rainy season has passed and spring is turning into summer. Birds would often move through the frame of that window as I worked. Commonplace birds: robins, blue jays, sparrows, cardinals. Not that I would have known a more interesting bird if I saw one. That day I wasn't using the computer screen, as I was reading through old notes, printed documents, and books. Maybe that's why I noticed the waxwings, even though I didn't know what they were.

There must have been twenty of them on that bush. Insanely close, since they didn't see me behind the glass. The bush was full of fruit, a berry I might be able to identify now if I went back to that place. I remember it was red and the size of blueberries. The perfect size for those birds, who, to my amazement, were passing fruits to each other, beak to beak, in a display of avian social grace I had never before witnessed. And the birds' plumage was as beautiful as their behavior: sleek, the feathers as streamlined in their layered attachment to the body as a work of fine porcelain. Except at the top of the head, where the feathers tapered off in a rough crest that reminded me of the New Wave haircuts some of us sported in the '80s—at least those of us who thought heading

----

out into the world looking like the guy they kicked out of Echo and the Bunnymen was a cool way to roll. The coloration was almost airbrushed: edgy pastels of lemony yellows and powdery browns with a black pulp-hero mask across the eyes, framed in bright white. And those astonishing spots on the secondary feathers of the wings that gave the species its common name—bright red dollops that looked every bit like drops from the wax seals that bound the ancient contracts I had been reading about in the arcane books open on my desk.

I watched them as long as they stayed there, which probably wasn't as long as it feels in my memory. Moments like that slow time and burrow in. Moments of passive communion with wild nature, in which you almost stop actively thinking and are just present. The questions come later, after the creatures have moved on, maybe headed far away in their seasonal migration. When you find yourself buying your first bird book, hoping to answer the first of those questions: What the hell were those?

You can look up the cedar waxwing in any guide to North American songbirds. *Bombycilla cedrorum* has only one cousin, the slightly larger and less extravagant bohemian waxwing, whose popular name has always made me like to think it can only be found around bookish '70s types with fern-filled terrariums and hexy macrame designed to hold capitalism at bay. The cedar waxwing is more social, and more likely to show up in any residential neighborhood where lots of berries can be foraged from ornamental bushes. They are not particularly picky. They have a reputation for frequently getting drunk, as they will happily eat berries that have fermented on the vine, and bird nerds report frequent sightings of waxwings flying erratically. They will also eat exotic berries. In the late twentieth century, many waxwings along the Eastern Seaboard were observed to have had the tips of their tail feathers grow in orange rather than red, an evident consequence of eating from European honeysuckles that had been introduced into American yards.

Cedar waxwings are not rare. They live year-round above the Mason-Dixon Line and are commonly encountered across the full range of the continent, at least below the Arctic. They move in big groups, such that if you see one, you will likely see twenty, fifty, or more. But they made their mark on me through the rarity of my personal experience of them, an experience that on the one hand was perfectly ordinary, but also charged with sublime wonder. Its coincidence with a key juncture in my life may be part of it. That ephemeral moment rekindled a connection with wildlife that I had lost in adolescence—or maybe never really had. An appreciation of the way that close observation and experience of wild nature, even as it exists in the heart of the city, can help you break through the haze of modern life. In time, it also helped me see the material I was mastering—the legal construction of our dominion—from a radically different perspective.

WILD BIRDS DO NOT abide by the boundaries we impose between legally distinct parcels of land. Like most species, they exhibit some territoriality, but only when nesting—and even then, only over a very small area. The rest of the time, they range freely across the continent in their big social flocks, looking for the next bush, drink, or bath.

Wild canids and other free mammals living in our midst also move across our property lines, but it may not be true to say they don't perceive them. They certainly perceive a fence or a road, and we might be surprised how much understanding they have of what those dividing lines represent. Animals learn—you can see it happen if you are lucky enough to be around younger animals. Perhaps the most striking thing you will quickly observe is that wariness of humans is something most species seem to learn as they mature into adulthood. How much of that is taught by their elders, learned from experience, or an instinct that only expresses with maturity, I don't know. Arctic explorers sometimes report how animals in depopulated polar extremes never acquire such wariness. Juvenile members of our own species are also oblivious to, or at least reckless about, boundaries. The idea of trespass is as learned as are the bounds of a playing field marked with chalk on a lawn. The boundaries nature defines, through geography and instinctive territoriality, and those the law defines, as an expression of human power relations and control of territory and wealth, are very different. To understand and experience urban nature at its richest, you need to follow the pathways through the former, which often means transgressing the lines of the latter.

In most of continental Europe—and in a more limited sense, in Britain—there is a right of trespass that allows walkers and hikers to follow paths through the private property of others, at least in the countryside. In the United States, no such right exists, though the law of trespass provides some refuge for those comfortable navigating zones of both geographic and legal ambiguity. To be guilty of trespassing under the laws of most states, you need to have reason to know the property you are walking on is private and that trespassing is prohibited. Much of the American edgelands where urban wildlife can be found are more ambiguous, pieces of private property that are infrequently used, generally unmarked, and often structured as corridors, like rights-of-way and empty lots. They can be parcels of public property not currently dedicated to active public use—zones of public infrastructure, lands acquired for future park use but not yet developed, or formerly private properties acquired through condemnation. Or the green margins of active uses, like the zones along the roadway. They can even be self-evidently private land, like the park-like environs of a corporate office park, that appear to be open to public visitors. Other places are more obviously zones you are not supposed to

go—places you can only enter by climbing over, crawling under, or pushing your way through the fence and going right past the "No trespassing" sign, as the animals do. Or, as the raccoons and opossums do, climbing right over the fences, an ability that may be one of the key reasons they are able to adapt so well to our urban realms. Even if they may not be able to perceive the extent to which they are existing in colonized space.

The history of our partitioning of this formerly unbounded continent reaches back almost a thousand years, to the conquest of England by William of Normandy. After his victory at Hastings, the Conqueror secured his control over the country by parceling it up among his followers, who held their lands by his grant, bound by the duty of military service. King William had around 1500 tenants-in-chief, who in turn divided up their parcels among the knights they would need to produce for war upon the king's command, all the way down to the peasants who were bound to farm the land. Prior to the conquest, a more primitive system of tenure existed, tied to the protection of the local Saxon lords. The conquest made the system national, centrally administered and supported by the Domesday Book of 1086, a detailed census of each property in the land, the heads of each household, and what service they owed for their tenancy. By the middle of the next century, when William's grandson Henry II was king, sophisticated legal and judicial systems had evolved around this system and the means whereby its titles and tenures could be enforced and transferred.

The idea of ownership—an abstract right separate and apart from the land itself and the duties of its care, production, and protection—did not emerge until the end of the medieval era, around the same time as the movement toward the enclosure of land took hold early in the sixteenth century. The enclosure movement accelerated in the seventeenth century as a means for more rational and systematized agricultural production, replacing the open-field methods of farming that previously characterized village life. Fences were used in service of pastoralism to meet the increasing opportunities for international trade in wool, and the fens and other wetlands were drained to create more arable land and pasture.

That was also the period of the settlement of New England, and the laws and modes of relating to the land came over with the Puritan colonists. Theirs was a mix of private and communal property, and the idea of each community having a commons shared by its members was also true of Spanish settlements in the southwestern parts of the continent. The commons in both regions were used for free-range animal husbandry—cattle and sheep in Mexico, cattle and hogs in Colonial America. That use of the commons, ironically, was the principal means whereby Indigenous Peoples, who had their own territorial dominions that usually included some low-impact agricultural use, were dispossessed. The interzone between colonial space and Indigenous space functioned as a kind of shared commons at the outset. But the pastoral monoculture that came from the open grazing of cattle, sheep, and hogs led to rapid ecological destruction, rendering hunting lands barren and displacing those who had long lived in balance with their bounty.

The partitioning of the land into increasingly smaller private properties accelerated once the forces of frontier settlement got over the eastern mountains and the Ohio River. In the countryside around that house in which I lived in Iowa City, the entire state was overlaid with a grid designed to facilitate its sale to settlers and homesteaders, many of them veterans of the war with Mexico who got warrants for land as the bonus prize for their service in helping to conquer the Southwest. A democratized variant of the system William the Conqueror invented for the land our laws come from, but not as free as we like to think.

The idea of the commons persists even in the most densely divided and enclosed metropolitan blocks of the American landscape. But it is an interstitial commons, defined by infrastructure. Even then, your freedom of movement is regulated by economic and social controls. The right of trespass did not make it across the Atlantic, nor did what the medieval lawyers called usufruct: the right to use the property of another without damaging it. But there are ways to hack our labyrinth of fences and other zones of exclusion. You can learn to do so by following the animals, by infiltrating the land with an understanding of its elaborate overlay of legal rights and their limits, and by learning from the people who have to find a little corner of the labyrinth where they can shelter without paying for the right to do so. The system we live under is not really so different from the one the peasants of medieval England did. The main difference is our tenure is mediated by money.

Yellowwood and Other Ghosts

In the summer, the tree at the top of our front steps drops balls to the ground that look like round, green brains. A little bigger and harder than softballs and the color of lemon-lime Kool-Aid powder, they are contoured with labyrinthine folds of hard flesh that recall the external structure of the cerebrum. When you first see them at your feet they are mysteries, even if you noticed them hanging from the branches. An object that seems too hard to eat, too big to be a seed, too weird to fit into any taxonomy you have been taught.

There were three of the trees that produce that fruit on our lot when we bought it. One did not survive construction, but two did. They were small, having been recently planted by my neighbors from whom I bought the lot. When they told me what it was, in the Navasota accent of my botanist neighbor Emily Lott, I heard "bodark," long on the "o." It took me a while before I figured out that was how the Anglo-Texans pronounce the French common name, *bois d'arc*, in the same way they flatten all of our Spanish placenames. It took a little longer after that to think about what *bois d'arc* meant: bow wood, a name given by French trappers and explorers who saw Indigenous Peoples making their bows from the wood of the tree.

Even with that knowledge, I didn't give much thought to the trees. They didn't seem that interesting. They were kind of stubby, surrounded by taller trees that displayed more beautiful attractions: the huisache trees that briefly burst with fragrant golden pom-poms you can use to make perfume, and the bark of which can be harvested into a potent hallucinogen; the hackberries that provide abundant winter food for birds; the cottonwoods that rise up from the floodplain taller than any others, floating white seeds that fill the air and cover the ground like summer snow. The bois d'arcs didn't fit in as well, as if they were not as native to this specific place—a pair of trees that had been planted rather than volunteered. By accident or serendipity, the spot where they had been planted ended up being along the path to our front door, and I found myself pruning them into a low canopy of thick, dark leaves to shade our entry from the summer sun. While the trees did not get much vertical height with the passing years, the young branches grew fast and were easily manipulated—green and malleable when young, with a fibrous hardiness that felt as strong as industrial cable. The only challenge was the branches also had thick, long thorns—super sharp and more likely to draw blood from an ungloved hand than the huisaches, which have a denser flourish of smaller thorns, or the mesquites, whose thorns are shorter.

I heard different things about whether the tree was native. Visitors who had grown up in places like Ohio and Indiana saw the trees as they arrived at our house and were reminded of their own homes. Emily told me she had planted them because they reminded her of her childhood in Navasota, which is halfway to Houston from here. Others said they thought the tree was more common in the Red River Valley that marks Texas's northern border, which turned out to be right. I learned from one knowledgeable source something I had already intuited in my seasons of working with those thorned, viny branches: that the tree was used by early settlers as the original barbed wire. They trained it to fortify hedgerows and to build natural fences and livestock pens.

Enterprising farmers in North Texas made good business selling seeds for that purpose to others across the country, marketing it as "horse high, hog tight, and bull strong." That's how it ended up being so common in the Ohio River Valley. I imagined an America in which metal barbed wire had never been introduced, as it was in the 1880s, where every home and business was picketed with living fence.

Visitors who saw the weird fruit hanging from the branches or lying on the ground called it by other names than the one I had been taught, which was also the name our friends at the Wild-flower Center used. Each name told a different part of the story: Osage orange, horse apple, hedge apple, yellowwood. A tree of the Osage Country north of the Red River, eaten by the horses of cowboys and pioneers, found in hedges, with a bright wood that grows too thinly to make good building lumber but is well suited to other woodworking uses, being one of the hardest woods to be found on this continent. But we had no horses, and the only creatures who seemed to eat the fruit were squirrels. I figured out that the fruits only fell from one of the trees, the bigger one, which must have been the female—the other, the male, hiding in her shadow.

We had been here close to a decade, getting used to that funny little pair of trees and seeing our toddler daughter curiously picking up those weird, green brain balls, when I learned that a more accurate name for Osage orange would be Mastodon Cheeto. A seed pod evolved to be eaten by those eight-ton American elephants that roamed the unfenced continent for millennia until they disappeared 10,000 years ago. And by

----

megalonyx, the giant ground sloth, a five-ton quadruped built like some cross between an anteater and a bear that could stand on its back feet and reach branches almost twenty feet high. A revelation that made perfect sense as soon as you heard it. When I held the fruits with that knowledge, they opened a window into the deep past of the land—conjuring images of those massive beasts lumbering across the ancient plains, down into the valleys of wild and scenic rivers, snarfing up these snacks littered across the ground like tennis balls scattered across the court after a practice session, then defecating the seeds out later to aid the plant's dispersal across the range. The seeds are a living remnant of those majestic, extinct animals, in the way a key can be a remnant of the door it once opened, even if the door is long gone.

SOMETIMES WHEN I WALK along the river down here, like a scruffy cousin of the mudlarks who forage the urbanized margins of the Thames, I find curious artifacts amid the expanses of river rock that cover the banks. The easiest to find are the fresh human trash, often brightly colored flotsam that stands out against the natural landscape: plastic bottles and toys, stuffed animals and fishing lures, beer cans and broken buoys. Sometimes the artifacts are older, the trash of an earlier era—the deep-blue glass of old apothecary bottles, the brighter blue and sometimes phallic glass of old transformer caps, the white porcelain fragments of antique table china that, when I pick it up, still shows the faintly colored patterns of its maker. And on occasion, I find something much older.

There are fossils all over the place around here, at what once was the bottom of a sea. Fossilized shells of marine creatures, some smaller than a child's fingernail, others bigger than your fist, curved almost like horns—what the settlers called "the devil's toenails." Where the creeks cut through the soil with every flood, you can sometimes find the teeth of dinosaur sharks that swam those waters. Becoming familiar with the layers of time visible in the landscape around you, you develop a different sense of the now. Maybe the ancient river helps trigger it, in the way it embodies deep time. You learn to feel the long now, a now in which your own life is as brief as that of an insect who lives, eats, breeds, and dies within days seems to you. A now in which the waters of the sea that covered the region where you are standing receded relatively recently, and in which the animals that walked into that landscape when it dried did so recently enough that you can still find their tracks. Sometimes you really can, in places like the Paluxy River southwest of Fort Worth, where Hugo and I stood in the watery footprints of ancient sauropods.

Sometimes you pick up a curious looking rock along the river and realize it is not a fossil, but also not just a rock. You can tell from the way it fits your hand. Rocks that once were used as tools, to make weapons or other useful things. Wedges and chippers. A visiting plumber once walked those banks with me after fixing our water pump and within twenty minutes had collected three such objects. Our neighbor, a production designer with an eye for useful objects, found an object archaeologists at the university museum identified as a 12,000-year-old Neolithic tool. When you hold such a thing in your hand the way you can instinctively tell it was meant to be held, you can feel the hand of its maker, a feeling almost more intimate than shaking a hand or holding it. A couple generations ago, you would have been able to walk those banks and find arrowheads laying around in plain sight, and such objects are still out there, especially in eroded creek banks, if a little harder to find with an untrained eye. Finding such artifacts of the people who once lived here lets you feel their presence in a very real way. Not like ghosts. More tangible and immediate, like the way you can feel the people who left their beer cans and toys to float downriver.

THE BOIS D'ARC TREE, *Maclura pomifera*, once ranged widely across North America, along with six other species of tree in the same genus, after originating in the Oligocene around 30 million years ago. It was only very recently, in the context of that epochal time span, that the other species of *Maclura* disappeared and the Osage orange withdrew to the much smaller regional range from which it got its name. Around 12,000 years ago, about the same time as the Neolithic hunter—whose closer ancestors might have walked across the land bridge from Asia—made that tool my neighbor found in the floodplain behind her house. Also around the same time the mastodons, giant ground sloths, giant armadillo-like glyptodonts, dire wolves, and saber-toothed cats went extinct. The mass extinctions of the North American megafauna, a review of the scientifically grounded literature will remind you, cannot be definitively shown to have been caused by the arrival of human hunters. It's just a correlation, in a period when climate change was also a factor. But the suddenness with which those big animals disappeared after we arrived can't help but make you think we had some agency in it, when you know how we roll.

Right after we moved here in the late '90s, I went to a meeting in one of the ugly, marbled high-rises downtown. Before I got in the elevator, I noticed a little exhibit of fossils in glass cases around the lobby—an unusual thing to see in the foyer of an office building. I went to look, admiring the massive tusks and huge femurs. When the foundation for the building was dug in 1985, the archaeologist on site discovered a mastodon burial ground had been there, on the upland terrace of the ancient river, around the time the first humans started ranging across this continent.

When my son was in first grade, we attended the inaugural installment of a series of open lectures the natural sciences faculty at the University of Texas at Austin put on to share their research and learning with the general public. The speaker was Tim Rowe, the paleontologist who had the genius idea to use magnetic resonance imaging to look at the fossilized bones of dinosaurs, a technique which more clearly showed how similar their skeletal anatomies were to modern birds. We had previously encountered Dr. Rowe in a National Geographic documentary Hugo was obsessed with, *Dinosaurs of the Flaming Cliffs*, about two smart-assed and adventurous field paleontologists from the Museum of Natural History in New York, Mark Norell and Mike Novacek, who get their Big Lebowski meets Indiana Jones on looking for feathered dinosaur remains in the Gobi Desert of Mongolia (also the subject of an excellent book by Novacek). Rowe explained his research, showing us some of the images that let you see the connections between dinosaurs and birds—especially between certain theropods, like the velociraptors made famous by *Jurassic Park* and the flightless birds of Oceania, like ostriches and emus. Then he told us the ecological story of how, very recently in geological time, humans figured out how to get out to those islands in small watercraft, where the birds descended from fierce reptilian carnivores had evolved into much gentler beings in an environment where they had no predators. The birds were so unwary of humans that we could walk right up to them, club them on their heads, and eat them. Most of those birds were soon gone the way of the dodo, the one whose extinction we know best because it was in the lifetime of our great-grandparents and was used as one of the narrative kernels of the modern conservation movement. Dr. Rowe's punchline was this: The dinosaurs, he had learned, never really went extinct. But they would in our lifetime.

In the brutally hot and dry summer of 2023, the weeks of triple-digit sun left our bois d'arc trees looking like they were struggling. They had branched out fast in the early summer rains, as always, requiring some pruning over the path. By mid-August, the fruits were smaller. They burned across the top, the lime-green color roasted like a marshmallow pulled too late from the fire. They didn't drop from the tree. It made me wonder whether this hardy survivor will be able to hack it in the harsher climate we have made. If the ghost plant will soon be a ghost itself.

Owls, Antlers, and Dead Animal Collections
To go from one room to another in the house we built here, you have to step outside. When I do so at night, walking across our

patio just a few feet from the darkness of the urban woods, I often hear the call of an owl. Usually four syllables, like four long notes played on a wood whistle, the third and fourth a little shorter than the first two. Most often when everything else is quiet—after the factories have sent everyone home and turned off all but the security lights, and even the traffic noise is minimal. The sound is eerie, almost alien, but also soothing. It's a reassuring sign, to know they are out there. Learning to see them is a lot harder. It usually involves the accident of being in the right place at the right time.

One morning, not long after we moved here, I went for a walk in those woods at daybreak, tracing a fresh path that followed the drainage ditch behind the door factory to a hidden lagoon where the runoff accumulates at the beginning of a creek. It was like a watering hole from some vintage nature documentary, a shallow pool of still water surrounded by mud and densely tracked with the footprints of animals who recently came to drink, but also littered with trash brought by the last big rains, and within earshot of the industrial cacophony above—the warning beeps of trucks and forklifts backing up, the banging of metal on metal, the rhythms of classic rock playing on a shop floor radio. Despite all that, the place had a stillness. Partly because of the way the little body of water in the urban woods made a kind of grove— an opening where tall willows bent over the lagoon, creating an almost chapel-like structure. A gritty postindustrial mirror of the sort of place our tree-worshipping ancestors might have considered divine.

As I took in the grace of the place, I saw a big owl sitting in one of those overhanging branches. It was backlit by the first light of

----

day, but the chalky white of its face was as clear as the daylight moon before it disappears. Its face moved when the owl sensed me looking at it, in that weird animatronic way owls' heads turn, as if separate from the rest of their bodies. It looked at me—this interloping human who had stumbled into the choice spot it was patiently stalking, or perhaps preparing to safely roost for the day—my presence ruining not only the possibility of its open-eyed slumber, but also the possibility that a small mammal would slink up to the edge of that skanky water for a morning drink.

I had never seen an owl of that size in the city before. It was what the people of the French countryside would have called a *chouette*—an owl with a smooth head and no crest, as opposed to the *hiboux*, which have two tufts of feathers like horns. A variation that has allowed the owl to be associated with both wisdom and hope—Athena and Christ—and with night, death, and evil. Looking into that face, you could see why our ancestors always ascribed intelligence to the owl. The bird that can see in the night when all other birds are blind, and which hides in the day, often in plain sight, such that we rarely see it even when it's right over our heads. This owl, which I later identified as my first barred owl, may have been planning to stay in that spot for the day. After sizing me up, it flew off, with a slightly annoyed rustle of big, strong wings.

After that encounter, every time I heard an owl—often the answer and response of two owls communicating with each other across the urban forest—I treasured the reaffirmation they gave of the persistent wildness of these dirty woods. And like seeing the fox running from the real estate scout, I couldn't help but feel that I had finally figured out how to experience and witness

- - - -

the presence of these ancient creatures, who mostly evolved long before we arrived on the scene, just as they were about to be pushed into more constrained habitats or maybe pushed out of the city entirely. I went back to that spot many times, hoping to see the owl again, but it was never there, and I would often wonder how much my appearance in that hidden space it occupied, with my alien eyes on its noble form, might have polluted that place for it.

The feeling that you have finally discovered real life just as it is about to be extinguished, in part because of your own intrusion into the wild spaces, is intense. Slow-burning, because the revelation takes time to accumulate. Especially the realization that the real life you have discovered is not just that of the animate beings we share this planet with, but your own real life as part of that ecological collective. You develop a sense of responsibility and agency, accompanied with a sobering fatalism, especially as you learn to see the signs more clearly.

THESE WOODS, LIKE ALMOST all American woods, are full of deer. The deer have adapted well to the urbanized forest we have made of this continent, the browsing it provides and the more challenging environment it presents for their usual predators. In Iowa, the state where I grew up, deer are the only large wild animals whose population has dramatically increased over the past century, and the same may be true in Texas. They are always there, as are their signs, and I often find antler shed on the forest floor. When you pick up an antler and hold it in your hand, it expresses strength, real and totemic.

- - - -

There are also coyotes in these woods, especially active in the cooler half of the year, and sometimes I come upon a deer they have taken. Walking up on the grisly scene of an antlered carcass here in this half-hidden, postindustrial woodland can be a little scary, the way it dials up the folk horror in the heart of Tarkovsky Park. There is always a story revealed—if you can look past the blood, the exposed bones still partly fleshed, the sheets of furry skin ripped from the body and tossed over there. It may be raining, everything wet. It may be fresh, something that happened just an hour before, or it may be days old and picked clean by vultures and bugs. Sometimes I find a corpse that has been beached after floating for some time in the river, bringing out the ghost in different ways, the way water bleeds color from the body.

On the first December morning of 2014, bushwhacking along the urban river, I picked up the scent of death and, with the weird instinct such walks developed in me, followed it. It led me into a place that didn't want me to enter—a patch of dense, weedy woods grown up at the edge of an old riparian backwater, a place that is not far from the highway overpass but feels miles from anywhere when you are down in it. When I made my way through the bramble with improvised simian yoga, I came upon a scene I was not meant to see, different than the usual struggle between predator and prey. An actual frisson of genuine horror ran through me, almost before I made sense of the distorted shapes. Which part was branch, which part bone, which part body?

Clear plastic coated the tangle of wire that had gigged the deer. It was a slasher movie torture scene, the way its big, long neck was stretched out in the V of the little trees, pulled taut by the cable that tied its rack to the branches. The front legs hung, barely touching the ground, while the hindquarters were starting to dissolve into the shadowed soil. I thought a human must have done this, strung the animal up for cleaning. Then I came around the other side and figured the deer must have gotten itself caught in a tangle of the human trash the floodplain is full of. No signs of wounds other than those left by animal scavengers. A plausible path for a fast-moving deer. A pose that could reflect intense struggle, then exhausted resignation.

The truth was, I couldn't really tell what had happened. I could only come up with postulates. And I couldn't get it out of my head, at the nexus of empathy, imagination, and shock. The knowledge that it was still out there, stuck in that position of total indignity,

- - - -

complete corporal violation. The mystery of how it got that way. The nagging sense that it was the result of active cruelty more than accident.

I told a writer friend about it over lunch. He said how our editor friend had seen strange people coming out of those woods, looking like they had been involved in dark rituals. He could not be more specific. You should call her, he said.

I composed an email, then deleted it before sending. When I mentioned it to the staff at the veterinary clinic while our dogs were in for a checkup, they said I should call animal control. At least they can take care of the body. I called animal control. The officer asked me to send her pictures. That's pretty disturbing, she said, when they came through while we were talking. She told me she would show them to her supervisor. She called back ten minutes later. She said her supervisor looked at the photos. It looks like the deer got its rack stuck in the wire, then got caught up in the vines. It happens pretty often, she said, as if to reassure me. No, she said, dead animal collection won't go out for something like that.

Only much later did I really digest the fact that the municipal government has a Department of Dead Animal Collection.

Of course it does. The city is a machine that sits on top of wild nature, and every edge where they intersect is also a wound, where the wildness that bleeds through is often extinguished in the process.

THAT SAME WINTER, AGUSTINA and I were driving back from dinner with friends when we saw something strange on the bridge—some creature in distress at the side of the road. It was a barred owl, maybe the same one I had seen in the swamp. It was standing on the pavement, huddled against the concrete guardrail in a high-speed left lane that had no shoulder. We circled back and drove past it more slowly to make sure we saw what we thought. Then we ran home, just two or three minutes away, grabbed some blankets, and returned with the intention of rescuing it. Agustina stopped our little red VW station wagon in the middle of traffic, blocking the fast lane with the hazards on as I got out with my interspecies samaritan mind on. This was not a road on which such an undertaking was safe—there was no real space but the lane, the traffic was moving at freeway speed, and the streetlights were minimal, above the ambient darkness of the wooded river corridor from which the owl had come. To step out like that and play in traffic with some sense of noble charity was the sort of thing country folks would have every right to ridicule as the folly of a soft-headed and naive city boy, longer on sentiment than good sense or understanding of how the world really works.

The owl seemed to have a similar view. It was clearly alive—still in the characteristic way of owls, but evidently edgy in a way owls generally are not. I gently tried to get it to take off, but it didn't budge. I had never been that close to a raptor before, close enough to touch it with my hands. It seemed both bigger and smaller than I expected—big in the way the unusual, flying tank proportions of all owls seem, and in the way you can sense what a powerful nocturnal presence they are in the forest. What it must be like for the creatures of the field when death comes from above in that form, suddenly, with no more noise than the movement of air and no more motion than some flash of feathers in the moonlight. And yet not really that big, by human standards—too big to hold with one hand, but not even as tall as my knees, even as you could see why there were owls in the paintings of Hieronymous Bosch that were bigger than people, because their presence makes them feel that way. That face—flat and light, with a beak like the sinister hook of some eldritch surgical instrument. And those eyes, which up close were like two ebon marbles, amping up the enigma.

The creature reminded me of the aliens in Whitley Streiber's *Communion*, a strange memoir of alien abduction that became a national bestseller in the 1980s, in which the abductions were always preceded by visitations from owls, whose faces the black-eyed and gray-faced extraterrestrials resembled. But in this weird waking dream, I was the abductor in the eyes of the owl, who must have been stunned by some glancing collision with a high-speed vehicle while flying under the spans of the bridge—maybe the top of a truck. As I raised our black fleece Ikea throw like Batman's cape, the owl turned its *Exorcist* head with evident alarm, and as I came in it raised its wings up and made clear that it would not be a willing subject of my half-baked plan. Soon I realized I was more likely to worsen the situation and cause the animal more harm. I finally got back in the car while the honking and swerving cars of others diverted, and we drove off, feeling the shameful failure of our noble effort at interspecies fellowship, calling the animal rescue hotline as consolation. When I spoke with one of the specialists the next day, they told me the best way to save an injured raptor is to put a big cardboard box over them and quickly close it. Something like a hollow tree, instead of a human hug.

- - - -

IN THE YEARS SINCE, as new development and human activity worked its way into this zone, I have listened to the woods, ever alert to the absence of our neighbor owls. And whenever I think they have gone for good, never to return, I hear their call. After our daughter was born in the spring of 2019, the first time I carried her down into the woods at dusk on a summer night, we encountered one of the barred owls in a floodplain tree, watching over us. The following December, I was walking alone in the morning, deeper in those same woods below the bridge, when I had another encounter. The owl flew over—I sensed the motion above and behind me before I saw it—and then alighted on the high branch of a nearby tree. I tried to get closer, stepping off the trail and into the brush. The tree it had chosen was in a somewhat hidden spot, rooted in the edge of a depression in the floodplain, a dry hole that may have been made by past movement of the river, or by the industrial operations of the old gravel mines. The tree was a sycamore, a big white tree that seemed endowed with its own magic. The owl tolerated my presence. Maybe it was settling in for the day after a long night's hunt, knew I couldn't harm it, and couldn't be bothered to relocate. Sometimes you get the feeling an animal has assessed your energy as nonpredatory, at least for the moment, providing a sense of detente. The feeling is deeply fulfilling. It makes you wonder if you could make a city in which such peaceful coexistence could be actively cultivated. One in which owls could feel as safe around us as grackles, foxes as comfortable around us as squirrels.

Maybe that's a foolish notion. Wariness of humans and wildness go together, tied up with the independence that makes animals like raptors and wild canids more noble. There's only room for one apex predator, and the others it crowds out have to take what they can from what's left. But it's reasonable to wonder what the natural landscape of the city could be like if we made room for wild animals in our margins with active intention.

Hot Chiles and Cosmopolitan Genes

Late in the year, when there's the right amount of rain, a strange fruit appears in the weedy gnarl of our yard and the empty lots around our house. It's the sort of plant you would not notice unless you knew to look for it. It's not showy. Just a wiry little bush with tiny green leaves that usually grows in the shadow of taller plants or fences. It's not picky about the soil conditions, and we often find it growing in dirt thickly mixed with old trash. When it blooms, the flowers are small, white, and unremarkable. When the flowers dry and fall off, in their place appear similarly small fruits, bright green in color, not even as big as peas, about the size of fat teardrops.

When they ripen on the vine, the fruits turn red, lending the plants the appearance of some kind of hot mistletoe. The red is the same red as jalapeños. Which makes sense, because jalapeños are likely descended from these edgeland chiles known variously as chiltepín, chile pequin, piquín, bird pepper, Indian pepper, turkey pepper, or, to botanists, *Capsicum annuum* var. *glabriusculum*. Chiltepín is the Aztec name, meaning "flea pepper" in Nahuatl, and among connoisseurs it denominates a different variant than the chile pequin, which is pointed and a bit bigger. All the variants are at least five times as hot as a jalapeño—30,000 to 60,000 on the Scoville Scale, though the burn doesn't last as long.

The chiltepín were first pointed out to me in the summer of 2013 by a moonlighting landscaper who worked as a foreman at the county housing services yard across the street. On the weekends, he was helping us build an outdoor fireplace from the old concrete rubble that had been dumped on our lot—and out of which the chiles sometimes grow. We were walking to the river, searching for rocks and artifacts, and he noticed a bush fruited near the path. He remarked on its spiciness, but not about its other unique qualities. I started finding it every season and harvesting it, picking the ripe fruits to make a hot vinegar and later my own hot sauce, concoctions that became more conceptually potent as I learned more about the plant.

Chiltepín can only grow from seed in the wild. To germinate, the seeds must first pass through the digestive system of a bird. There's a Texas forager who provides a speculative recipe on his blog for a method to mimic that process using battery acid, but that seems like a bad idea. Wild chiltepín are easy enough to find most years, and once you know the secret, each plant tells a little story about the movement and behavior of songbirds. And you learn where to look. For starters, only in places where no one has cut the grass. Shady, but not too shady. And most commonly, along fences or under the branches of trees. That learned intuition is a better guide than your eyes, because the plants really do disappear visually in the landscape, often hidden by other plants. Even the red of the peppers ready for picking is hard to notice, perhaps because the peppers are so small and the color still has so much green lurking behind it. Some people propagate the plants from cuttings or replant a whole plant in a pot at home. In the wild, especially as the climate becomes more unpredictable, the plants rarely reappear in the same spot the following year, at least around here. Some years I worry they won't come back at all, but then it rains and there they are.

Botanists say that most of the peppers we enjoy in the North American diet—from the bell pepper to the serrano—are descended from chiltepín, and that the variation in size, flavor, spice, and color we enjoy in the peppers on our table was achieved through human manipulation of the plants. The discovery that the weedy little fruit that comes back every year in the unmowed edgelands behind the factories is the ur-pepper of the Americas, an ancient form of life that precedes our intervention, was a rare and wondrous gift. So was the revelation that we somehow figured out how to grow our own versions of a hot fruit that seems immune to domestication.

HUMANS LOVE TO PLAY with their capacity to control the reproduction of others, to see what we can make with that godlike power. I remember a fishing guide Hugo and I went out with into Matagorda Bay in the fall of 2007. Back in Texas after years overseas with Halliburton and KBR, from the Yugoslavian civil wars of the '90s to the post-9/11 Afghanistan and Iraq wars, he told us stories about hunting feral pigs, a pastime he had learned growing up in the South Texas town of Seguin, getting paid to clear hogs from ranches and golf courses. We got to talking about the dogs they take on those hunts. He explained how pit bulls are too small to be

----

good boar-hunting dogs, and bigger breeds like Rottweilers are too heavy—they get worn out running through the woods chasing the hogs for hours. For better results, he and his friends on the Texas coast had started breeding their own, mixing pit bulls with Presa Canarios, Rhodesian ridgebacks, mastiffs, and the Arkansas giant bulldog—itself a cross between the English bulldog and American Staffordshire terrier. Imagine, he said, a pit bull the size of a Great Dane. He told us about some of the individual dogs that resulted: Big Jake, a 250-pound beast who once walked into the bar after chewing his way through the metal airplane cable his owner had used to tether him to his truck bed; Little Jake, around 225 pounds, who was unkillable, sustained through several mortal accidents by his desire to sire pups; and Watermelon Head, under 200 pounds, who liked to puncture the tires on UPS trucks with his teeth.

The conversation made me think of an article I had read earlier that year by Freeman Dyson in *The New York Review of Books*. In the article, Dyson recalled visits he had recently made to a garden show in Philadelphia and a reptile show in San Diego, remarking on the artistry and ingenuity human beings deploy to remake the natural world as their instrument and means of self-expression, expressing his enthusiasm for what will happen when the tools of genetic manipulation become widely available to garage hobbyists in the same way computing technology did in the '70s. Once that threshold is crossed, argued Dyson, we will approach a kind of genetic singularity, in which the sharing of genetic material across species boundaries mediated by the human imagination will accelerate into unknown territories. He was not alarmed by this prospect, but hopeful and excited, and as a reader you were

----

quick to remember he was also a climate-change optimist who had advocated for detonating large quantities of nuclear weapons in space as a way to get to Mars faster.

Dyson was riffing on the work of microbiologist Carl Woese, who had redrawn the taxonomic Tree of Life in the 1970s after he and a colleague discovered what they called "archaebacteria," a third kingdom as distinct from bacteria as plants and animals. Building on these discoveries, Woese advocated a new biology that started with the radical recognition that most of the history of life on Earth has been one of evolution propelled by horizontal exchange of genetic material between single-celled organisms. The very concept of species, Woese argued, is almost useless when applied to microbial life—a realm of cosmopolitan genes that freely move between organisms as environmental conditions dictate, realizing "a continuum of genomic possibilities" rather than discrete genomes. Against this intuitively persuasive and revelatory background, Dyson's assertion that our current "Darwinian interlude" was likely to end in our lifetimes seemed remarkably plausible, even probable.

I grew up around families who had made fortunes through their mastery of genetic mixing. Two of the boys we sometimes played with were the sons of the chief executive of Pioneer Hi-Bred, a company cofounded by FDR vice president Henry Wallace, which was one of the world's leading innovators in making more productive corn through selective breeding and genetic engineering. One of their competitors, DeKalb, had a more memorable logo: an ear of corn with Pegasus wings. You would see it on ball caps and in the signs by the sides of fields advertising the brand of seed in use.

By the time I was an adult, those signs marked the patented seed in use on the farms—coupling the powers of genetic manipulation with the exclusive right to profit from the results.

Here in Austin today, there is a start-up called Colossal that aims to bring back the woolly mammoth, using techniques of genetic engineering not far from the homegrown means of chimeric production Dyson envisioned. The basic idea is to crossbreed them with living elephants and grow a new breed of elephant that is as adapted to cold climates as the mammoths were. They will then be allowed to range across the arctic tundra, aiding in the restoration of grasslands and thereby combatting climate change. A partnership between laboratory geneticists and rich technology entrepreneurs, fueled by venture capital and hubris—one can't help but think this interventionist and anachronistic approach to rewilding is destined to have the pop-Faustian ending of a Hollywood creature feature. What else is coming?

It's intuitively scary stuff, the basic ethical conundrums of which are compounded by our sociopolitical angst about the people who have access to those powers and the absence of regulatory checks on what they do with them. But after two decades in the field, witnessing how blurry the boundaries we try to enforce between species are—and between humanity and nature—I've learned to interrogate our reflexive reliance on using those boundaries to irrevocably order my reality. The distance between those who tell you which species that free canid must be and those who would divide humanity into races or castes, or tell others what gender they are based on their sex characteristics at birth, is not as far as we might like to think. Testing and transgressing those boundaries is far more "natural" than enforcing them.

Much of our thinking about how to correct our currently disastrous climate trajectory is tied up with Restorationist Romanticism. The dream of Arcadia, of the idealized wild world that preceded permanent human settlement into city-states, echoes in our yearning for ecotopian possibility. We codify it in our policing of native versus invasive species and in our conservation strategies that focus on setting aside large swaths of land protected from active human use. Bringing back as much of the biodiverse life we have destroyed as we can—and saving the pockets that have somehow evaded our machines—is self-evidently worthy. But on an overheated planet marred by the sprawl of 8 billion humans, the path to ecological health will take a lot more than islands of conservation.

I wasn't looking for pathways into the future when I started exploring the interstitial urban wilderness. I was just looking for something that felt more like real life. I found it, and learned how to walk right through the barriers we construct between ourselves and our natural environment. It made me want to break down those barriers in the fabric of my own life and see what different ways of living might be possible. Starting at home.

Part Two

Rewilding Domestic Life

5

Making Camp

Hermits and Muscle Cars

You could only find the Impala by accident, the kind of accident that happens when you get lost on purpose. I found it on a sunny Saturday in May 2009, exploring the woods behind the lot I had just bought. It was not long after capitalism had collapsed—or so we thought at the time—making it weirdly plausible to find one-self in a scene from some end-of-the-world movie ten minutes from downtown. And the minute I saw it, I knew it was not a sign of the end, but a window into a new beginning.

An abandoned car is not the sort of thing you are supposed to be excited to find next to a piece of real estate you have just purchased with borrowed money. But for me, in that moment, it was a sign that I had found a way to escape. A landmark that beck-oned across time and space from a more emancipated version of the world, instead of the misery masquerading as affluence I saw everywhere I looked, including in the mirror.

Buying the empty lot yoked me to the rat race in fresh new ways, compelling me to scramble to figure out a way to financially make it all work. As evidence of how collapsed capitalism really was, at least the real estate sector, all the banks I talked to told me they were prohibited from lending money to buy empty lots. The only way I was able to consummate the deal was on a contract from the sellers, the biologists who were now my neighbors, that gave me six months to come up with a bank loan to cover the balance, which was more than my salary. But when I went over and walked the place, followed the trail through the forested floodplain down to the blue-green wonder of the urban river and then deeper into the mysterious forest beyond its banks, I was able to forget all that, if only for a couple of hours. And when Monday came, it would give that work new meaning, by tying it to the path to liberation that the lot represented. Even if I didn't fully appreciate all of its layers at the time.

The old Chevy was way off trail, tucked into the back part of an expansive wetland that somehow managed to exist behind the factory and below the overpass, surrounded by the kind of woods no one is really meant to roam, in the trashed-out floodplain near the edge of town. A place that felt authentically secret and unexplored. An intact remnant, it seemed, of what had been here before European settlement irrevocably marred the landscape.

When I first saw the wreck as I bushwhacked through the tall water grasses, it looked like it might have been there for thousands of years. But I could also remember when cars like that cruised the streets, cars with Batmobile lines forged from Rust Belt steel sometime after the assassination of JFK and before the resignation of Nixon. The sun had baked it down to the color of primer, speckled with fungal green. Aquatic plants grew up out of the seats and the engine block, watched over by dinosaur birds perched in the tall trees that ringed the secret swamp.

I couldn't tell how it had gotten there. It might have washed downriver in a big flood, or been driven down some time before, when the river channel was different. I went back again later,

----

many times, and it was always there, but every time I had to intuit a different path through the impenetrable vegetation and knee-sucking muck. It manifested different forms with changes in the river, sometimes almost completely submerged, other times almost ready to fly off, its hood and trunk popped out like asymmetrical gull-wings. A mystical motorhead Ozymandias that transported you in ways its designers never intended.

I had spent a decade exploring these kinds of places. In a way, I had been doing it my whole life, with varying degrees of active intention. I had seen enough empty lots, urban woods, and involuntary parks to know this one was the pure shit, and that the atemporal vignette I found that Saturday afternoon was the proof. I also knew how risky—maybe even crazy—the idea to wager my

finances on buying a little slice of the postindustrial ruins was, thinking I could take a brownfield bisected by a petroleum pipeline and make it into a home for my broken family. On the other hand, my son's realization that he wanted to be a designer meant this could be a project we could collaborate on—the project of making our own new home together, one that made use of the things we had learned together, exploring the wild city.

I had a lawyer's reflexive confidence that there's always a way to make a deal work, coupled with a science fiction writer's yearning to invent different realities than the one we find ourselves in, and a pronounced deficiency at making authentic, vulnerable connection with my fellow humans, which was what drove me to seek solace in urban nature in the first place. As I looked back on the domestic and workplace stress I had endured in those long, hard years, the only time I could remember crying was watching an in-flight movie on my way home from a business trip—the brief scene in *The Queen* where Helen Mirren lets Elizabeth II uncork a few tears when she encounters a majestic stag in the woods at Balmoral, after resisting the pressure to show feeling instead of strength in the wake of Princess Diana's death. My endgame, to the extent I had one, was to get my kid through middle school and high school; set myself up in a place where I could live modestly enough to spend more of my time writing, gardening, and exploring; and have the rewards of living in nature without giving up the cultural and professional riches of the city.

I was okay with the fact that the storyline sounded likely to end up as some variation on the solitary old guy in the weird house at the end of the street. I kind of liked that idea. I loved first-person

----

narratives of exploration and discovery, and fictions of marooned astronauts and wanderers of the wastelands. In the Icelandic sagas, sometimes the unknown authors mention how, when Norse settlers first crossed the cold sea to make new homes on that barren island in the ninth century, they found Irish hermits already living there, in caves along the coast. For reasons I probably never interrogated closely enough, that always had an intuitive appeal for me. In the same way that the seventeenth-century postcard of Saint Onuphrius as painted by Tzanes, which arrived in the mail around the time I started looking for a place to buy, ended up tacked above my desk and is still there today—an icon of the student of jurisprudence and philosophy turned ascetic wild man of the desert. Or Radagast the Brown, the nature-loving wizard Tolkien invented in his world-building but couldn't find a place for in the story, because the character knew how to stay away from the human drama. Proclivities I had learned from my mother—who, as middle age drifted into retirement, revealed that she had always preferred mushrooms to people—and her own mother, who went off in her seventies to look for weird birds in the jungle.

The Impala eventually disappeared, in November 2013. No one knew how. The municipal authorities disclaimed involvement. Maybe the floods of that Halloween carried it away. You can still find its digital ghost on the online maps, if you know where to look.

But I kept going back to that spot. Even after the muscle car was gone, you could always find something new and interesting there: a weird plant you had never seen, a rare bird, some backyard detritus made enigmatically wondrous by its change of context. In time, I learned the wetland was not, as I had naively assumed,

----

a remnant of what once had been. In my childhood, it had been a gravel mining site. You could see it there on the topos from the early '70s, and if you looked on older maps and aerials you could see the road that had run through there before World War II. It was a place where, in the years since I was in college, an industrial site left to its own devices had completely rewilded. Through the prism of that revelation, the apparition of the Impala seemed more certain to be a sign of a greener world that could be.

Urban Birds and Bachelor Pads

One of the surprising things I've most learned to appreciate living at the edge of the urban woods is the strange bounty of real darkness. It's especially intense if the sky is clear, the moon is down or mostly shadowed, and the only light from above is that of the few stars you can see in the city, which usually include at least one planet and sometimes three you can see with the naked eye. There are streetlights outside the fence, but just a few. There are security lights around the perimeter of the nearby industrial facilities, but none of their beams can really compete with the power of the riparian forest behind the fences, hidden acres of floodplain mostly vacant of human activity. Our house is tucked back closer to the woods, and in the early morning before sunup, when I finish making the coffee and walk out to the trailer where I work, I never know what surprises await. A spider in my face as I walk into a fresh web spun from the branches over the path. An armadillo foraging at my feet. Raccoons screaming in the woods. The white face of an opossum, maybe baring its teeth before it scrambles over the fence. The startling snort of a deer. Low-flying bats near my head, working their way home to the undersides of downtown bridges after a long night eating insects from the air.

In August 2023, as the new moon of peak summer brought the first feeling in the air that our brutal weeks of rainless triple-digit heat might eventually turn into the cool of autumn, I walked out every morning over three days to find big owls cavorting in the trees along the street: one announcing itself with a loud hoot right next to my head as I unlocked the gate; another in the old mesquite tree; and then, on the third day, the rare sight of a pair, making even stranger noises in the darkness behind the maintenance facility across the street. Calls so strange, different than the usual four-note hoots, almost like cries or screams, that I wasn't sure they were owls. I walked slowly in the direction of the sound, and then they flew out in front of me, low across the street, alighting in the shadows of the tall sycamore behind the door factory. I tried to call back, in my bad imitation of their most characteristic call. Sometimes it works, in the forest. But these owls could see me standing there in the street trying to fake them out and get them to reveal their location. The experience made me see how owls, animals I had always thought of as solitary figures, are never really alone. Or, at least, that they always know how to find each other, even in this brutalized habitat we have left for them. The urban wild has a way of helping you see the truths you work to hide from yourself.

IN THE DAYLIGHT, WHEN I step outside from our house, I often see a lone animal on the roam, traveling through this spot where the woods intersect with the machined city. A coyote outside the fence at first light, in the field behind the door factory, looking back at me before it disappears. A young stag in the morning mist while the trucks loudly unload nearby. A falcon that has just discovered the perch the old telephone pole provides. Sometimes I wonder if it might be one of those animals at a life juncture where it must seek a new home. That plotline recurs in many tales we tell children, drawing on our real-life observations documented in field guides and nature shows that relate how young hawks, beavers, bears, stags, and members of other species must go off to find their own place in the world, a new territory to hunt or forage. Sometimes that burden falls not on a new adult, but on a mature animal that finds itself broken off or cast out, maybe after a fight or natural disaster. They often wander far, like the lone Mexican wolf US Fish and Wildlife staffers tracked covering 775 miles over two months across the western half of New Mexico, from the Gila National Forest to the outskirts of Albuquerque and south to the Mexican border, until it settled not all that far from where it had started.

I remember a day in the summer of 2007, when I was looking at a house for sale in the neighborhood near campus without knowing I would need to roam farther. The place was in a kind of pocket edgeland, where a street dominated by student apartments dead-ended in the green space through which an old but still active railroad track ran under an elevated freeway. After the walk-through, as the realtor drove off and I walked toward my car, I noticed birds in the closest tree. Almost spectral, the way their motion and color seemed an ambient part of the landscape, even as they flew. They were waxwings, the first I had seen since that law-school vignette sixteen years earlier.

They didn't share any fruit, maybe because there wasn't any. They just stopped for a moment, maybe to see what they could find there, maybe for a rest. Quickly, they moved on. But they stayed in my memory, as I kept an eye out for them and wondered where I might see them again, as if it would mark the place I was meant to be.

I DIDN'T BUY THAT house. I rented a downtown apartment instead, with room enough for Hugo and me. We greened the place up, with a huge planter of far-out ferns by the picture window and tomatoes and basil on the balcony. We put up feeders, and the birds appeared quickly. House finches and sparrows mostly, sometimes pigeons. In midwinter, the grackles would arrive in insanely huge flocks, filling up not just our porch but seemingly every space visible from there, lined up on the power lines and crowded into the little trees that downtown allowed. Black birds with blue-metal iridescence and boatlike tails, the males prone to crazy feather-fanned dinosaur dances in the mating season, and a long, high-pitched call that makes the city sound like a jungle. Jackdaws of the American borderlands, who you would sometimes encounter in similarly prodigious flocks during a twilight run to the mall or the hardware store, filling up the sky and covering all the parked cars in fast-drying excrement. Urbanized birds of a southern clime, whose obnoxious charisma I couldn't help but appreciate—especially when they stole someone's French fry or tortilla chip. Maybe it was the wandering birds who helped us realize we weren't really home.

We were just making camp along the way to a destination we had not yet figured out.

Hugo and I explored the creek beds, railroad woods, and abandoned infrastructure around that apartment, saw our first urban coyote, and went on farther excursions, sometimes paddling the river, sometimes road-tripping to the Trans-Pecos and beyond, into epic landscapes of flare-offs, UFO museums, and land art. We saw tarantula migrations south of Balmorhea, tracked bobcats in the snow at Big Bend, and had a close encounter with the Coen brothers at a motel swimming pool. Right there, in the downtown blocks around our place, we had close encounters with ancient trees, but we—or at least I—did not yet have the capacity to really see them. If I had, maybe I would have found my way here sooner. I was happy to have a kid who still wanted to hang out with dad, even as he became a teenager. And I was lucky that the things we liked to do together usually got us out in the real world, which he had helped me learn to see in the first place.

On the weekends Hugo wasn't with me, I went out on my own. Not always away from the crowd. There were club shows and music festivals, a community garden plot I tended with former colleagues, writing workshops and lunches with friends, and dates with friends and strangers. But the time alone in the woods—trail running, paddling, and exploring—was what lasted in my mind. I started wondering if there might be a way to live in the urban wilderness, instead of just exploring it. To find a retreat without leaving town.

THE IDEA OF SOLITUDE in nature stands large in the romantic imagination. Not just in the West—I remember being struck as a high school student by the commonalities between Chinese paintings of small, solitary human figures in vast and wondrous landscapes and the German landscape paintings I had grown up around, including the ones my own great-grandfather and great-aunt painted that hung on our walls. But in American nature writing, that idea of the lone figure in the wilderness is seminal, and permanent in its allure. It's there in Thoreau especially, the way he married the idea of pastoral solitude with personal virtue. It may have been in that period when I was flirting with the possibility of my own hermitage that I read how Thoreau's mom would bring him food and do his laundry while he was living in supposed isolation and self-reliance, in a cabin that was a twenty-minute walk from her house. The seed was planted of what a pernicious lie that myth is, even as it also tells the absolute truth. Learning to see how invested that archetype is in white privilege and patriarchy, an investment that deeply infects the literature and culture of the American outdoors, would take longer.

As my path clarified and I found this empty lot, I set out to make my own sci-fi Walden on the Colorado, thinking I was breaking out on my own. Alone in nature in the interzone of my own life, I'd had some of the most profound experiences of my life, experiences that were like a religious awakening. I wanted to cultivate that wonder, that possibility, in the everyday fabric of domestic life. What I didn't anticipate was how that pursuit of solitude in nature would obliterate the very idea of solitude, exposing it for the Cartesian delusion it is, a conjuring of language and the objectified self that the deprivation of human company can help you see through.

166

What we experience, alone in nature, is the opposite of solitude: the revelation of our connection and community with the nonhuman life and animate elemental energy that surrounds us, infuses us, and is us. It is best experienced without other people, because that's when the channel opens widest. Nature does not reveal itself as easily to a group of humans as it does to a lone figure—especially, with animals, a figure who manifests no aggression or fear. It helps if you are in a frame of mind that aids your openness to it, whether through the natural grace of a child or a wizened elder; through the aids nature provides in its mind-expanding intoxicants; or, in my case, through the exhaustion that life sometimes hazes you with. When you learn to see the natural world that is all around you, even if you're in the city, you also learn to see the human world more clearly.

I learned, for example, that the hermit and the parent and the spouse can be the same person, and the servant and the artist, the neighbor and the advocate. I learned that the boundaries between the city and the natural spaces are largely an illusion. Not just because there are so few, if any, truly natural spaces, free of our imprint. I learned how to find my way home, wherever I was. Even if I didn't really belong there.

The signs of where we are all meant to be were right in front of me. It took me time to learn to see them.

Sacred Groves and Cityscapes
On the outskirts of the city of Oaxaca, right by the main highway, between the town hall and a cathedral, stands a tree god. The signs around the tree do not call it that. They call it *el Ahuehuete*, which

is the Nahuatl word for the species of tree, *Taxodium mucronatum*, commonly referred to in English as the Montezuma cypress. The Aztec name means something like "old man of the water," and as you walk up and try to take the tree in with your eyes, you realize how old they mean.

The tree is so huge that it cannot really be photographed, not in a way that truly expresses its scale. Not just tall, but volumetrically expansive, like a crazy cross between a live oak, a redwood, and a willow, its gnarly trunk working its way up twelve stories high and spreading out long branches that create a canopy like a jungle unto itself. The trunk is thicker than it is tall—a circumference of 42 meters (138 feet), so thick that when you get close to it, it shatters your conception of what a tree is. You cannot touch it, because it is just out of reach behind a short fence. On the fence is a metal sign in hand-painted cursive that reads *"Soy un ser vivo, no cortes mis ramas."* A first-person declaration by the tree that it is a living being, and you should not cut its branches.

The age of the tree is not really known. It is at least 1400 years old, and some say it could be 6000 years old. The story among the Indigenous peoples of the area is that it was planted by a priest a thousand years before Columbus and consecrated to the Aztec wind god Ehecatl, a manifestation of Quetzalcoatl whose power delivered the rains that made the crops grow. There is another specimen of the same species across the courtyard, not quite as big. Standing there between them, one cannot help but sense what a sacred place it is, expressing something profound about the majesty of trees that live longer than us, about our connection to trees, and about the way such trees embody the entirety of our experience of nature, the cycles of life, the elements, water, light, and earth. The cathedral is there next to it on one side, and the office of the civilian authorities on the other, but they cannot really compete.

The idea of the sacred grove runs deep in human culture, across almost all cultures, even though to find a living example of such a place as one can around the Árbol del Tule is very rare. In Northern Europe, many of the first Christian churches were built on the sites of sacred groves that originated as ancient places of pagan worship. In Japan they are often preserved as Shinto shrines, sometimes in the heart of the city. I stumbled upon one in the middle of downtown Seoul in 2018, around a Buddhist temple, surrounded by modern buildings where once had stood a forest. In West Africa and India, many sacred groves have been preserved to this day. In the United States, you might think there is no such tradition, the veneration of certain forest sites by the Indigenous Peoples of the continent having been largely erased and the wilderness the colonists found having been replaced by farms and great cities. The truth is more complicated.

You can find echoes of the grove all over the American landscape, even in its most urbanized corners. When my brother Alex, a painter and musician, died of an aneurysm at the age of fifty-two, among the things I found going through his stuff was the ornate old brass plate from his mailbox at the apartment he rented in Manhattan's Lower East Side in the early '90s. Located on Forsyth Street, in the zone between Little Italy and Chinatown, it was one of those double-illegal rent-controlled sublets that were common in New York back then, a form of informal tenancy in which there may have been three or four different people writing checks to each other before the one of them whose name was actually on the lease wrote a check to the building's owner. A beat-up and barely maintained turn-of-the-century tenement, it had the roaches, horror-movie plumbing, and peeling palimpsest paint jobs that suited a young punk rocker, with no air-conditioning and old-school radiator heat that would wake you in the night with those heavy metal pings and klangs straight out of *Eraserhead*. But if you went to the windows—big windows made of high glass, where the pigeons cooed on the fire escape and reminded you other life was around, even in that dystopian urbanity—you got a view from three floors up of an expansive, blocks-long park named after FDR's mom. A paved park, granted, but that wasn't a bad thing if you were a skater like Alex. And there were plenty of trees: tall sycamores that created a kind of concrete arboretum, an urban clearing amid the shade of those broad-leafed ghosts of some forest from another place and time, in a zone where the buildings across the street were not very tall, and you could see the sky.

Walking through that park on a hot and muggy summer day, I could almost feel how the pavement under my feet covered what had been an expansive saltwater marsh not that long ago. And there were many birds, especially on the weekends. Exotic birds, which I would hear before I saw them. As we stumbled out to find a cup of coffee, we would encounter elderly Chinese men gathered around the beautiful carved bamboo cages in which they kept their pets—*Hua Mei*, a fighting thrush native to China and Southeast Asia characterized by reddish-brown plumage, a white band around the eyes, and a beautiful and wide-ranging song. The men would carry the birds to the park in their cages, covered in white cloths to protect them from the eyes and sounds of the city as they traveled, and then take them out of their cages to socialize with the other birds as the men socialized with each other. Turning the urban grove into a living one, filled with the sounds of nature imported from faraway homes.

Sous les pavés, la fôret.

Upstate from downtown Manhattan, around the same time the Zapotecs say Pechocha planted the Árbol del Tule, the sacred texts of the Latter-day Saints relate how the prophet Moroni secreted golden plates—recording the history of his people's emigration from Israel to North America—in a cave in a hill in western New York known as Cumorah. In the 1820s, a teenage boy named Joseph Smith—if we are to believe his stories—went to pray at a grove near that site, which was also near his family home, seeking guidance on which flavor of Christian faith to follow among the cornucopia of choices early Americans believed themselves to have. The result was a visitation from two heavenly beings, which recurred with lessons from an angel who eventually led Smith to discover those plates, translate them into the Book of Mormon, and found his own faith whose sense of mission led his later followers across the continent to make a new home in the wastelands.

Smith's theophany in the Sacred Grove, often ridiculed by nonbelievers as a classic American tall tale, has a certain resonance with the truth of its historical moment, when the Puritan association of the wilderness with savagery and the devil—a place they thought was best dealt with by cutting the trees to fuel civilization and bring the earth under the plow—was evolving into something

----

different. While the instrumentalist view of nature has never gone away, the seeds of a more Romantic conception of the forests of America became evident in the emergence, around the same time as Smith delivered his new gospel of the secret history of the wild American continent, of the transcendentalist movement—the idea expressed in the works of Emerson and Thoreau that nature is the locus of the divine and that spending time alone in the woods is the path of moral rectitude and personal revelation in a fallen world. A tension emerges in that generation between two competing imperatives: the instrumentalist belief that the land is there for our sustenance, and that to fail to put it to work is a species of moral failure, a sin of waste; and the intuitive appreciation of the beauty of untamed nature and biodiversity, where true life can be found, from which springs the urge to preserve and restore what wilderness we can. These competing urges remain unresolved and ever in conflict in the American landscape, and in our own lives.

When Hugo and I lived in our downtown apartment, we had a view of a sacred grove, and often walked through it, without seeing it as such. In our defense, the city had made it hard to see: in the corner of a scruffy park across from a surface parking lot, catercorner from a monstrous concrete parking garage and next to an empty lot, where the unfinished frame of the Intel building stood as an unofficial memorial to the '90s tech boom the pundits had promised would never end. The trees known locally as the Auction Oaks are Texas live oaks, *Quercus fusiformis*, more than 300 years old. When Republic of Texas president Mirabeau Lamar visited with a small troop in the fall of 1837, just one settler and his family were living here among the Indigenous peoples, and the trees were part of an expansive savanna of wild rye and oak groves. In the morning after their first night camped on the Colorado, Lamar and his men were awakened by the young son of their host with the news that a huge herd of buffalo was gathered in the prairie, foraging, which they promptly set to slaughtering, Lamar purportedly killing a record-size bull with his pistol. Lamar advocated for this to be the new site of the Republic's capital, and named it after Stephen F. Austin, who the biographers report took tremendous joy in the sound of trees coming down to build towns, as he accelerated his mission to "redeem Texas from its wilderness state by means of the plow alone." Under those oaks in 1839, the first 301 lots the Anglo settlers carved the land into were auctioned off for $180,000.

Not far from the spot where Hugo and I encountered a coyote behind the Amtrak station stands the last remnant of an even more magical grove that had been here for hundreds of years, until the Anglo-American colonists and their descendants got to work. The tree sits in the middle of a parking lot, behind a '90s strip mall at the western edge of downtown and across the street from an AT&T store, West Elm, the Amazon/Whole Foods headquarters, and a Starbucks—a landscape that renders it almost invisible, even as thousands of people pass by it every day in their cars. Locals call it the Treaty Oak, after lore passed down from the early settlers that the tree is where the Comanche and Tonkawa would hold their war and peace councils, a story that sounds like projection on our part of what might have been a very different connection those peoples had with the ancient trees that stood there. Back then there were fourteen of the Treaty Oaks, but only one was still standing by the 1920s, when it was deemed the finest specimen of its species in the country.

In the late 1980s, right as the Cold War was ending and the Satanic Panic was in full bloom, a guy claiming to have occult intentions poisoned the tree with the arboreal herbicide Velpar. The tree was saved but only a third of what had been there survived, and the perpetrator went to prison for nine years on a conviction of felony criminal mischief. I had passed by that tree countless times over several decades—walking to lunch meetings, driving back into downtown, shopping in those soulless retail centers—but never fully noticed its greatness. I could blame the way the developers and the city planners and the attempted arboricide reduced the majestic oak to the invisible status of just another landscape tree, but I also need to blame my own persistent capacity for seeing the city without also seeing the natural landscape it has not entirely erased. If I go there now, and get up close, I can see the massive scars of necrotic growth up one side of the tree, right by the entrance to the beauty salon.

There were no majestic oaks on the lot I found, not even hidden ones. There was the one lone mesquite up front, some younger native trees my neighbors had planted around the cottage next door, and in the back, a thick stand of hackberries—maybe the least loved of the native trees down here, derided as a thirsty tree prone to disease and premature collapse. The hackberry's mottled gray-brown bark is unexceptional, its leaves small and unremarkable, its branches often tortured, and its fruit a tiny, hard berry that blackens the patios and cars beneath its shade. It is often infested with mistletoe and wrapped in poison ivy. But here, in

- - - -

this blighted lot, the hackberries seemed different. Tall and grace-fully branched, they formed a complete canopy along the edge of the bluff at the back of the lot, where they grew despite the mas-sive quantities of trash mixed in with the soil. They gave the lot the feeling of a grove, more dirty than sacred, but perhaps with the potential to be nursed back in that direction.

6

Making a Green House in the Brown Lands

Little House on the Petroleum Prairie

The US Environmental Protection Agency maintains the official definition: "A brownfield is a property, the expansion, redevelopment, or reuse of which may be complicated by the presence or potential presence of a hazardous substance, pollutant, or contaminant." It's accurate but bureaucratic, simultaneously precise and vague, powered by the deep understanding encoded in our language of the idea of brown lands and wastelands, while somehow obscuring the horror it describes: land that has been poisoned by us and rendered uninhabitable.

The modern human idea of home is deeply tied up with our ancestral connection to healthy nature. Whether you ask a group of kids, an advertising agency, or a selection of digital bots to show you a picture of a home, you can bet they will come back with an image of a conventional house with a pitched roof, windows, a front door, one or more trees in front, and a green lawn. They won't show the toxic ambience of pollution somehow deemed safe for us all to live within. We designate as off-limits the most poisoned sites, the ones where we know the adverse impact to our lives and health would be a certainty. But humans ignore the everyday toxins all around us and rarely allow ourselves to see how much we have ravaged the whole world to make it serve us, razing entire ecosystems, sometimes covering up the scars with

----

manufactured landscapes designed to simulate nature without actually letting it in. Most of us can't see that truth, if we want to get through the day. We learn to filter it out, along with all the other everyday horrors and injustices we numb ourselves to. The choice to see is also a choice to feel the pain. And as such, every generation grows up more isolated from real life. As we began working on this project, the National Park Service launched a campaign, featured on billboards around our neighborhood, to lure children to parks with digital images of frogs and furry creatures photoshopped onto photographs of real hands, as if virtual animals were the only ones they could find and the only ones they thought kids could believe in.

The idea that our home *is* nature, not the commodified struc-tures we make to protect ourselves from it, is one that rarely emerges. In his 1972 book *On Adam's House in Paradise*, Joseph Rykwert documented the deep obsession among architects, all the way back to Vitruvius, to deduce the shelter made by man or God that they assume must have existed in the Garden of Eden. The idea that there was none is never considered as a serious possibil-ity. And there are few dualities harder to shatter in our thinking than the concepts of "inside" and "outside" that are so integral to how modern humans think about the world. At least until the air-conditioning fails.

There was a time when our ancestors slept in trees. Almost 2 million years ago, before *Homo erectus* learned how to make its own safety by sleeping in groups around the campfire. An innova-tion that also made it easier to dream, much more than our pri-mate cousins, though we still don't spend as much time in REM sleep as the platypus. Evidence from chimpanzees and orangutans suggests our first beds may have been stick platforms our hominid ancestors learned to make when they got too big to safely sleep on branches. That development quickly got us down on the ground, though, which led to our evolution into the hunters and foragers that walked out of Africa to every corner of the planet. We can make camp wherever we need to. We can sleep in an open field, in a cot tied to the side of a cliff, under a bridge. But while we have left the trees, we like to stay close to them. Even in the suburbs.

The empty lot where I decided to make a home had not been formally declared a brownfield. It had been tested for petrochem-ical contamination and passed. But the pipeline was there, valve

box and all, as was the trash, and the ugly industrial uses that surrounded the lot. Some of the damage you could see, and some you
could not. The access to wild space the lot provided in the heart of
the city was more clearly evident. The two qualities went together.
You couldn't have the one without the other.

It was an unlikely place to try to find one's way into the
twenty-first-century version of that imagined proto-house, the kind
of house that tries, as best it can, to build shelter from the Earth,
instead of on top of it and in opposition to it. If I hadn't been doing
the project mostly on my own, aided by an intermittently interested seventh grader who would soon be moving on, the toxic
taboo would probably have prevented it. As a place for a retreat
without leaving, it was hard to beat. Even if, contrary to my early
expectations, it would end up as a fortress of solitude for four. I
could see the path, more or less. It had checkpoints and obstacles,
known and unknown. I had some ideas of how I could alter my
relationship with the land, but I didn't anticipate that it would end
up changing me just as much.

IN THOSE YEARS I had developed a fascination with land art,
partly from visits with Hugo to the West Texas town of Marfa,
whose old military base had been transformed into a gallery of
site-specific works by writer-turned-artist Donald Judd. Works
that were in conversation with the landscape, with the history of
place, and with deep time, effecting minimal interventions. Subtly
carved stone blocks set in the tall grass that interacted aesthet-
ically and maybe energetically with the enigmatic purple mountains along the horizon, the kind of mountains where you might

----

encounter a Castaneda-grade *brujo*. Milled aluminum boxes in an old armory building, each slightly varied, reflecting the weirdly angled light of the Marfa plain, across which people famously see dancing orbs along the horizon line after dark. **SEE MYSTERY LIGHTS**, as the old sign advertised by the highway through town. Crushed cars sitting on the floor of an old agricultural building that recall abandoned vehicles in the desert, where nothing really rusts. A lone building at the edge of the old base, overgrown and battered, remade as an abandoned Soviet schoolhouse. Exercises in amplifying our anchoring in place and time that situated us much more deeply in our true environment. I read up on other works of land art, like Walter De Maria's *The Lighting Field* and Robert Smithson's *Spiral Jetty*, and started imagining speculative works of my own in the short stories I was writing for anthologies and magazines.

I began following the work of the L.A.-based Center for Land Use Interpretation, just as they launched their Houston Field Office—a trailer in an old junkyard along Buffalo Bayou in an industrial area east of downtown, right before the river opens up into the Ship Channel. They were conducting investigations into that insanely Anthropocene urban ecology, where primordial Gulf Coast swamp meets the fossil-fuel industry. They even organized canoe trips through those zones, an idea that resonated with me. The work culminated in an installation and gallery exhibition on the same weekend as one of my favorite jazz trios was playing there, so I convinced Hugo to check it out with me.

The exhibit was amazing, framing, almost implausibly, the energy infrastructure of Texas as a species of unintentional corporate land art. Mostly through a mix of photographs and maps, and one remarkable video installation of a flight over the Ship Channel that showed how that most intensely developed and toxic industrial corridor of refineries, depots, and tanker traffic was just as intensely wild and green. A handful of objects showed the tangible components of that infrastructure. One gallery of photos showed the money end: the shiny office towers of the big oil companies, downtown and on exurban access roads, simultaneously luxurious and boring. Another gallery showed maps of the infrastructure of collection, transmission, and distribution across the wider landscape and the way it tied into the natural contours of the land, as rights-of-way almost always do. It accelerated the way I was already starting to see the blighted yet beautiful world around me wherever I went. To see how simultaneously absolute and illusory our conceptions of the boundaries between human space and wild nature are, and to appreciate the weird dividend of how the grim zones of the most intense industrial activity can inadvertently preserve or create rich pockets of interstitial habitat.

When I saw the pipeline site, I saw, against conventional wisdom, how it could be a homesite. Maybe even the most beautiful homesite you could find, if you approached it as a portal to the urban wild. As a science fiction writer, I had learned the power of narrative as laboratory, in which you can safely explore speculative permutations of the possible. This seemingly unbuildable empty lot was an opportunity for a kind of applied science fiction, one that explored the possibility of building a home that worked to obliterate that boundary between toxic industry and free ferality, and maybe even bring it back into harmony.

I was not a land artist. I did not have an institutional patron willing to fund my folly. I was an oddball bachelor dad with a half-baked idea for a different way to live and barely enough extra cash to pay for a down payment on a normal house. It was a challenging prospect, even without the added complication of having to enlist the help of Chevron, which had acquired this pipeline when it merged with Texaco in 2001.

THE FIRST ELEMENT OF the plan was to keep the building project simple and small. The house would be no bigger in its square footage and layout than the two-bedroom apartment my son and I shared downtown. The constraint was both financial and conceptual: to end up with a monthly mortgage payment that was the same as the rent I was paying, and make the land the real living space. To live in the edgelands.

To do that, I first needed to figure out how to get the pipeline out of the ground while, in line with my conceptual premise, preserving the memory of that past industrial land use. I ended up calling Chevron. They were, it turned out, quite willing to have me pay them to remove their environmental liability from my property and vacate the two easements they owned. It made sense, and as a business lawyer myself, I had a reflexive confidence that it could be done, because it was in their interest. The cost was not trivial, but a fraction of the value it would add to the land and within range of what I could cash flow. How to build a house on such a site was something I had less confidence about.

As I debated how to proceed, I walked the site after work one day with a friend who worked in the construction business. When we went for drinks afterward, we ran into some other friends of his, including Thomas Bercy, an architect who had been transplanted from Belgium to Texas as a teenager when his father's job in the oil business brought him to Dallas. We all ended up drinking together and then grabbing dinner across the street. Thomas and I got along well, and we got to talking about possibly collaborating on the project.

A few days later, Thomas visited the site with me. When he saw the trash, he suggested we bury it. I shared my conceit that the trash and the pipeline were part of the history of the place that should be remembered, even as we cleaned up the land. We met with his partner, Calvin Chen, a native of Taiwan who had spent time in Australia before relocating to Texas. They were young and hungry, having left an established firm to go work for themselves just as the Financial Crisis hammered the construction business, and they seemed to get my screwy ideas. They would be able to move fast, which I thought was important to keep the project in line with my budget. We agreed to try it out. I would pay them $1500 to develop some schematic designs.

I wrote some design notes for them, which combined notes toward an edgeland manifesto with photos of how we lived in our downtown apartment and clips of overgrown concrete bunkers and modernist treehouses. I got them reading J. G. Ballard and Paul Virilio. Hugo and I met with them a couple of weeks later at their offices, after school. They presented three rough concepts. Two were modern but conventional, but one stood out, simultaneously leaning into two different and extreme directions—primitive and sci-fi futuristic. It looked like a crashed spaceship—as if you tucked

----

a little apartment in under the scar left by the removal of the pipe-line, the linear cavity providing a memory of what had been there in the land, as well as expressing the idea of healing the scars of a broken home. The roof would be green, an opportunity to experi-ment with phytoremediation, cultivating plants that heal the soil. And it was small, the conditioned space no bigger than our apart-ment. It was a brilliant integration of the input and constraints we had provided with their own ideas as young designers excited to take bold risks. We all agreed that was the way to go and that we should push it further.

Actually buying the land was a more challenging undertaking. The big bank where I had my accounts was now prohibited from making any loans against empty lots. Calling around to other banks, the answer was the same. The market had dried up after the crash. The brokers, eager to get their commission, came up with a solution: persuading the owners to sell it on contract. I would have six months to line up financing, paying them principal and interest in the meantime on a promissory note for the purchase price we negotiated, which was a good price for a used and abused acre of land on a beautiful river, but still a big number for me. As we worked on the detailed design, I worked on figuring out how I would pay for the whole thing.

THE AMERICAN WAY OF making new homes is not friendly to doing things differently. Especially if you want to do so with bor-rowed money. The history of the empty lots of the United States is a model of colonial settlement, premised on the grand lie that the lands were empty when acquired, an illusion whose persistence is evident if you look at the annual reports of the Bureau of Land Management, which read a lot like the annual reports of a business corporation. That some of the deals are listed as having been free encodes some of the truth about what kinds of transactions those really were—acquisitions by force from the prior occupants or colonial owners. To consummate the deal, the sovereign needed to populate it with its own productive taxpayers—often in transactions directly related to the means by which the land was acquired, as with the veterans' benefits given to soldiers in the Mexican War of 1848 upon their discharge: a warrant redeemable for 160 acres of land anywhere in the country. In Texas, veterans of this territory's earlier uprising against Mexico were entitled to first-class headrights, and a wide menu of other land grants were available to anyone who would put the land to work. Widespread homesteading of the Great Plains and the West was stymied by fights over whether slavery would be permitted, until 1862, when Congress passed the first Homestead Act. From then until 1934, 270 million acres of federal land were given away for little more than the cost of the filing fees to men, women, and recent immigrants, as long as they had not taken up arms against the government. As a consequence, loans to buy homesites were uncommon until the 1930s. Maybe because they were not needed to promote productivity in the populace—a homesteader was, by definition, a farmer or rancher who was living off the land through the application of their own labor, eventually turning it into property that would generate surplus they could sell.

That's not to say that everyone owned their own home. Only 40 percent of the population did in the early 1930s, with most of the rest—especially in fully colonized urban areas—living as renters. The first wave of home mortgages, which were provided by insurance companies, were typically limited to 50 percent of the property value and a three- to five-year term with a big balloon payment at the end. Massive foreclosures resulted, leading to massive federal intervention. When the New Deal government put in place institutions to stabilize this, buying the first million defaulted mortgages, the fifteen- or thirty-year mortgage backed by insurance became the standard. Soon, in the era that followed World War II, home ownership became a middle-class entitlement. In time, the single-family house became more than home, transformed into a financial asset whose greatest value is not how it protects you or how it makes you feel, but how much money it makes you when you sell it.

The modern financial model of home ownership in the United States is one of the most effective machines for the manipulation of human behavior ever invented. The dream of the basic security and comfort of a nice shelter in line with the images that the media trains us to pursue is only attainable if you play the game. First, you have to build a good credit score, which means you need to take on debt just to show you are capable of handling it. That usually means having credit cards in your twenties, which for many of us leads to spending more than you have and being trained to think of having more money as the path to happiness. You need to build a good, reliable income, which means learning to be a good employee, ideally one who earns a salary and has a track record of raises. Finally, you need to buy a house whose value is predictable—a house that is as much like the other houses around it as possible. That allows your mortgage to be sold by the bank that originates it, packaged in a portfolio of similar mortgages and sold as institutional securities. The impact of this system on how we live our lives is profound and rarely examined. Ecologically, it abstracts our homes from the land, and makes it very hard for people to finance the construction of homes that innovate greener design. Economically, by tying our living place to our labor, it produces a neofeudal system of tenure well adapted to consumer capitalism, which expends much of its other energies selling us things to fill the house with and diversions to make us think we are happy while plugged into this matrix. The emotional stresses this system produces are immense—even if, when the game is working out okay for you, they simmer at a low level. The difference between a home mortgage and a payday loan is not as great as the institutional custodians of the former would have you believe.

The only way out is to figure out how to pay for your house without a mortgage, or to plan your life in a way that pays off your mortgage, in a society of values so inflated and supported by the promise of tomorrow's surpluses that even the idea of paying off one's car is mostly illusory. And if you ever have the discipline or wealth to pay off your mortgage, almost anyone you consult will tell you not to, in a culture that promotes the financial benefits of tax deductions and the servile behavior home-based debt produces instead of the freedom and happiness that comes with liberation from that debt.

The homeowners who get the best outcomes in our society are the ones who learn to treat their houses not just as home, but as their primary investment. A way, through the appreciation of value,

----

to generate real wealth when you sell the property—surplus that can be put into an even nicer home or perhaps some other investment. Keeping everyone invested in the economic model, and the way of thinking about the land, that the American real estate business embodies. The environmental impact of this system is far more devastating than the pampered variants of human indenture it enables. In a nation unique for the easy availability of land over the course of three centuries, the evolution of mortgage financing has enabled a landscape of sprawling suburbia, of essentially identical homes that bulge forth from terraformed little lots, oblivious to their footprint on the Earth.

I was a white male lawyer with a good income, even if encumbered by the financial setbacks that come with a failed marriage. That made me presumptively creditworthy, with a privilege unafforded to most. And I understood, more or less, how the game worked. I knew that there were still banks that would keep the mortgages in-house, if they thought there was a long-term relationship they could profit from or if they were just hungry to build up their balance sheets, maybe as new entrants to the market. I asked around, made calls, had meetings, and eventually found a bank that would loan me the money to finance the lot purchase I had already made. Being able to finance the construction would take more time, but the portal that hatch in the middle of the yard represented had started to open.

Interstates, Ecologies, Artists, and Lovers
The first place I experienced in Austin was the landmark that is most often, and most surprisingly, used to define its ecology:

188

Interstate 35. This road connects Laredo to Duluth and, halfway between Austin and Duluth, my hometown of Des Moines. The stretch of I-35 that runs from the Colorado River to the north of the University of Texas is a double-decker monstrosity—probably on purpose, as it was built in a way that reinforced the Jim Crow dividing line across which people of color were segregated, on the path of a wide boulevard called East Avenue. I did not know of this history when I arrived at the old airport one Saturday evening in the spring of 1998 for my first visit to the city, just as a storm had blown through. Rain always makes paved landscapes look prettier than they are.

My wife, Agustina, saw some of the same things, long before we met, around the same time as I first visited Austin. She had moved up from Houston to go to school, studying painting at the university. Hanging on our bedroom wall are four oil-on-canvas images she painted as a student, of the upper and lower decks of I-35 at night. Mostly, the paintings reveal the beauty of the sky—crepuscular pink, ebon dark, the lights of the cars streaming through like plastic stars. Now every time I look at those paintings, I am reminded of how we found each other in large part because we saw the same world, and felt the same yearning for the possibility of beauty and wonder amid the ugliness, a search that brought us both to this zone on the other side of the dam that holds back nature.

I-35 is more than a freeway and more than an urban wall. It is also an ecotone. Various practitioners of the natural sciences refer to it as such—most notably, the meteorologists of the National Oceanic and Atmospheric Administration, who regularly forecast

----

189

major and minor weather events and patterns as occurring east, west, or along "the I-35 corridor." Their doppler radar sometimes captures large swarms of bats or flying ants along that corridor, which, like many major highways, follows the path of much older roadways along ancient paths made by nature. North out of town, and most of the way to Fort Worth, I-35 follows the route of the Chisholm Trail, and a stretch south of Kansas City tracks the Santa Fe Trail. The pioneer trails were almost all Indigenous Peoples' trails once, and likely animal trails before that. In 2015, I-35 was declared the "Monarch Highway"—a zone in which six states agreed to collaboratively seed native wildflowers that would aid the eastern monarchs and other butterflies who have long followed the highway's approximate pathway on their way south to the oyamel fir forests north of Mexico City, where they winter. The I-35 corridor travels north and south, but as an ecotone it marks the transition between the woodlands of the east and the plains and arid topographies of the west. The Wichita people were one of the main occupants of that liminal territory before Europeans arrived, ranging from Central Texas through Oklahoma and Kansas into Nebraska. In Austin, I-35 marks the eastern edge of the originally platted town and approximates the dramatic shift between the prairies and the Hill Country.

The connection between I-35's topographical character and its sociological implications is one of the first things a newly arrived modern homesteader is taught by those who are already here. There is a "good" side and a "bad" side—or was, until the forces of gentrification swept over it. The lawyers in the firm I moved here to work for in the late '90s taught me the dividing lines, in a well-mannered way, as they tried to explain one's options regarding where to live. In the office, which occupied the high floors of an '80s office building right on the river as it passes through downtown, people jockeyed to get views to the west, where you could see the beginnings of the rolling hills and palatial suburban homes that sprawl far beyond the horizon, instead of the views to the east, flat as a table and interlaced with the landscape of infrastructure—airport, power plants, highways, tank farms, and working-class housing. For some reason that view seemed more interesting to me, not just because it was the one I was stuck with. It seemed more real.

Long before I found my brownfield lot, I found myself drawn to this zone that lurked at the edge of the view from my office window. I had found my way through on the river with Hugo, and I wondered if there were other ways in, other contiguous zones that remained undiscovered to me. I put on my running shoes and jogged the unmarked trails through expanses of old ranchland along the south side of the river that seemed to have reverted, officially or unofficially, to commons. The portals proved elusive, but there were signs I was close.

At the base of the dam, there was a park with baseball fields and a big parking lot that was probably packed on weekend afternoons but empty when I was there. Behind the ball fields, I could find the woods and the kinds of paths through them that had been made by ranch hands in trucks and neighborhood kids on foot. Sometimes I'd notice rows of trees in the woods that had once demarcated a lane, but whatever road had once been there—or structure it had once led to—was gone, overtaken by wild foliage. Down

----

one path, I found a massive concrete structure above a riparian creek, a bunker that looked abandoned, its original purpose unclear. Occasionally I would see markers of buried pipelines and gas lines. I could follow a path that ended up in a pocket prairie behind an expanse of cheap apartments, or one that terminated at a hurricane fence topped with razor wire, or another that came out between two little houses at the end of a cul-de-sac. I would often get irretrievably lost, sometimes disoriented or even a little scared. Sometimes I would see a coyote, or a hawk, or a stray dog. Rarely would I encounter any other people.

At the edge of the parking lot behind the ball fields, right where it bumped up against the woods, stood a mysterious tower. A nine-story concrete edifice, with windows and balconies, weirdly abstracted, like a sketch toward the idea of a high-rise trying to emerge from a lookout keep of yore. Its official purpose and design are straightforward: to provide a place for firefighters to train. Its enigmatic promise—viewed through the right frame of mind—is as a landmark that points the way to the portal, maybe as the portal itself. A place where everyday life morphs into the surreal.

Not long after she painted her quadriptych of I-35, Agustina had managed to engineer an intervention in that fire tower: an installation of fabric into its empty windows that expressed the motion of air moving through, captured on video. When I saw it, not long after we met, I knew I had found someone on a similar search, one that had brought us to the same weird place, even as we saw it and experienced it through the prism of our own perspectives.

We met in a more ordinary way: in the offices of Thomas and Calvin, one afternoon following a design meeting. Agustina had a

- - - -

studio down the street from the lot, in an old fishing camp remade as maker space, populated mostly by designers she worked with. As newly minted masters of architecture in a broken economy that had no jobs for architects, Agustina and two of her grad school class-mates partnered up to buy a laser cutter and use it as the means of entrepreneurial architectural production. She produced a line of lamps from corrugated cardboard and cut coroplast, finding it easy to get design attention and awards but harder to get commercial distribution and production scale. If you dropped by the studio, the first thing you would notice was the smell of burnt paper.

That started the conversation, which ended up going into differ-ent territory over the course of the following six months. Aesthetics first, about naturally occurring surrealism, the idea of the uncanny, and the way it manifested in the strange zone we had both found ourselves in. About the fire tower, the abandoned muscle car, and the meanings they encoded. About the possibility of aesthetics to conjure magic from a broken world. She was edgy and cool, beauti-ful and athletic, smart and elusive, more than a little witchy. Medi-terranean, South American, and Texan all at the same time. Like an artsy Artemis, with a deeply liberated sense of independence.

Our first date was at Justine's, a hip little brasserie that had just opened in an unlikely location near the lot, across the street from the oxygen tank distributor and a cantina called El Agasajo. We talked about our life trajectories. She was, like me, an introverted loner, who had been single for seven years, focused on a search for meaning in her life that was about other things. Born in Paris to Argentine expats, she'd been transplanted as a girl from the weird wonders of Buenos Aires to the brutally soulless landscape

----

of suburban Houston, a dislocation she had been trying to find her way free from forever. After she finished her painting degree at UT she moved to Venice, talked her way into work as a glass-blower based on her experience working at a bong factory north of Austin, and managed to find her way into the interior life of that city, living with friends in the old Jewish quarter, the daughter of Spanish Sephardim and Italian immigrants somehow finding her way to one version of home.

When we stepped outside after dinner, a brutal wind had blown into town. We went for a long drive in the dark in search of concrete monoliths and abandoned buildings. At the end of the dead-end road by the police training facility past the edge of town, we got out of my truck to look down into the wild ravine below. The wind had grown so intense we could barely hear, and when we opened the truck doors, we feared we'd blow off the edge. We had each found a companion in our search, maybe a partner. Now we had to find our way through the darkness and into the wonder.

I decided to give up my apartment and move into the one-bedroom rental house next door to the lot, as a declaration of com-mitment to the project. I quickly learned this brownfield was special, even without the extra enhancement of a house designed to tune it in on its own frequency. We had fun—Hugo, Agustina, and me—maybe the most fun any of us had ever had. It took the pressure off the timeline to build, even as it also made us realize: This was it.

The Architecture of Cardinals
As February turns into March, the cardinals get busy. Ordinary birds, exceptionally common, yet always a welcome and beautiful

----

194

sight, thanks to their scarlet coloring, crested heads, and persistently comforting call. When we first moved into the cottage,
we noticed how many cardinals were living in this zone between
the factories and the urban woods. We didn't start noticing the
nests until a few years into our occupancy of the house we built.
As the cross vines began to grow down from our roof and cover
the upper parts of the windows, reaching all the way to the ground
in a few spots, some pairs made their nests there—hidden from
danger behind the leaves, their domestic life visible to us from
inside. One Saturday afternoon while studying in the living room,
Agustina looked up to see the commotion of two fledglings as they
dropped from the nest onto the concrete. She was alarmed, until
the parents both quickly flew to their aid, showing their juvenile
progeny by example how to use those wings. And then it worked,
and the kids clumsily flew off to the trees by the pool.

The nests of the cardinals are astonishingly well anchored on
what would seem the flimsiest of foundations—a few strands of
vine hanging like thread next to a vertical architectural plane.
They usually last for many seasons past their use as incubators
of new life. But sometimes they fall. One that hung over our front
door dangled for weeks after it lost its anchor on one side, leaving
us the view of a single speckled egg on the edge of tumbling to the
ground. Others take years after their abandonment before they
finally end up on the ground where we can take a closer look.

If you look it up in one of the bird books that provides guides
to nests as well as the species that make them, you may read how
cardinals often use bits of string or cloth in their construction.
That curious note is true, albeit dated. When a nest ends up on our

- - - -

patio, we can see how our neighborhood cardinals have upgraded, taking advantage of their lives in the trees next to a long row of industrial operations. The outer rims of the nests are the usual strands of dead grass, woven in a way that seems super taut when in use but quickly falls apart when removed from its context. And when we peel it back, we find the things humans made.

The cardinals especially love the white polyethylene open-cell foam that is used to wrap hard objects shipped inside corrugated cardboard boxes. It's easy to imagine how much of that there is around the loading docks of the factories and warehouses near our home, all the slivers that tear loose in the wrapping and unwrapping. We also find a lot of clear plastic wrap, and sometimes bits of white printer paper, usually inscribed with fragments of some shipping order or invoice.

In February 2022, as the cardinals were getting ready for the new breeding season, our young daughter, Octavia, and I found an abandoned nest on the patio and decided to see what all was in it. As we disassembled it, we were amazed at how complex the construction was, with multiple layers of varying materials woven into a snug little bowl you could hold in the palm of your hand. The core structure was made from seemingly endless spools of long, thin stems of dried-out tall grass. Inside that, a layer of clear plastic that seemed to have been crumpled up by a human hand and then flattened by a boot or a tire, printed with bits of blue ink, one piece with the letters **T-EXHAUST.** Another layer of wider blades of grass, maybe inland sea oats. A fourth layer of white paper that looked to have once been wet and unfolded to reveal a thermal printer pharmacy receipt from 2018, the items sold too obscured to read.

Further in, two different bits of the cellophane that originally packaged some snack foods—maybe packs of crackers or cookies—their ingredients and warnings still legible, if incomplete. The part of a beige Subway to-go bag that had some of the logo on it. A seamed piece of a gray plastic bag, printed in French with part of the address of the California banana farm from which it came, zip code 91361. A few bits of that open-cell white foam insulation. The clear plastic wrapper of a Black & Mild cigar. The long, thin tear-off strip that was used to open a different smoke, one packaged in gray and printed along the entirety of its length with lawyerly verse:

> *aging, or color should be interpreted to mean safer. Nothing*
> *about this cigarette, packaging, or color should be interprete*

I don't know to what extent the cardinals rework the materials they find beyond the remarkable weaving they do, but I know other birds convert found materials through the application of their labor into something very different. Some take paper and chew it into pulpy insulation. Others do similar things with the threads of fabrics.

In Mexico City, sparrows and finches frequently tear up cigarette butts to use the cotton fibers for their urban nests. The jury is still out on what effects the toxins in those fibers—ethylphenol, titanium dioxide, propylene glycol, insecticides, and even cyanide—have on the fledglings. In Antwerp, magpies have recently been found to be stealing plastic strips of aluminum anti-bird spikes—metal arrays installed to prevent birds from nesting or roofing on the edgeforms of buildings—and using them to fortify their nests, creating structures that blend natural and manufactured materials in a new cyborg form that looks like the product of an Easter egg hunt curated by H. R. Giger.

The use of human materials for avian nesting is not new. But their adaptation to thermal insulation and waterproofing made possible by plastics seems a different kind of leap. And if ornithologists are right that the typical cardinal only lives for three years, it seems the knowledge about how to insulate nests with industrial materials is somehow being passed on between generations of birds.

The revelations that slowly settled as we observed the birds with whom we shared our space was profound. Their choice of locations to build their nests affirmed the potential of one of the half-baked utopian ideas that drove the design: the belief that we can blur the boundaries between human and wild habitat in a way that lets us share the same space. We were able to watch the birds raising their young outside the rooms where our own children slept, bringing food to the open mouths of babies within sight of our infant daughter as she nursed. Their repurposing of discards of human industry as materials to build a better nest blurred the boundaries in a way we didn't expect, revealing a survival advantage obtained not through the generosity of our supposed stewardship, but through canny adaptation to the world the birds found themselves in. As we learned to pay closer attention, we saw they were not the only ones.

- - - -

7

How to Live in a Feral House

Harvester Ants and Internets

In the middle of our supposedly empty lot, a secret metropolis was hidden—a big, barren patch of dirt along one side of the valve box, with a hole in the center from which ants were coming and going. Big ants, with heads the size of lentils and mandibles big enough to clamp down on your fingertip. If you watched them, you would soon see they had built a network of roads—wide dirt paths blazed through the wild grass, jammed with foragers heading out and returning with seeds of grain for the commune. The patterns of their activity, there in a lot just off the cloverleaf of an old highway, weirdly mirrored our own.

Our neighbor Tom Atkinson, an entomologist who met his botanist wife, Emily, because the bugs he studied were eating the plants she studied, estimated the colony numbered as many as 160,000 inhabitants. They were fascinating creatures, not just because of their roadbuilding. Hugo and I would watch them for long periods of time. Sometimes he would drop a little leaf into the DMZ around their entry holes to see how quickly and efficiently they would remove the vegetative interference. A couple of times we encountered battles between invasive fire ants and the harvester ants, who were several times bigger and whose bite was much more intense, at least to human recipients.

One morning in 2010, when we woke up and looked out of the bedroom window of the cottage, we saw people in blue hazmat suits digging up our yard. It was the pipeline remediation crew Chevron had dispatched on our dime, arriving with all the drama of one of those movies about a viral outbreak or alien invasion. Except they were the invaders. At least from the perspective of the native ants, whose mound the crew ended up designating as a "biohazard" to be dealt with accordingly.

They tried digging up the mound with a backhoe, but quickly realized that would only aggravate their problem, as the ants would make it impossible for them to go in and remove the valve box. They tried over-the-counter insecticides from the hardware store, but those proved ineffective. They were working on getting stumped, but they also had the can-do, trial-and-error, "better to ask forgiveness than permission" attitude characteristic of Texans. In the end, they came up with a solution that was incidentally more humane. They just put more dirt over the ground, and busied the colony with that problem while they extracted the valve box and pipeline. It worked.

And when they were done and gone, the ants returned.

A year later, when we had finally been able to line up the financing to build the house, the crew from the design-build firm had the same issue with the ants. The colony was right at the edge of the area they needed to excavate for the foundation. When they were done, the entry stairs—poured concrete—came right up in the spot where that valve box had been. And the summer after we moved in, the ants returned. We were happy to see them.

Beneath their colony was a small utility closet where we accessed all our domestic infrastructure controls, including the router for our home Internet, which was connected to a long ethernet cable fished through a pipe buried in the yard. The cable probably went right through the colony.

Not long after that, I learned scientists had deduced that harvester ants control the comings and goings of their foragers using a method that is mathematically identical to TCP/IP, the protocol that regulates the packet switching of data on our modern digital networks. The number of new foragers sent out by the colony is directly regulated by the number coming back with food. Not long after, we changed the name of our network to *Anternet*, and began to wonder when the human networks we brought and the biological networks we were striving to coexist with would begin to merge. The truth was, they already had. We were just living in a way that made it more immediately evident.

The harvester ants were everywhere, once we learned to look for them. Usually in places made more hospitable to them by our own networks. Along the sides of roads, especially at elevated points, like the berm-supported highway on-ramp a block from our house or the raised area where the sidewalk crossed over the dam. We would find them along the man-made trails, especially in spots maintained as rights-of-way for telecom infrastructure, like the buried lines that followed the feeder roads. The harvester ants were flourishing, because humans had created a habitat they were well suited to, one that made their basic community-building easier and provided ample food in the weedy grasses that grew after our bulldozers moved on. Most importantly, we had, in a very short time, driven their main predator to the brink of extinction.

My dad used to tell us the story of the summer he went to the Boy Scout Jamboree in Washington, D.C., not long after World War II. How he rode on the train with boys from all over the country, many of whom brought talismans of their homeplace to show off, and some of whom brought animal familiars. The Texas boys, he said, all had horny toads they kept in their pockets. Even when he was old, you could still see the juvenile wonder in Dad's face as he remembered seeing those strange, beautiful creatures, once as common as squirrels. While not extinct, they are exceptionally rare now, their populations decimated by our overtaking of their range. They didn't adapt as well as their main food source to that change.

When the harvester ants reappeared at the top of our stairs in the first warm season after we finished construction, it was a sign we might succeed in our crazy goal: to build a home that also provided a home for the other species that did or could live there. One where we could coexist without too much discomfort. One that recognized that the line between our habitat and theirs does not really exist. That just as they work hard to adapt to us, we could return the favor and reap the rewards. Dividends that paid in wonder and in the energy and health of real, biodiverse life. It also provided a platform where we could figure out how to build our own new family, in a place where the other life that permeated the domus made it easy to break out of our own self-absorption and see the bigger picture.

Country Living in the City

The cottage we rented next door while we built our house was a funny little place. The outside was painted the same green as the feathers of the monk parakeets who would come around to snack on the mesquite pods, and the interior floors were eco-friendly orange tile. It was tiny, with one little bedroom that could barely hold a queen bed, a single closet to share, a little bathroom with just a shower stall, and a kitchen with an electric stove, a spot for a washer-dryer, and a few open shelves. We put Hugo's bed in the corner of the living room with a screen for privacy if he wanted it, and I found a 1978 Airstream Land Yacht at a used camper shop and parked it in the driveway as an extra hangout space for him. Ever the analog kid, he immediately latched on to the weird,

cheesy wonder of the 8-track tape player built into the living room end, bringing home $5 boxes of random tapes from Antone's while appreciating the special awesomeness of the tapes the previous owner had left behind, including a compilation enigmatically titled *A Phone Call from God*. We put our last TV in the trailer, so Hugo could play games with visiting friends, but we didn't get a new cable subscription. We had a record player in the house, but our real entertainment was the life outside. Not so much by active intention, as slow realization that was where we wanted to be, and where we belonged.

Almost every night, we would hang out there on the porch or in the backyard—sometimes all three of us, sometimes two of us, sometimes one of us home alone. If it was cold, we would build a fire in the pit, up at the edge of the bluff that graded down to the floodplain of the river, sometimes roasting marshmallows, other times telling stories. It was mostly hot, though, but not too hot to sit outside after the sun went down. We were each working really hard—Hugo with an intense school and the emotional challenges of adolescence and parental division, Agustina with two businesses of her own and a part-time office gig, me with an IPO and a book to deliver—and the place proved a perfect sanctuary where we could forget our worries. We soaked up the life energy of summer, which got unexpectedly more intense every night as it got darker and later. Sometimes aided by intoxicants, sometimes stone sober, we would alternate between laughing, reading, and listening to the cacophony of life from the woods and the river— the chorus of frogs, the insanely loud skronks of horny herons, the banshee howls of the coyotes.

In the daytime, we went back to the land. We planted a vegetable garden, learned the names of the lizards from Hugo, made terrariums, and explored. Walking along the river with Hugo, I learned you could just as easily walk *in* the river, with or without shoes, if you let go of your uptight obsession with not getting wet unless you are wearing gear made to get wet. That revelation opened up new expanses of territory—astonishing quantities of wild space hidden in the edges of the city. Maybe it was the access we each had to that space—mental space as much as physical space—that made that quirky little home such a good platform for figuring out how to build our relationships as a modern family.

Living in the rented cottage next to our empty lot, we learned how easy it could be to live in nature without leaving the city. A simple little shelter, sited at the edge of the woods on a side street behind the industrial park. It made me realize how accessible that way of living is, if you can find one of those funny old houses or apartments that occupy the edge between human space and an urban creek, woodland, or involuntary park. In another version of the story, we might have stayed in that cottage for years. But we had already elected to amp up the experiment, by seeing if we could build a house that brought nature all the way home.

How to Make a Prairie on Your Roof

Agustina had been the one who envisioned the house as it could be when it was done and fully landscaped, in a rendering that dialed up the utopia—a Texas prairie dappled with wildflowers, in the middle of which the earth has erupted at two sharp angles, opening a small entrance to some mysterious underground structure.

A house that supplicates itself to the land, expressing its boldness with restraint and balance. As we settled into life next door, we worked on the task of figuring out how to make that vision real. In a project riddled with confounding obstacles, that effort to invert building to nature, truly wild nature, was the biggest challenge, in part because it was the real victory condition.

Green roofs are a common thing in northern climes, as are partly buried houses that let the green roofs turn white in the winter, insulating the house with the warmth of the earth. Some of the Indigenous Peoples of the Southwest built pit houses, which followed a similar plan on a smaller scale, and that was one of the precedents Thomas and Calvin had in mind with their design—shelter made from the Earth itself, trying to adopt Indigenous knowledge to modern conditions. But adapting the European-style green roof to the hot and dry climate of Texas was a challenge that had stymied many until a British ecologist named Mark Simmons figured out a way. The answer was as simple as it was beautiful—instead of the golf course monoculture that is typical of a Northern European green roof, plant the roof with native prairies that were adapted to this climate. To do that, you needed to figure out how to make a growing medium they would thrive in, and over more than a decade of research, that's what Mark did. Two of his protégés, John Hart Asher and Emily Manderson, were landscape architects Agustina had gone to school with, the former one of her business partners. She brought us all together one day at the Wildflower Center to talk about the options. I brought a skepticism about redemptive restorationist strategies, wary of the idea of bringing back our imagined version of the ecological past, and more interested in imagining a sustainable path into the compromised future we can see coming into being around us.

The categorizations we make about which species are native and which are invasive have a political dimension. The people who urge the strictest policing of invasives often, it has been my impression, do so in a way that is wrapped up with conceptions of social class and the weird way that gets expressed in supposedly classless American culture. The way it is so often highly educated middle-class white people advocating the doctrines of ecological purity makes it feel sometimes as if the eugenics many of our grandparents and great-grandparents advocated for the human race got transferred to the plants that we live around. At a deeper level, perhaps more subconscious, it is often the people whose forebears were the earliest European settlers of these lands who get the most caught up in restoration efforts that aim to bring back the botanical ecologies that were here before, as if to atone. I have a reflexive wariness of such ecological puritanism, even as I recognize it has a lot of benefits.

There is wonder in the alien. The wonder of the weird future that is aborning, as nature adapts to the world we made. Like finding escaped parakeets taking over the cell towers above the 7-Eleven, houseplants gone wild along a rocky riverbank where they used to dredge gravel, a naturalized pomegranate tree fruiting in the secret woods below the overpass, rich honey made by invasive bees in an old tire half-buried in the dirty soil of an empty lot. Emerging research indicates it is non-native animals, terrestrial and marine, that show the greatest ability to tolerate

----

the extreme weather events occurring around the world with increasing frequency.

To me the real problem with "introduced species" is when conditions allow them to crowd out the natives. Like in spring, when the downy brome grass comes in not long after MLK Day, so early and with such prodigious reproductive efficiency that it crowds out the indigenous wildflowers and grasses that are also in the seedbank and would otherwise flourish. Even worse, the rhizomatic Johnson grass that overtakes open fields all over our region, choking out all other life—even making it hard for mammals to move through—and stubbornly resistant to even the most aggressive weed-control efforts. Species like those, and the manicured ornamental grasses that dominate American lawns, are a core ecological problem that would be easy to fix with a little effort. They limit biodiversity at the base of the food chain, and when you change that, the benefits are immediate, profound, and wondrous.

Our lot was a mix, with exotics dominating the sunny areas and native grasses thriving in the shade—a common variation in edgeland environments around here. With our roof, we had the opportunity to create a model restoration. Only it wasn't really a restoration—more like a simulation of the ecology that dominated the area around us before European settlement. Even though our actual lot, as we came to learn over time, did not want to be a prairie so much as a riparian woodland.

My skepticism of the bias toward native plants versus so-called "invasives" was countered by my experience of the biodiversity that comes with a native prairie. In the '80s, while I was away at school, my parents had bought an acreage in southern Iowa, where my mom had the idea that they could retire. She saw the potential of the heavily wooded, mostly unfarmable site and had stubbornly heretical ideas about how to restore it to its natural condition as an oak savanna. Every year of my adult life they burned it, and the resulting transformation, without a single seed ever brought in, was remarkable. Every visit, especially in summer, I would experience the intense and undeniable life energy that a recharged ecosystem brings. The idea of experimenting with something like that in the heart of the city intrigued me, especially if we could balance it with my own heretical views about the virtues of weeds. So when Mark told me the growing medium could include used vacuum tubes from old televisions, I was sold.

Driving on the highways that connect San Antonio, Austin, and Dallas, you can see the ghosts of the prairie that once covered this land. Sometimes you can find tiny remnants. Two hours west of Austin, outside the town of Junction, where the forks of the Llano River meet at the edge of the Hill Country, a sage named Bill Neiman and his family operate a business called Native American Seed, using the techniques of production agriculture to save the seed stock of not just the Blackland Prairie, but all the other native grassland ecologies of the region. For decades now, Bill has been traveling around the region, finding pockets of wild plants that have survived or reasserted themselves in untended corners, harvesting seeds to take back to his place, where older and simpler tractors and farm equipment help him turn the floodplain of the Llano into an incubator of a greener future. An eternally hopeful undertaking, even if it often feels like you are losing.

Making a prairie out of your yard is not quite as easy as ordering a bag and spreading it across the ground. But really, it's not much harder than that, and you can do it on any piece of land where prairies once grew, even as small as a little side yard. Planting our green roof was a more complicated undertaking, involving the importing of a European specialty green roof sealant that came in giant drums Homeland Security detained as suspicious for several months until we finally liberated them. Sourcing and mixing all manner of weird soil inputs—from rice hull ash to crushed pecan shells—and layering the growing medium in a lattice of plastic cells. Planting live plants and plugs and huge amounts of seed, and

watering it copiously despite the drought—something you can get a permit for here, if you are using precious water to establish drought-tolerant natives that won't need it in future seasons. We started planting in June 2012, and by the end of the first summer, we had an early successional prairie growing over our heads.

For the second phase—the wider yard around that—we did not have the luxury of a bespoke growing medium, just the dirt where that pipeline and trash had been, dirt that was full of the seeds of invasive plants. So, we went to the hardware store, bought huge sheets of black plastic normally used by house painters, and laid it out over the land in advance of growing season. The invasives would come up on cue, but find no sun. If you peeked under the tarps, you would see the sprouts, white like subterranean mammals or cave fish. After a few months of that, we rolled up the tarps, put out the native seeds, and watered. And the next season, we had more prairie.

Keeping it that way requires constant vigilance. The invasive species always appear, and to try to keep them completely at bay, especially when working with an urban plot surrounded by properties that are not so maintained, is a Sisyphean undertaking. It helps to be someone who grew up doing yardwork, turning what was a miserable chore and then the source of comic book money into a meditative practice—the joy of weeding. A yardwork that is about bringing biodiverse life back into the world, instead of machining the land into a simulation of life. We can never get rid of all the invasives, especially not on our little plot of urban land, but we can achieve some measure of balance.

- - - -

The first summer we cultivated our green roof, a weird plant dominated—tall, dusty green, with sharp seed expressions at the ends like an insanely thick pipe cleaner. I wondered if it was a native, even though my intuition told me it was not, and I learned it was a thing called hogweed that needed to be pulled as fast as it appeared. In the heart of our new prairie, thick stands of reedy rye appeared, which looked beautiful, but I was admonished that they were invasive and needed to be eradicated immediately before their seed spread. That proved pretty easy to do, over a few seasons. Entirely eliminating the patches of Johnson grass proved more challenging. And in time, the brome grass found its way in. First at the edges, then quickly, over a few years, working on taking over. The only solution, when that happens, is to start over, resolarizing the soil under plastic; or deploying the technology Indigenous Peoples used when they wanted to dial up the biodiversity of the land on which they lived: fire.

On the advice of my dad, a retired dentist who singed his own eyebrows off the first season he and my mom burned their acreage in southern Iowa, I bought the garden tool every all-American lawn boy secretly yearns for: a backpack flamethrower. It's really a simple propane torch—a small tank you carry in something like a 1970s backpack frame, with a rubber hose attached to a long metal nozzle whose flame you can control much like a garden hose. Working in small patches, with the torch in one hand and a water hose in the other, I tried that technique, and it worked. I did not burn my eyebrows off, or my mustache, or start a fire I could not control, but I came close, and decided to mostly leave the torch in the shed. As the seasons added up, the life in the yard constantly

----

changing with them, I learned the greatest joy came from tending the yard on my hands and knees. With the work came the wonder.

Snakeskins and Fangs

To find the invasive plants growing in our pocket prairie, I work my way through the tall grass and wildflowers, combing it back like the unkempt hair of Mother Earth and pulling out things that don't belong by grabbing them at the base and (hopefully) ripping out all the roots from the soil. I have learned the textures, colors, and anatomies of the plants well, through a dialed-down version of close observation that comes to span seasons strung out over time. I have made hundreds of decisions about what to leave and what to remove. I have made mistakes: sometimes finding the beautiful bloom of an extravagant wildflower only after it revealed itself from the bunches of invasives I just pulled out. I have learned how the plants interact with each other—sometimes providing each other support, sometimes crowding each other out—and encountered all the other life that appears in the prairie once we cultivate the habitat for it. Once in a while I have realized I just pulled a plant from an anthill—only after they started to bite under my sleeve or pant leg and I had to quickly rip off my clothes. Lizards, grasshoppers, ladybugs, bumblebees, dragonflies, butterflies, walking sticks, mantises, lacewings, and all manner of curious beetles abound. I have seen which creatures like which plants. I have seen how the birds take advantage of the cover and the abundant food. I have begun to be able to tell, intuitively, which plants in the prairie would make good food for my family.

As I comb through the wild plants, I often find the remains of life transformations—the chrysalises of butterflies, or the empty exoskeletons left behind by the molt of a big bug, which look like a mold. On the ground I sometimes find snakeskins recently shed, reminding me of one of the apex predators of the wild garden. When I started finding snakeskins in the yard I was blindly probing with my hands, it was a little intense. Over time I came to appreciate why, for the ancients and the early Christian mystics, snakeskins were a symbol of human transformation. The druids, it is said, saw the very image of life in the snake and its traces—a creature of the earth that is also the knower, and perhaps teacher, of its secrets.

One night, as we returned home from seeing a movie, I almost stepped on a coral snake by our bedroom door. I immediately remembered the mnemonic rhyme someone had taught me not long after I moved to Texas:

> *Red on black, friend of Jack.*
> *Red on yellow, kill a fellow.*

The Texas coral snake, *Micrurus tener*, is considered the most potently venomous snake in the United States. It's not a big snake—even when you encounter a big specimen, as we often do around our house—but it's a scary-looking creature. Something about the colors: the red, yellow, and black rings, like the stripes you might see on some '70s pickup, slightly dulled to a flat matte for night hunting. Some way in which nature has preprogrammed you to know that if you fuck with that little animal, it has a good shot at killing you.

That first one we found was there on the concrete patio between the living and sleeping sides of our house, slithering around in the dark. Hugo was with us that weekend, and as we stood there watching the snake, he told us what he had learned at camp the summer before—that the likelihood of getting envenomated by a *coralillo* as a human adult is very low, because their mouths are so small that it would be hard for them to get a bite unless you served up a fingertip or toe, and the way they deliver the poison requires a chewing motion that is hard to complete if you are that much bigger and fighting back. But that conventional wisdom, it turns out, is wrong—coral snakes can actually deliver quick bites with substantial venom. And when they do, you better seek immediate medical attention. Though the doctors may not be able to do much to help you, as the bites are so rare that pharmaceutical companies stopped making the antivenom years ago, concluding it was not profitable enough. The freshest available stocks, if you can believe Wikipedia, had an expiration date sometime in 2020.

Over the years, we have seen many such snakes on our patio. Usually at night, but not always. I found one by our front door one Thursday in May as I headed out to give a talk at a technology law seminar. I made a video, and to induce it to move, I dangled the red-and-blue tie I had not yet put around my neck, creating a curious dance of stripes on stripes. I found another one curled up around the sole of one of my snake boots as I went to put it on. Of maybe a dozen such encounters, I only killed one—to protect our dogs—but I may need to do so again if one appears when my young daughter is around.

The architects who designed our house did not intend to create an optimal habitat for deadly serpents between the bedroom and the kitchen. But that's what they did. The house is divided into two pavilions: kitchen, dining, and living rooms on one side; bedrooms on the other; each with its own door to the outside, the uncovered patio the only way to get from one room to the other. It's a small space—around 700 square feet on each side. The patio is narrow, like a canyon, with glass windows rising twenty-five feet at the peaks on either side, wild plants dangling long from the roof. At the front, the house is buried, and the patio leads to a staircase up to the front yard. At the back, the patio opens level with the ground at the edge of the woods. The ground back there is covered with thick foliage and leaf litter, depending on the season. The house was designed as a platform for plants, without really anticipating how that would amplify its capacity as a biodiverse habitat for animal life. Cultivated with seventy species of native grasses and wildflowers that nature added to over the seasons, the green roof attracts all manner of insects. The insects attract lizards, who often hide in the tiny nook that runs between the base of the windows and the concrete floor of the patio, waiting for bugs who come down from the roof to crawl through that wide-open DMZ. The coral snakes come in to hunt the lizards, and perhaps other, smaller snakes.

The coral snakes thrive in those wild, dirty woods behind us, growing bigger than the guidebooks tell you to expect. Sometimes I see them there, moving through the grass as I walk, right in the spot I am about to step. I once returned from a walk to find one coiled all the way around the trunk of a hackberry, seeming substantially larger than the four feet said to be the upper end of their likely length. Of course we always make them bigger in our minds, because it amps up the wonder. The marvel of a deadly, mythic creature sharing our realm with us. Coexisting, maybe even finding a sort of welcome.

The red on yellows are far from the only snakes, and not the only deadly venomous creatures, around our house. One summer day I found a king snake in our swimming pool, so big that it covered almost the entire length before it slither-swam over the edge. I once found a bright-green grass snake crawling out of a recess in the concrete wall of the bathroom, next to the toilet that I was at that moment using. In that same bathroom, my early-morning encounters have included a black widow spider behind the tank and a mama wolf spider waiting for me as I opened the door and turned the light on, with a hundred tiny babies on her back, all of whom suddenly scattered when we bumped into each other. I found another black widow in our utility closet, waiting for prey in a bundle of clear plastic that I was about to pick up. We did not really set out to create a house that harbors creatures that can kill the humans who are the home's principal inhabitants, and over the years we have tended to see fewer of them inside the house or on its high-traffic verges. But the revelation that you can coexist with the full ambit of the food chain down in the postindustrial hobbit hole you have made your home is potent affirmation of the possibility of cultivating biodiverse life in a little corner of our urbanized world.

Even as we are often reminded that life is sustained through the death of others, the aesthetic and existential experience of the place is mostly the wonder of being surrounded by other life. The effect of the design is like a terrarium that somehow folds in on itself and expresses a boundless universe inside. The living room windows are a gallery for the unceasing parade. Butterflies flitter by, including every variation of swallowtail—pipevine, giant, tiger. Dragonflies hover along the edges of the green roof, their heavier-than-air energy reminding me of the bio-mimicking machine dreams of prog-rock album covers. On summer evenings the swallows come in from their nests along the side of the bridge, buzzing the roofline to take the bugs from the air. So do the bats, flowing out from their roosts under the bridges downtown. The first summer, when the green roof was new, I hosted a visiting writer for a European art magazine who walked in and said the house reminded her of a Tarkovsky film. As we talked about that insight, there was a loud bang on the window. We looked and saw a hawk flying off with the dove it had chased into our canyon, as if on cue from nature's director—proving what might be possible if we worked harder to make our built structures more about the landscape than the humans that live in it.

Brujas and Devil Riders

When we lived in the cottage, Agustina and I started making little terrariums—glass boxes full of plants better suited for a rainforest, arrayed to soak up what sun they could through our north-facing windows. The terrarium as symbolic space had long been a persistent symbol in my mind, an image I would draw in my journals—a miniature house under a tree inside a vitrine. I drew such an image one afternoon in the cottage, with a cigarette butt smoldering on the edge and a Valentine's heart arising in a thought balloon next to the smoke. We still have that picture in a little photo frame on our living wall, faded from fifteen years of sun. And we still have two of the terrariums we started back then, filled with mementos of the life we have lived together here, building our own version of family on our own terms. We also built a terrarium to live in: partly out of active intention, partly by accident, all as a kind of dream conjured into reality through some improvised *brujería* whose effectiveness surprised even us.

Growing up in that era when the '60s lurched into the '70s, stories of people going back to the land were always close by. It was always, in my memory, about becoming a farmer—the cool version. The hippie farmers who grew their own food, communally, to be liberated from the capitalist rat race through small-scale agricultural production. In Iowa City in the late '80s, the ghosts of that scene were all around, some as successful cooperative businesses that had opted back into the mainstream economic system, maybe on terms they could stomach. My aunt and uncle there have lived that way, she as a worker at the food co-op and he as a wizardly bicycle mechanic, modeling a kind of hedonically rich austerity—in their younger years living like migratory birds, bicycling from Iowa City to Austin for the winter and back again.

In the little 1920s brick house at the end of a cul-de-sac in Des Moines we lived in when Hugo was a toddler, the ghost of the prior owner—someone who had lived through the Depression— was evidenced by the horror-movie basement packed wall-to-wall,

----

floor-to-ceiling, with jars of foods he had preserved for when he would need them, only to have them outlast him. When we planted the first season of vegetables in his raised beds of soil, so well composted and turned you could shove your arm in them up to the elbow, I learned some of the wonders of small-scale agriculture myself.

In Austin, in the aftermath of the Financial Crisis, urban farming became a bona fide movement, on little acreages where millennials and members of Generation X would rekindle that same utopian dream, growing produce to sell in local farmers' markets and health-food groceries. An old neighbor and former client of mine, one of the world's leading experts on animated holography and 3D imaging, was an intensely committed advocate of urban farming and introduced me to the guy behind one of the biggest operations, who had made an idealistic organic farm on old floodplain land across the river from where I had bought my lot. You could tell the people working on the project were having fun, living in old trailers by the farm, with access to the river and a sense of communal mission that felt very real. Maybe it was my Iowa expat's bias that made me want to walk away from the farm, down to the river. The instinct that farming is, in some fundamental way, not about returning to nature, but enslaving it, no matter how few chemicals or machines or capitalist business methods you use to bring the green from soil to table. The learned lesson from a childhood in the heart of the Corn Belt that, in the heart of the heart of the country, everything is green but nothing is wild. And really, at a certain level, there is no authentic life. That is not to deny how essential agriculture is to the rich lives we lead, nor the joys that come from tending one's own garden and eating food you have grown from the dirt where you live. It is to interrogate whether the practice of it really brings you closer to nature, or just to a greener variant of human instrumentalism.

The instrumentalist idea of the green home is more commonly expressed in the way we talk about change through the prism of engineering: the urgent goal of lowering our carbon footprint. The term "green building" refers to building systems—the infrastructure of electricity, heating, and cooling, of homes as centers of consumption. It is about how to maintain the comfort of the building's human inhabitants in a way that consumes fewer of nature's available resources. Thinking about how we lower our atmospheric impact is one of the most critical challenges facing humanity, and the green building movement and the standards it promotes are deeply important. But ultimately it is focused on how to get there through technological change, without making any real changes to the way we live.

That's not to suggest I would gladly live like the characters in the novels I have written about near-future versions of America, where Texans find themselves living without air-conditioning, often because of endemic brownouts and failures of the electrical grid. But I've gone without air-conditioning in the worst summer heat and humidity, and survived without heat in severe winter conditions of cold and ice. Those experiences provide surprising windows into how else life could be, and how much our climate-control systems are the barrier between us and real life. The means whereby we maintain the illusory boundary between "inside" and "outside" that defines our lives.

- - - -

Our house is about a different sort of experiment in green living. At its essence, it is about letting the yard—even the house itself—go truly wild. Or as wild as you can reasonably manage. And about living in that wildness, in the natural elements of the outdoors. Living behind glass and being outside at the same time—or at least having to go outside to go to another room. It is not the same as living without shelter, but an experiment in altering the boundaries between us and the outdoors.

The wildness of our home has its limits. We put a fence around the main part of the yard, primarily to keep our dogs in, but also to keep uninvited humans out—which when you live where we do is, we learned, prudent and perhaps essential. That also keeps the big terrestrial animals out. The coyotes and the deer come right up to the fence, but not through it. And while the life that does exist inside the fence is rich, especially in the warm months, we try to keep it outside of the interior spaces. Mostly, we are successful. But not always.

THE INSECTS THAT LIVE on our green roof often appear on the glass windows that frame our rooms, usually when undertaking private activities that they seem to think can more safely be conducted on that glass: sleeping moths; juvenile Aztec spur-throated grasshoppers, with their green, yellow, red, black, and white stripes; dancing mantises. They come there to rest and to reproduce. We find all manner of strange eggs laid on the steel frames around our doors: the pendular drops of lacewings, the marvelously camouflaged little wigwams of bagworms, the amber pupae of mud daubers. Along our front fence, passion vine grows wild in the warm season, with its insane flowers that look like they were designed by some sci-fi art director imagining the bloom on an alien planet. *Passiflora* is the exclusive larval host of the Gulf fritillary butterfly, and those caterpillars like to build their cocoons on all the rigid man-made structures nearby. I have found them on the unused padlock by our front gate, under the lip of the trash can, on the steel frame of the old shorty shipping container we use as a garden shed, and even on the wheels of my 1987 Toyota Land Cruiser in the season when I hardly drove it. And when they hatch, they flutter around behind the factories like tangerine fairies, bringing grace to a world that does not deserve it.

Once in a while we find a giant walkingstick, *Megaphasma dentricus*, clawing at our front door—the biggest insect I have

ever seen outside of a museum, almost too big to hold in your hand, and when you do, a marvel of almost machine-like body and movement, with its heavy exoskeleton and the awkward geometry of its joints and body hinges, designed for slowly navigating through foliage, not the pressed steel and milled aluminum where we find them on display as we go about our day. Then there are the phasmids, whose reproductive practices caused the pioneers to call them "devil riders."

The females, who are about as long as one of your fingers and almost as thick, are the ones who earned *Anisomorpha buprestoides* the name "musk mare" among earlier generations of Americans who encountered these strange creatures in the country they had just taken by force. They were also sometimes called the "witch's horse." The cowboy-era settlers adopted so many equestrian analogies because these walkingstick bugs are most often seen with the diminutive male on the back of the female, usually for many days, as the insecure inseminators try to block any potential competitors long after the main work has been done. All through the warm half of the year—really any time it is not cold—we find them mating on our doorframes, and try to nudge them gently aside so we can enter or exit without harming them. The female has a special power: to shoot a malodorous cyclopentanyl monoterpene dialdehyde compound from a pair of glands at the front of her thorax, a spray that can be accurate as far as five feet away, often aimed at the eyes of its threat and capable of causing temporary blindness in humans. So far, we have not been sprayed.

The first summers here, our pool would be covered for one or two nights in the ghostly white larvae of some flyer I have never

- - - -

identified, a thick layer of life that glowed on the underlit water like some uncanny nymph ballet underway just outside our living room. Sometimes we experience the hazards to our habitat that come with the absence of boundaries between us and the creatures we share the space with. As winter ends, the ants get busy, often finding their way in, sometimes running convoys from under our kitchen cabinets through our daughter's play area. The wasps and hornets love to build their nests on the frame of the house and other steel foundations. Usually conspicuously, but the yellowjackets have a knack for nesting in boxes I need to open, as I have learned the hard way with a breaker panel, the charging station for an electric car, and the canoe I store upside-down on a pair of sawhorses in the yard.

In spring, when it rains, the millipedes sometimes come out. Little crunchy critters, variant in size but usually around an inch long, simultaneously fast and slow as they move across the polished concrete floors inside the house. Our first couple years, it didn't really rain that much. In 2015, it rained a lot, bringing the millipedes into the house in larger numbers and compelling us to better learn about their habitat and behavior. How they live in the leaf litter, are nocturnal, and like to stay dry. In the early morning, we would find hundreds of them crawling around on our living room floor, and huge masses gathered on the outside of the doors, trying to get in. We tried spraying insect repellent around the thresholds, but it did little to deter them. We bought a Shop Vac and started just vacuuming them up off the floor every morning, part of the routine between coffee and breakfast. We bought natural chemical insecticides, mostly made from menthols, which

I attached to the end of a hose, and then aimed at the swarms of millipedes piling up outside our doors, mitigating the interior infestation with the smell of mint murder. Anything to avoid the feeling of them crunching under our feet and being there, creepy crawling in the dark as we slept.

The third weekend in May that year, we went to New York for the launch of an issue of a journal I had contributed to. My talk was about borders and the idea ascendant at the time that the US-Mexico border could be secured with a virtual barrier comprised of the machines of electronic surveillance. When we returned home, we found our own domestic border had been thoroughly breached. Our living space was almost entirely covered with the corpses of millipedes that had entered the house seeking dry shelter (which was there) and food (which was not), resulting in their death. The stench was horrible, a weird odor of insect death, totally different from the smell of the slaughterhouse when the wind blows the wrong way. The smell of scents released by tiny glands that might serve to repel or attract, depending on your species. We vacuumed them up, too.

A reasonable response to this development would have been to bring in an exterminator. I joked that the end of the movie version would have me, alone in the house after my family has abandoned me, taking on an army of bugs with that backpack flamethrower. Instead, we tried to solve the problem without deviating from the philosophy of the house. I worked to reduce the quantity of dead plant matter left each fall by our rooftop prairie. We enlisted the aid of the folks from the door factory next door to help us better secure our thresholds from creatures small enough to crawl right through the gap. And amazingly, after a season, it worked.

We knew there would be other similar issues to come, but as long as there was no risk to our family's safety, we were okay with that. The dividends of natural wonder in our everyday domestic life were worth it. In time, we would even learn to recognize individual insects who had moved in with us for good.

8

Living in the Wild City

Foraging for Meaning

On a low table by our front door sits a large, round glass terrarium that soaks up the morning light and attracts the curiosity of our daughter with its collection of edgeland mementos. On a base of white gravel are displayed small artifacts that encode the history of our life in this place and the history of the place that preceded us. At the center is a piece of beautiful driftwood, with pointy knobs well suited to display bits of lost jewelry. Leaning up against one side is a fading Polaroid of Agustina and me when we were dating. There are rock-encrusted crystals Agi found on her searches next to blue chunks of antique transformer glass I found glistening in the river bottom. Two raccoon skulls, along with a 3D-printed facsimile of one produced with a scanner. There are two rubber hands made as finger puppets, both found on the street, one darker than the other. The "R" from a 1990s Chevrolet, a shard from some settler's teacup, an "O" from a Toyota. Part of the mandible of a small mammal and the leg of a bird, talons intact. Feathers—the black-and-white tiger stripes of hawk wings, the herringbone down of a woodpecker, the rusty red of a cardinal, the unearthly green of a monk parakeet. A bushy fragment of fox tail I found on the trail, which Octavia likes to use to transform herself into the animal. Superman's left leg and Spiderman's masked head. A blue plastic policeman and a beige frogman posed to hold onto a personal submersible. A roach clip that looks like the Venus of Willendorf. A twelve-sided die left behind by some wayward kitchen table half-elf. An empty aluminum canister I found half-buried in the front of our yard that once contained a half-ounce of Mr. Prolong—"A TOPICAL SPRAY TO PROLONG THE ACT OF LOVE"—branded with the silhouette of a dude holding his arms atop his head to show you all he's got. Spent brass cartridges from a .45 and a .30-06. A dog-eared Jack of Clubs picked up off the sidewalk outside the oil jobbers' on a gray Sunday morning. A nickel, an origami crane, the rusted fragment of an old metal camp cup. The sealing cap of a bottle of champagne we drank when we moved over here. A river rock we laser-etched with a petroglyph of a Predator drone and other rocks made beautiful

by the movement of water in the river. A scale model of the fire tower across the river that encodes the creation myth of our union, and two unused stamps with black hearts Agustina printed to mail the old postcards we sent out as our wedding invitations. A repository of memory embedded in objects, and of the existence of life outside the self.

When we moved here, even before the house was built, we started exploring every day. Usually in the company of dogs, starting with Hugo's dog Mothra, a terrier who went wherever he was; Agustina's familiar Lupe, a black mouth cur we rescued as a stray puppy in 2010, our first year living here; and Katsu, a Kishu Ken we adopted and trained in 2011. The dog walking was mostly my job on the weekdays, and I developed a routine whereby the dogs and I would get up at 5, I would write until 8, we would walk for an hour no matter the weather, and then I would have breakfast and attend to my law practice—all subject to modification for the day's other mandates, like taking a kid to school or going to a morning appointment.

On our walks, we would range far. We tried to go a different way every day, and mostly succeeded, in part because every day the world was different. We found new corners of the woods, different ways to cross the river by walking in it. We found wild pockets and secret creeks behind run-down subdivisions. We followed animal trails that led to the back side of aggregate mines, including one old quarry where a dirty oasis grew around a pool of scary water at the base of a mountain of asphalt. We followed another trail that led us to three urban wizards standing around a fire. We encountered a brown ranger in the woods in the rain, with a posse of ten German shepherds he must have rescued. We found spilled blood, spent candles, and chicken feathers on a muddy riverside promontory on a Sunday morning, evidence of an animal sacrifice to an old god gone underground. We found a remarkable teepee behind the dairy plant, made from pillars of cut bamboo and big sheets of synthetic insulation harvested from the industrial landscape, and a hundred other improvised camps of the people—mostly men—who live outside and usually alone. We got to know some of them. We saw atemporal visions of riders on the berm, and mounted police officers in the river. A pair of duck hunters in Vietnam-grade camo wading in the shallows on a Saturday morning, shotguns at the ready, apparently unaware they were minutes from downtown. A fossil hunter who greeted us from the far bank as he poked away at its eroded face, hollering a copro-paleontological encouragement to look into the amazing world of "dinosaur poop." We found the after-party remnants of Saturday night raves in the jurisdictional no-man's land under the bridge and the spent shells and used fireworks people would sometimes pop off on top of it. We met owls, whitetail, coyotes, caracara, herons, egrets, kingfishers, coral snakes, water moccasins, Texas water snakes, turtles and frogs, big fish and small ones, armadillos and opossums, scissortails dancing along the frontage road and rare songbirds in the riverine brush, and all the tracks the woodland nightlife leaves in the sand at the water's edge. We pulled ancient bones from the water and watched the ephemeral beauty of new butterflies flittering through the shafts of sunlight that break through the forest canopy in springtime. We walked in the thick fog of winter mornings and the insane heat of the rising

- - - -

summer sun, into a past before the human discovery of this continent and a future after we are gone.

We explored the streets, too, of a neighborhood we had passed
through many times but never really known. Past the hot pink
crape myrtles in bloom outside Double Tuff, where two brothers designed and installed bespoke truck tarps to keep your loads
locked down. Down quiet asphalt side streets, where the summer
foliage grows thick in the chain-link fences, yellow blooms of
trumpet vine, piles of old machines visible through the apertures.
A truck spring shop with a hand-painted logo of Atlas holding up
the world and the motto "Service is our Strength." In the back, a
1940s Plymouth awaiting its rebirth as a hot rod. An indie convenience store with a mural of Astro Boy on the side and the logo, in
big Aztec pride serif, **EL OTRO LADO**. Shady bungalows rich with
displays of familial identity and self-expression. Outside one, at
the edge of the concrete creek, huge handmade birdhouses in the
style of the great buildings of America: the US Capitol, the Alamo,
the White House. Across the street, an old farm still running, now
under the stewardship of twenty-first-century urban farmers.
And behind the house, rows of union halls, aggregate factories,
an ironworks, a used truck tire yard, an old fire station, the cell
tower with its parakeet condos. A neighborhood of trailer parks
along the frontage roads, of quiet streets patrolled by fearless chi-
huahuas and scary-ass pit bulls. Old bridges spanning expansive
empty lots protected from redevelopment by their designation as
toxic brownfields, where petrochemical facilities once leaked their
product into the soil. Little businesses advertising their products
and services in hand-painted signs, many in Spanish—specialty

haircuts, auto paint, tire repair, prepaid phones, high-interest loans, tacos from la Chilanga. Used car lots full of high-mileage pickups and sedans, flags of this country and others proudly displayed next to big signs saying "no credit needed." A bus depot made from an old shed on stilts, where patient passengers await long, slow, and uncertain rides to the other side of the border. At night, no matter what else has changed around them, the big freight trains blow through the darkness of the sleeping city, blasting their horns in a way that awakens memories of the past.

You can follow the train tracks down under the bridge and on into the woods. Or you can follow the desire paths that diverge off the busted-up sidewalks, into the young forests that have grown up in the rights-of-way. One branch of the concrete creek is shallower and covered in graffiti. If you follow it, you get to the spot where the creek returns to wild and then joins a bigger creek, the one the early colonists would follow north from their farms in the ancient floodplain to the hilly area they called the mountains, a path that must have been an Indigenous trail before they got here. At the base of the old trestle that crosses the creek at its boggiest section, there are trails leading deeper into the secret interior, trails on which you are guaranteed to get lost the first time you explore where they go. You might end up at the far reaches of an urban creek, in the backyard of a family home, in the vast treeless right-of-way where the power lines have cleared a path that turns into a tropical green prairie in the summer. Or you might find yourself in the weirdly quiet yet mechanically humming everyday dystopia of the municipal infrastructure facility, whose fence you can somehow end up inside of without ever crossing a barrier. At

----

the top of the bluff behind that there once may have been a Span-ish fort—and, more recently, an outlaw landfill—and in the late afternoon now can be found an atemporal vista of the sun setting over the distant high-rises of downtown. Down every trail, under every bridge, there are secret lairs off the official registry—some of them made by wild animals, others by men.

Learning to travel through time while walking what by one measure are very ordinary streets, you see history unfolding before your eyes, in the backlots of American reality and in the vignettes that accrete as you move through the world, plant-ing in your memory with an object permanence similar to the way the wildlife encounters stick. A black limousine motor-cade with police and Secret Service escort roaring down the boulevard. Riders on horseback traversing the concrete des-ert. A mariachi at rest, carrying his big guitar and waiting for the bus. Murals on the sides of tire shops and taquerias that memorialize the heroic ancestry of the people that run them, merging the aesthetics of chain-mail-bikini paperback covers with the codices that got burned by the *sacerdotes*, valorizing the strength of a conquered people who first came from a place not far from here, before they became the empire that built pyramids of the sun. Sometimes you'll see those images on the hoods of cars, like the late '70s Fleetwood parked outside the abandoned lighting factory, the word **UNSTOPPABLE** inscribed in decal across the top of the windshield. On weekends the low riders come out, in slow-rolling convoys. So do the real estate scouts, in waxed black Range Rovers, driving just as slow and taking notes.

Vultures and Pavement

The animals that love the twenty-first-century city best may be the vultures. I don't remember seeing many vultures as a kid growing up in the Midwest. Not until I was in college, when I would see them when I was home on summer break, gliding on the thermals above the interstate. You could see what efficient flyers they are. Birds built for an overheated world burning its way into a loop of necrotic entropy. Those were turkey vultures, with red heads and condor wings. We have those down here, too, but they seem a little secretive, more likely to show up on a trailcam than in front of your eyes. They often are the first to find carcasses, showing up for their close-ups with faces that look like they've been skinned. But in the southwestern city, it's the more social black vultures that rule, patrolling the zone in soaring biker gangs, watching over the roads from streetlamps and freeway signs, defecating and sometimes puking on themselves to keep cool in the concrete heat of the Anthropocene landscape.

The birds Audubon knew as carrion crows are around all year, but in my mind they are especially associated with the heat of high summer. In my field notes they seem to make the biggest impression in the season between winter and spring, when the mammals of the field are most on the move. I see them at all times of day, but especially in early morning, when they discover the remains of the night, and in midafternoon, when they find the casualties of the peaks of human traffic. I encounter them along the urban river, where they dine on the big fat grass carp that the overnight water releases sometimes leave stranded on the banks, and on the bigger deer carcasses the coyotes leave. I also see them just

----

as often on the street, scavenging roadkill, which comes in every terrestrial flavor—house cat, dog, opossum, skunk. They gather in big groups, jostling for access to the prize. I can usually see the ones that are up in the trees or the telephone poles first, before the smaller gang gathered around the corpse. There seems to be a correlation between how long they've been pulling at the find and how close they'll let you get—if they just found the carcass, they won't fly off until you are steps away, and even then they don't go far, watching you from the nearest perches. When they finally feel compelled to move, you can hear their hisses and grunts, and the sound of those big, thick wings with the white understripes. But they are otherwise quiet, having none of the organs other birds use to sing. They find death around them by watching, waiting, and following each other. And even when you get close to them, their faces are hard to see in the flat-black monotone of their feathers and skin. If you happen to be carrying field glasses or a zoom lens, you might be able to see that the first thing they eat is the eyes. Then you can witness their design for disembowelment: how they use their entire heads and necks to insert themselves through the hole where the skin stretches tight across the abdomen, using that hooked node at the end of their beak to pull out the long, soft organ tissues inside. The chalky white stains you sometimes see on their wings and necks are of more uncertain origin, but the evidence of dirty business recently done suits their role as dark angels who carry the creatures the city kills back into the food chain.

Over decades of interstate driving, I came to assume that the seeming ubiquity of vultures in the American landscape is directly related to our highways and roads—the roadkill they generate and the way our paving of the land generates intense thermal updrafts the vultures can ride all day long. Many scientists have tested similar theories, and while they confirm a correlation between the northern expansion of turkey vultures and the exploding population of white-tailed deer, the consensus seems to be that a connection with roads cannot be scientifically proven.

Vultures, especially black vultures, have always thrived on the cities we have made in the centuries since European settlement, and the mass-production of death for which they are designed. Especially in the South, where it never really gets cold. Audubon related how common carrion crows were in antebellum Charleston, Savannah, New Orleans, and Natchez, especially around the slaughterhouses. He later reported how, in the period when he was studying them—sometimes shooting or trapping them—particular black vultures seemed to be able to recognize him and the horse on which he rode.

They are not the only animal that sees us with that level of understanding, of who we are and what we do. By paying closer attention to them and seeing the city and the countryside through their eyes, we can better understand ourselves. Apex predators who have remade the world into a machine to feed us, leaving our leftovers, waste, and nonhuman accident victims for other creatures to survive off. We talk about the dream of colonizing other worlds, but rarely note how colonized the one we live on already is.

As our scientists learn to better find the story of the past as it is embedded in the land, new revelations appear that help us better understand who we really are. The best evidence indicates that the earliest humans first learned to eat meat by acting like vultures themselves, feasting on carcasses left behind by the large predators of the savanna before other scavengers like hyenas got to them, taking advantage of primitive tools to harvest parts of the carcass like bone marrow that the hyenas could not get to. This was likely the means whereby *Australopithecus* grew itself 2.8 million years ago into *Homo habilis*, who then figured out how to cook meat with fire, an innovation some now theorize was intended to make our food safer to eat. It also did much of the work other animals need to do through extensive digestion, freeing up energy and space for human brain development. Walking the edgelands, one gains a fresh appreciation of our ancestral gifts as scavengers, able to make use of whatever surprises the postindustrial city leaves along our path.

Trailer Parks and Ancient Oaks

Until the end of the pandemic, if you walked from our lot across the bridge to the other side of the river, the first thing you would see was an old sign atop a tall metal pole advertising a place called The Grove. It did not explain what The Grove was, and if you followed the narrow lane past the sign, you would find nothing but woods. Along the way, the drive branched off into the woods, cutting loops through the tall trees, but the only structure you would find was a mysterious metal box covered in graffiti, right before the last steps down to a side channel of the river. If you did a little research—or asked your older neighbors—you would find out that The Grove was a trailer park. According to some, back when the '60s blurred into the '70s, it became a commune, where people lived more intentionally, perhaps giving the idea of The Grove deeper truth. Or maybe that's just an urban legend that tells a truth about the laid-back Austin that's long gone, if it ever really existed the way the cowboy stoners and cathode-ray slackers would have you believe.

The western end of The Grove is bounded by a dry creek. The creek was not always dry, until a failed effort to redirect it to facilitate development. If you follow the creek up from the river, as I once did not long after we moved here, you will come upon a spot that looks like the ruins of some ancient lost city, where spires rise up from the earth like tiny towers, as if a colony of intelligent ants has erected a high-rise metropolis. Upon closer inspection, you would realize it is an outlaw BMX course, made in a secret location that would be almost impossible to find if you didn't know where you were going—or, like me, got lost on purpose.

Across the valley of bike jumps, you would come upon another empty lot that is as green and Edenic as the BMX course is brown and alien. There's a trail there, which didn't used to be marked. And if you followed it, you would find all manner of young plants growing along its side. One of them, growing in the seeping water of a recently recovered spring, is a fresh spawn of the Árbol del Tule, cloned from a tiny clipping someone managed to smuggle back here.

The spot where that sapling grows is at the base of a bluff, at the edge of a basin where trash was dumped for many decades after World War II—sometimes illegally, sometimes legally, including when it was the city that was doing the dumping. There are all manner of toxic chemicals in the soil, though you wouldn't know

----

it if you went there today, as the spot has been cleaned up and restored by volunteers who have turned it into a beautiful urban grove. Phase one of the cleanup was, at its core, a cover-up, where earth was moved to cap the old landfill. Even now there is so much methane trapped in the ground that the city forbids us from conducting any controlled burns to stimulate the prairie ecology that is establishing itself on the surface.

The place now known as Circle Acres comprises around ten acres which are more like an oval than a circle. It's a landlocked parcel, tucked behind a row of houses on a side street in what was, not that long ago, an unincorporated neighborhood at the edge of town. On the opposite side is a municipal park made from old ranchland that abutted The Grove. Topographically, Circle Acres is a bowl in the land, a secondary floodplain where a creek cuts through the grade down to the nearby river. The deepest part of the bowl is a backwater off the creek, a swamp circled by exceptionally tall trees. If you walk down in there, you will always find the trash the waters bring, unless you happen to visit on a day after one of our group cleanups. You will also likely encounter one of the majestic birds that like to hunt in that secret sanctuary, though they will probably fly off when they see you or hear you, whichever comes first.

On higher ground are the more visible remains of the land's history as a dumpsite. Huge sections of concrete sewer pipe are scattered across the acreage like tubular monoliths. In the face of the bluff behind the restored spring where the *árbolito* grows, you can see more substantial quantities of rubble, ready to break loose when the next big rain comes.

Right after 9/11, a collective of young activists organized as the Rhizome Collective took on the Sisyphean project of restoring the site. They then passed it on to an older environmental nonprofit, Ecology Action, that had run a recycling center for decades until the city finally started doing that job itself. My friend Eric Paulus became the caretaker and recruited me to join the board. The land hosts an outdoor mycology lab, a nature camp where kids learn to connect with their inner hunter-gatherers, and an apiary run by a former CIA agent. It also hosts a lot of ghosts.

If you follow the trail, you will end up on a road, which is also called Grove. It goes up a hill, connecting to a residential neighborhood of small wood-frame houses on one side and community uses on the other side—a neighborhood activity center, a

----

community college campus, a public library, and a municipal golf course. Right across the street from where the buses turn around at the end of their route is a stand of scrubby trees behind a low fence. Walking by, you might notice a spot where the fence is interrupted by a cable wrapped in orange plastic that hangs between two metal posts. There is no sign to explain, or any other suggestion that there is something worth investigating on the other side. One of those spots where the only way you find it is with a slightly dangerous curiosity and a willingness to step over a barrier whose only real impediment is in your head.

There is a dirt path there, made of the fine, dusty earth ant lions like to make into traps in the season of their hungry larval bloom. The path cuts through scrubby foliage, initially unremarkable: brushy ground cover, a big patch of tasajillo, some young oaks dropping tiny acorns and Spanish moss, and lots of mesquites. If you keep going, a quarter-mile or so, the path cuts around and the trees start to get bigger and greener at the edge of a steep grade. And then you come upon some of the biggest trees you have ever seen. Live oaks, ancient and gnarled, rising up out of a secret corner of town. There are three of them spread across the little zone. One in a recess in the ground, a deep bowl that has grown up around it, that gives you another measure of its age. Another, the furthest in, has one of its big branches bent as if it had once been tied down as a signal to mark something notable, perhaps a spring. The middle tree, which is also the biggest, has a nook at its thick base through which the high-rise landscape of downtown, two miles away, is perfectly framed. An atemporal vignette that interposes two divergent visions of how the world could grow, and makes you wonder if we could find the equilibrium in between.

There are stories that Indigenous Peoples used to camp at that spot, when the city of Austin was new. Those kinds of stories are always fuzzy, as the colonial erasure of tribal history and identity in Texas was so aggressive—especially in the period when this was its own independent country, ungoverned by even the idea of setting aside marginal lands for the prior inhabitants being displaced. But when you see those trees, it's easy to think you can feel their presence. Maybe looking down through their branches to see the new town being erected from the trees that met the saw.

THE THICKEST OAK TREE in the county—and perhaps the most magnificent—is not in a park, or in a parking lot. It is hidden in plain sight, sitting there in a spot where tens of thousands of people drive by it every day and night, yet secreted so completely that you would probably never be able to find it, even if you had a map on your phone that was telling you exactly where to go. My friend Bill lives under its canopy, but the place where he lives is even more invisible than the tree to the ways we have been taught to perceive the urban landscape, even though it is right there by the side of a major road, with a door you could walk up to and knock on.

I first met Bill on a Sunday morning in late winter, when I heard my dogs barking at the fence. I went to see what they were agitated about, expecting to find an animal, and instead found a man and a dog standing there in the rain trying to figure out how to get through the gate from the woods to the public street. I helped

- - - -

him out and we got to talking there, on the verge between pavement and wild. He explained himself without me asking, saying he had walked from his place back there, pointing imprecisely to the endless zone between industrial operations and the river that I knew that gate was the entry to. He asked me my age as he started to size me up. It turned out we were born the same year, a few months apart. That fact provided permission to share more.

Over the year that followed, I ran into Bill often, always back there in the edgelands. At a spot where the trail terminates at the river, bathing in his boxers. Coming the other direction across the field behind the factory. On the path by the dirty wetland, wearing a handmade ball cap that reminded me of the German army field caps you used to be able to buy at surplus stores, the kind the Billy Mumy character wore in *Bless the Beasts and the Children*, the movie our English teacher had us watch in middle school about summer camp kids who intervene to save a herd of buffalo from being shot. I complimented him on the hat, and a few weeks later he left me a similar one he had made for me, from old denim, cardboard, black vinyl, and remnants of plastic woven placemats. He told me where his place was, and I found it so I could express my appreciation by bringing him books, which were the thing he said he could use.

Bill's place was another spot I had driven by countless times and walked or biked by a good number. It was in a little one-story building right by the side of the old highway, a building that looked like a house but had most recently served as the office of the asphalt yard behind the house. The surrounding area was a mix of industrial waste and feral interzone, with an unlikely oasis

----

of native plants that had somehow grown up around a concrete containment pond, a hundred-foot-high melting mountain of old shingles and tar, a forest of thorny green retama, and the thickly wooded sliver of floodplain along the river. Bill's place was almost completely covered in green, especially during the warm months, helping ensure its remarkably stealthy presence. The house was completely hemmed in by the highway on the front, the staging area of the asphalt factory in the back, and a row of storage containers along one side. On the fourth side was the only bare dirt. And there, in a kind of scruffy courtyard with trashy little volunteer trees, stands the ancient oak.

The last time I visited, Bill had made a strange and charismatic totem on one of the little trees that faces the oak. The smiling green troll face of the animated movie character known as Shrek, framed perfectly by the circle of an old motorcycle tire. The tree is not as thick as the Árbol del Tule, but it shares some of that same intense gravity at its base, an anchoring in the earth so complete and permanent that you can't help but imagine the massive roots below that have grown and matured over hundreds of years, maybe a thousand. Even bigger than the four huge trunks that grow up above, branching out into a low, expansive canopy that is so big and yet so hemmed in that you can't really see the tree in its entirety. The tree is legally protected, in more ways than Bill himself, living there in the structure that probably only survives because it is next to a tree a new building could not encroach on. He's a lost forester in a desecrated grove, there by the ancient animal trail that has been turned into a high-speed tollway.

- - - -

245

Bill found his way to that unlikely spot, he told me, when he walked back from Missouri, sometime during the Bush administration. He has lived there continuously ever since, with the personnel of the surrounding industrial operation aware of his presence. In law school, after you learn how to turn a fox into your personal property by killing or wounding it, you learn how to take real estate from others through the doctrine called "adverse possession"—continuous and conspicuous occupation of and assertion of right to a place long enough that the law will treat you as its owner. The fancy jurisprudential version of squatters' rights. Every time I go to make a delivery to Bill, I half expect him to have finally been evicted, or the building to have been razed. And I have wondered sometimes whether that doctrine of adverse possession might be applied to protect Bill's tenure there in his abandoned shack full of the things he has found and the things he has made, living off the city in the way of a forager, making cash when he needs it by collecting cans. But I know that kind of argument would never prevail, because we live in a system that ties your right to live in your home to your labor just as effectively as did the feudal system it purports to have replaced. The city does not abide space no one is paying for, and is constantly looking for ways to make you pay more.

Natives and Invaders

When our daughter, Octavia, was old enough to hold her neck up without support and begin to see the world around her, I started taking her into the woods in a back-borne baby carrier. While my years walking the urban woods had mostly exorcised the gear fetishism I was prone to when my son was young, I was excited about the Deuter Kid Comfort Pro when it arrived on my birthday, and the ability it gave me to share with her the world I had learned to see.

Our first walks were in the autumn evenings, when the owls were coming out, and the sun would cut through the canopy at low angles that brought details of tree trunk and leaf into higher relief, with an intense yellow crispness. A world of imminent shadow, and danger. Then we started walking in the mornings, with the dogs on long leads, a rather intense kind of multitasking. A world of new light, for new eyes, full of wonder. Through woods and riverbanks that are dirty in their ways, but still feel cleaner than the streetscape.

Being parents of a newborn helped us see how blighted the world is. We wondered what foul atmosphere we were exposing her pure lungs to the first time we pushed the stroller down the street, past the door factory, the tollway on-ramp, and the air supply depots where they blow pressurized gases off the giant tanks—in a neighborhood that does not pretend to be cleaner than it is in the way suburban subdivisions do. We felt the days get hotter that first summer, watched the news get scarier, and wondered what kind of future we had brought her into. But nature has its way, and new life is maybe its greatest gift.

Bringing Octavia home made us see our feral house in a more dangerous light. The wild qualities that made it feel more alive were also things that posed danger to her. The little spiders in the corners, the snakes on the patio, the coyotes just outside the fence, the people who sometimes breached the fence. It gave us a different kind of awareness of what was going on around us, and a fresh appreciation of why the human domus has evolved in a way so effectively designed to protect our food supplies, water, and persons from animal and elemental threats. And it began to make us think that maybe the changes we saw going on around us—changes certain to erase much of the wildness from this weird corner of the city—were ones we might welcome, even as their imminence filled us with a sense of anticipatory loss.

"There's always a grieving process," said Austin's preeminent lawyer for real estate developers, looking me right in the eyes. We were talking about his client's proposal to build a shiny new high-rise mixed-use development on the site behind our home, where the old dairy plant collides with and even protects the riparian wildlife preserve. He said it in a friendly enough way, or so he probably thought—friendly in the way of a dad telling you he's leaving your mom but they both love you, a boss telling you about the layoffs of which you're a part and from which you will find unexpected benefits. The effort by the agent and facilitator of the colonizing forces' unending expansion of their dominion— now recolonizing zones they briefly forgot—to put a human face on, even as the real client he serves is an impersonal collective expression of financial and political interests. One that rewards him well for his service and immunizes him from having to really feel the impact of his work on the communities it destroys. Neighborhoods and families long consigned to the downzoned part of town that has now been targeted for redevelopment as the coolest part of town, and who will need to move to the next county to be able to afford anything similar. Wildlife communities that may find their way to some other pocket of urban or exurban habitat, or be extinguished. Even the stars that will no longer be visible in the night sky. There's always a grieving process, but for you, not for him. A process that becomes more complicated as you reckon with your own role in the change you see around you.

The American popular library is full of stories of people who went to the frontier, made homes from the wild land they found, and helped turn the empty plain into a prosperous, bustling settlement full of commerce, culture, and imposed order. That quintessential folk narrative has a way of echoing through our contemporary lives and the other stories we tell. Rarely do we interrogate whether those kinds of stories have a happy ending. Or whether there might be a better one we could write, or live.

It's a strange process, whereby you ruin a place by moving to it. The term "gentrification" doesn't really do it justice. It's colonization. No matter how ethically you try to do it—even if you undertake the crazy idea of doing it in a way that amps up the wildness rather than domesticating and destroying it. By making a place "fit" for human habitation, you pave the way for others to follow. In our case, we did so in part by deciding to participate in publicity about our project, the unique qualities of which had elicited attention. We convinced ourselves it was worthwhile to do, to share the ideas that drove our approach and the wondrous results people could be inspired to achieve in their own environments. We didn't really like the attention on ourselves, even as artists who might reap some benefits in the consequent attention to our other works—especially since we always found people got our stories wrong, whether because we weren't good enough at sharing them, or because people tend to impose their own preconceived narratives. I had the foolish idea—the kind of idea that compels one to write speculative fiction instead of works of so-called literary realism—that you could get people excited about new ideas when what they really want are personal stories: stories that generate the emotional investment the consumer economy really runs on. Most of which is about giving attention to the infinite mirrors of the self.

The house's photogenic qualities and unusual narrative got more pickup than we expected—design magazines, features, and even TV. The publicity drew attention to this neglected corner of the city. The attention would have come anyway, eventually; the things that made Austin cool had been successfully appropriated as a consumer brand, combining with the tech economy that paid my bills to make this the fastest-growing city in America. We weren't the only professional couple who had made our home in this neighborhood, and the industrial blocks of East Austin were already being remade as maker spaces long before we arrived, including the space where Agustina had her groovy studio when we met. Our project exposed a different kind of undiscovered secret, one that was very compelling to real estate types: the wild edges of the city that we had set out to save. One of the richest families in town, beneficiaries of and contributors to the 1990s tech boom here, bought the undeveloped land to our east. Another group of rich guys bought the old warehouses that hid the heron rookery, as the site of a new hotel. They bought the machine works across the street and turned it into a beer hall. As the town grew and real estate values exploded, out-of-town money began to pay attention and much bigger parcels of industrial land got snapped up to soon remake the neighborhood around us with shiny new towers full of offices, apartments, and places for people who have money to spend it. In the summer of 2020, the richest man in the world announced his plans to build a futuristic electric car factory on the banks of the wild river a few miles down. He said he would remake the riparian zone around the factory into an "ecological paradise," when the truth was, at least by urban standards, it already was. And in the first years that followed, as the factory went up at a speed that even a nation-state would have trouble matching, it became clear those plans were a ruse, or a grand idea that was easily deferred when the technobaron got distracted.

Australian environmental philosopher Glenn Albrecht coined the term "solastalgia" to describe the emotional pain we feel as we witness the deterioration of our natural environment. It's a more precise and powerful neologism than terms like "eco-anxiety" and "climate grief," because of the way it roots the feeling in the home-sickness you feel for the place you live, as it slowly and frighteningly degrades before your eyes, and you come to sense more clearly where it is going, and your limited power to influence that outcome. Living here, we learned that feeling in a hyperlocal way, before I ever learned any of those terms. I felt the loss of the wildlife around us before it was gone, as I saw the plans the machine had to expand the shining cyber-city into this corridor, and fill the empty lots with monolithic buildings designed by spreadsheets to turn the outdoors into the indoors. As I learned to see our little moment here through the prism of deep time, I came to appreciate how unevenly distributed that feeling is, from the frat boys turned developers who were incapable of seeing the social and environmental costs that were not priced into their deals, to the women of Indigenous heritage whose intense emotional connection to the land and water drove the way they spent their days. I found myself wondering if there might be a way to reconcile those divergent perspectives, in the same way the house tried to reconcile industrial waste with ecological balance.

By retreating from the world in our search for the last corners where its natural wildness persists, we learned how the world really works, under the dominion of its human masters. We also began to imagine the ways in which, aided by the things the urban wilderness had taught us, the future might be different.

Part Three

Rewilding the Future

9

Blood in the Land

Maoists and Muralists

There is a deserted traffic island near our home where the roads from downtown converge into the feeder ramps for the old highway. On it has grown a tiny forest. Unlike the pocket forests being planted in cities around the world to restore some urban biodiversity, it grew without human curation. But it is still full of life. For a few seasons a pair of red-shouldered hawks nested in its cover at the point of the triangle, making home in a few hundred square feet of woodland surrounded by the constant circulation of high-speed vehicular traffic, above a weedy forest floor littered with the remains of old homeless camps and the trash people toss from their cars. The saddest aerie in the world, you might think. But over the course of those seasons, as I saw them hunting in the mornings from the metal lampposts and high branches above the on-ramps, I wondered if maybe they hadn't found an ideal spot. A rodent DMZ, where the mammals of the field were at their most vulnerable as they crossed the road.

One spring afternoon during the pandemic, I saw the nested pair of buteos mating on a low branch in that unlikely redoubt, right by the enigmatic basketball hoop that stood there in the tall grass of the clearing. A year later, they had moved on. Maybe they got tired of the noise after squatters took over the old warehouses behind them, or got spooked by the plans to turn that empty lot into an office park. The signs promised the coming of a complex that called itself The Eclectic, even as they and you knew it would be anything but.

At the southwest corner of that triangle stands a pair of buildings well positioned to soak up the afternoon sun. The structures are old, at least by the standards of this part of town: one completed in 1940 and the other in 1944. The walls, made of old-school masonry with art deco detailing and arrays of glass bricks, are beautiful—all the more so because of the way the layers of paint that cover them take on new fades in the relentless sun. There are a few doors big enough for a truck to back in, but they are rarely open, making one wonder what's inside. When they are open, you can see, but it still doesn't make sense, as the interior is crammed with endless stacks of used hospital equipment, stainless steel and white plastic slowly fading to beige.

Those sun-blasted old walls provide a popular platform for graffiti artists to paint their works, and for young bands with dreams of stardom to have their pictures taken. Sometimes the owners of the building leave the art up for a while, if it's especially good or funny. More often they quickly paint it over, for the next tagger to hit, and for the sun to freshly discolor, turning the walls into palimpsests that record some secret cultural history of the edge of town.

We often walk by there in the morning, as daylight is dialing up and the new works painted in the night first become visible in their full colors. And every once in a while, instead of the usual expression of urban cool or territorial marking, there will be a message from the East Austin Maoists. Like the one that appeared one Wednesday in September 2020, in block red paint accompanied by the hammer and sickle:

ELECTIONS NO!

PEOPLE'S WAR YES!

Within two days, someone else had altered the slogan with selective deletions:

ELECTIONS ··!

PEOPLE·· ··· YES!

Six weeks later, right before Halloween, a new call to action appeared, this one a poster that had been printed elsewhere and pasted up. The text was arrayed around a drawing of a woman in hard hat and safety vest, her right foot using her lunchbox as a soapbox and her right arm holding up a power fist:

WORKING WOMEN KNOW ALL

POLITICIANS ARE OUR ENEMY!

BOYCOTT THE SHAM ELECTIONS!

OUR PLACE IS IN THE FIGHT FOR

REVOLUTION!

There are similar slogans elsewhere around here. On the walls of convenience stores, on the cinder-block fence outside an old gas station awaiting its remaking into a hipster cocktail lounge, pasted over the political campaign signs that get erected on the wild green lawn of the abandoned lighting factory. The most remarkable one I have seen appeared on July 4, 2019. Another poster pasted to the wall, this one a portrait of two women seated in chairs, holding hands. On the left, Frida Kahlo in a white dress, her heart exposed, her free right hand holding Mao's Little Red Book and a knife from which drips blood. On the right, a revolutionary in olive-green dungarees and combat boots, face hidden by a red scarf, eyes shaded by the visor of her field cap, her left hand holding a copy of *The Origins of the Family, Private Property, and the State*, from which also drips blood. On the yellow wall behind them, portraits of Marx, Engels, Lenin, Stalin, Mao, Madame Mao, Rosa Luxemburg, and Camarada Norah, the words *Marxism will heal the sick,*

and an image at the base of the infinite multitude of the people. The dripping blood pools into three words on the floor:

CAPITALISTS

ABUSERS

REVISIONISTS

The creators of these calls to revolution in the margins of the fastest-growing city in America do not call themselves the East Austin Maoists. They may have no true name, or many. Their exhortations to the barricades do not produce much popular response, other than annoyance from more mainstream groups who think they discredit them. Maybe you have to be a science fiction writer to experience them as alternate futures bleeding into our own. Even if the truth is less fantastic.

The group of people behind the murals were originally known as the Red Guards, a movement with affiliates around the country—from Los Angeles to Kansas City to Pittsburgh—that started in Austin. The Austin Red Guards were said to have disbanded at the end of 2018, according to Wikipedia. Then I saw them on a Saturday afternoon in January 2019, operating under the new name of Defend Our Hoodz, protesting the opening of a rotisserie chicken joint from a local hospitality company that had taken over the neighborhood tire shop and appropriated its murals of Aztec warriors as part of its brand. I happened to stop for lunch that day at the vegetarian Mexican restaurant across the street and was surprised when I sat down to see the scene through the window: men and women with their faces masked by red bandanas, like Camarada Norah wore in that poster, brandishing picket signs and megaphones, and doing a pretty good job of shutting the place down and shaming its owners.

That I knew some of the principals behind the project—smart, strong women who have had a huge and positive impact on the culture of Austin and West Texas—only made the scene more compelling, like some borderland variation on *The Bonfire of the Vanities*: liberal, highly educated white folks trying to do something self-expressive and cool with their talents and money and the world they find themselves in, confronted with the uncomfortable truth that they are agents of what we call gentrification, but is really just the twenty-first-century continuation of the colonization of the Americas by European settlers. I'm in on it, too, no matter how much I try to heal the land and ally with my neighbors in the fights against the displacement of both human life and wildlife.

Contemporary gentrification may be less violent than the first couple of centuries of colonization in the United States, operating as it does under due process of law; but when you dig deeper into what's really going on, the differences are not so easy to parse out. For smart kids in working-class neighborhoods that were long dominated by factories and power plants, and then made rapidly unaffordable by redevelopment pressure, the seemingly unlikely attraction of Chinese theories of industrial Marxism as an ideology of peasant revolution, as further reworked by South American intellectuals into a framework for Indigenous resistance to settler colonialism, makes sense—especially when you come to appreciate how many of the neighbors white culture labels as "Mexican" are really descendants of Indigenous Peoples of this continent.

The Shining Path leads from East Asia to East L.A. and East Austin, by way of the Andes.

The East Austin Maoists are not the only revolutionaries walking these streets. And not all of them are looking for a popular uprising from the Left. I've encountered Tea Party mobs marching on the Capitol—including the unlikely figure of my son's orthodontist, who I had only experienced as an exceptionally sweet, kid-friendly, and medically effective health-care provider, turned sweaty and frantic as he saw me on the street and urged me to join the uprising. I've seen men with assault rifles and venti lattes outside a downtown Starbucks on a Saturday afternoon, a mass mayhem cosplay that is simultaneously laughable and terrifying. And I've seen the more authentically scary stencils and woodland encampments of a homegrown white nationalist cell that calls itself the Patriot Front, whose violent vision bleeds through much darker.

Glimpses like that remind me how the Second Amendment is the underexamined third rail of American politics, deeply linked to the idea of the right of revolt that is both the holy fire of our national creation myth and the thing the federal state has to vigilantly work to keep bottled up—even as it exploits it to convince people to rally behind the power, and even die for it. And in Texas, the idea of the right of revolt, coupled with the right to bear arms and the right to occupy and exploit this land, is so integral to the way of thinking and the existence of the state that they mandate its teaching to all fifth graders—and, just to make sure it sticks, a second time around for all seventh graders. They call it Texas History, but there's a lot more going on than that snoozy name suggests. Including the aspects of Texas history and American

----

history we like to avert our eyes from, like the way gun rights are also deeply tied up with both our control of nature and the ability of some of us to exercise control over our neighbors.

A year after my encounter with the insurrectionist orthodontist, when we moved into the cottage next to our empty lot, we found a different band of radicals organizing for revolution. Across the street was another weird old lot, this one a metal warehouse in a big yard full of salvaged neon signs for forgotten stores and brands, attended by one white-bearded old hippie dude and his tiny white dog, who would sometimes zip around in an electric golf cart. The lot was another brownfield, and right after we moved in, they began a government-supervised remediation of the subsurface hydrocarbons that had leaked into the soil. In 2011, the lot became the staging area for the Austin chapter of #Occupy, and every night, we would hear them planning the uprising that would never quite achieve the change that seemed certain to be coming. It was the year of the Arab Spring, not long after the revolution in Ukraine, a period when images of popular masses retaking their capitals and starting new governments filled our news feeds.

The romance of revolution had an intuitive appeal, as one who grew up reading about popular uprisings against unjust systems as the progressive engine of history. All American kids get some of that, with the Declaration of Independence as national manifesto. As a student of political economy in college before the end of the Cold War, I got a lot more, from both sides: the communist dream of life liberated from work, inequality, and property; and the neoclassical economists' blackboard vision of a mathematically perfected distribution of all the value in the world in a way that maximized the happiness of all. Both of those utopian dipoles collided with reality in the following decades and, in their absence, I wondered what new theory would replace them as the idealized vision of a better tomorrow that counterbalances our pragmatic resignation to the world as we find it. I explored those possibilities in my work, advising Internet dreamers in my law practice and conjuring speculative alternatives in my writing, but the very idea of the future—or at least of one that would be more just—seemed increasingly elusive.

My midlife retreat into the urban wild started as an escape from these dismal certainties. But as the long walks into nowhere accumulated, I started to see fresh clues in the rewilded ruins of the recent past. In the way nature reframed my experience of the city, and blurred the barriers between the two, I started to see how the social and economic injustices that characterize contemporary American life are rooted in the damaged relationship we have with the land on which we live. Slavery and its legacies, the genocide and dispossession of Indigenous Peoples, wealth inequality, imperial war, borders, and the use of force by the state were all tied up with the systems whereby society extracts surplus from the Earth to maintain human dominance and prosperity.

I could see the system's design flaws everywhere I looked, once I started seeing the world around me through that prism. Out there in the heartland, driving back and forth between Texas and Iowa, across Oklahoma, Kansas, and Missouri, the horizon-spanning vistas of ancient buffalo range turned into prosperous farms and cattle ranches 150 years ago, now showing the unmistakable signs of economic and ecological exhaustion. Walking in the old cemetery behind the storage-locker facility, I realized that the neighborhood across the river had been a cotton plantation not that long ago, and transformed into a freedmen's community after many of the people buried there were emancipated. The semiotic landscape of names on the land, names of the people and images of identity, encoded the history of the last 500 years, from the places named after military outposts to the common names for plants and animals inherited from cultures thought long erased. The extremes of wealth inequality were ever-present, and I started to understand how even the seemingly ethereal technology transactions I stewarded as a business lawyer were rooted in the same system as those plantations. Social and economic inequality could never really be overcome without awakening to its roots in our systems for appropriating the natural bounty of the world.

ON JULY 4, 2023, we went with our extended family to spend a week on the beach at South Padre Island, at the end of America where the Rio Grande spills out into the Gulf. There's an 1850s lighthouse right before you leave the mainland, with an ornately faceted giant glass bulb that once guided mariners and is now a tourist site. When you pay the fee to walk up and check out the view, they give you a little brochure that explains the history of the place. It also includes, in tiny print, a list of "101 Things to Do in Port Isabel":

> *Number 28. Check out the wetland behind the H-E-B [grocery store].*

So I did, even though I had been sent out for provisions. But there was no wetland. The open acres behind the strip mall were more like a desert, an expansive empty lot of cactus, low brush, and wide channels of bone-dry brown dust. I realized I had already driven through it earlier in the trip, headed to pick up Hugo from the Brownsville airport on a road that passed through a landscape of coastal flats and estuaries. The signs marked a national wildlife refuge, and I saw a few wild birds, but the marshlands had degenerated into wastelands, filled with hundreds of weekend warriors tearing it up on ATVs. They reminded me of the Mad Max reenactment clubs that used to take over the highways outside San Antonio. Maybe the apocalypse already happened, too slowly for any of us to realize.

The next day, on the beach, out along the horizon, past the border blimp tethered above the kites and crowds, its electronic eyes scanning the horizon for intruders, you could see the launchpads, factories, and towering rockets of SpaceX, a vision as straight out of the science fictions of my childhood as was the sense that the sun and air were reaching a level of intensity that would soon be too dangerous to go out in. You couldn't help but believe that the yearning to colonize another planet those rockets expressed was driven by the recognition of how badly we have trashed this one. No one can own the Moon or Mars, at least under the treaties currently in place, but in 2015 US law was changed to allow companies to own the mineral resources they find there. And in the shimmer of those silver rockets in the summer sun, you could see how unlikely it is that we will avoid doing out there what we did down here.

Zebulon Pike and the Courts of the Conqueror

The real estate scouts are easy to spot. They have nice cars, the kinds of cars you don't often see in this neighborhood, or at least didn't used to, and they roll slow, sometimes backing up to take a second look. Working their way through the side streets of "transitional neighborhoods," looking for opportunities to realize profits from properties that are ripe for redevelopment, or at least repackaging to a different demographic. Not all of them are pros. On Sundays, couples roam around looking for investment opportunities or new territories to explore together, with the same eyes on the land. Some of them take notes. Every once in a while, one will get out of their car and investigate on foot.

The tradition reaches way back, in a way we rarely acknowledge. Perhaps because the scouting used to be so much harder in the days before motor vehicles and paved roads, when the land was wilder. George Washington, the mythologized patriarch of our country, was a real estate guy, who went out as a young man to the Ohio River Valley and surveyed sites for new settlements, making nice maps. Looking at them and imagining Washington as a colonial-era preppy business bro, I wonder if the skills that made him successful in real estate were also what made him successful in war. It's easy to imagine all of the propertied men of his generation realizing the value they had lucked into on this (to their countrymen) new continent—so much value they were willing to spill blood to have more freedom to manage it as they saw fit, and keep more of the profit.

Thomas Jefferson was pretty good at the game, too, dispatching Pierre Du Pont, James Madison, and Robert Livingston to put together a deal with the agents of Napoleon to acquire the critical port of New Orleans from the French. To their surprise, they got the entire territory of the Mississippi River watershed, almost doubling the size of the United States, for $15 million—an amount that would equal less than $350 million today, not even a dollar an acre.

A year after they closed the deal, Jefferson's army chief General James Wilkinson sent a young officer named Zebulon Pike to take a closer look. Pike was twenty-five, the same age as many of the commercial brokers I encounter hunting for deals at the edge of town. His first expedition set out from St. Louis on Friday, August 9, 1805, in a seventy-foot-long keelboat crewed with twenty men and four months of provisions. They were tasked to find the headwaters of the Mississippi, scout sites for military bases to assert the new sovereign's dominion, attempt to broker peace between the Sioux and Ojibwe, and take informal census of what British and French trapping and trading interests remained out there. Upon his return, Pike published the journals of his expedition, beating the other presidential expedition of Lewis and Clark to press.

Pike's book was a bestseller, despite a wooden style that reveals its author as a bit of a stiff (maybe even a bit dense), and history was not kind to him, as he was caught up in the scandals around his commanding officer, General Wilkinson, and Aaron Burr. Pike was suspected of having been an agent in Burr and Wilkinson's conspiracy to make large portions of the West into their own new country, especially in his second expedition up the Arkansas River and into Colorado, where he found the mountain that got named Pike's Peak, got lost around present-day Salida, then got captured by the Mexicans. The best edition of Pike's journals is the one

----

annotated in 1895 by naturalist Elliott Coues, whose footnotes are much longer than the underlying text, making fun of the author, riffing on the ways we change the names of peoples and places in their passing between different language groups and understandings, and obsessively tying the sites Pike records to those of the world of Coues's day. Through this metatextual mess, a picture of the country as it was emerges. Edenic and open, the rivers and streams clean and free, the prairies and forests rich with life. And yet the land was also full of human activity—not just of the members of Indigenous communities who seem far more sophisticated than the condescending Pike, but also the English, French, and American settlers who were already out there engaged in commerce. Pike reports seeing Indian villages and settler trading posts all along the river, visiting with Julien Dubuque at his lead mine in what became northeast Iowa, and remarking on the Sioux and white pioneers living in longstanding settlements at what is now downtown St. Paul, Minnesota. He meets Indigenous People who maintain crop fields and others who mine lead to make ammunition for firearms. He learns the local names for places and the stories they encode, like the swampy creek near present-day Galena famed for giving people smallpox and other fevers, and the places where the bones are literally buried. The true wilderness you expect to see described is elusive. To find a time when the American land and the life it harbored were free of human impact, you have to travel back thousands of years, maybe tens of thousands.

The land through which Pike paddled was a place of many nations. Three different European kingdoms had asserted claims to all or parts of it, treating with the Indigenous nations and bands

- - - -

who they found there. Across the river from Pike's starting point in St. Louis stood the earthen pyramids of Cahokia, a Mississippian civilization that traded across the continent, including in Mill Creek chert, the mineral preferred to make hoes for the agriculture widely practiced across the region. At its peak, during a period of warmer climate, the settlement at Cahokia, whose true name we do not know, may have been as large as 40,000 people, building wooden henges that aligned with the celestial objects and connected with nodes of settlements all up and down the networks created by the rivers. I've seen the mounds north of Dubuque, mysterious presences in the land whose purposes we don't really understand, reminding us how much deeper the history of the continent is than we tend to acknowledge. By the time Pike arrived, the populations of the major tribes had been decimated, but they were still everywhere. Some of them still are. Even now, the land on which we live is comprised of many nations, each with its own traditions for how the community interacts with and gets sustenance from the environment. And what was another country once could be so again.

For those of us born into the colonial occupation of this continent, it's easy to avoid giving much thought to the means whereby the sovereign of the United States obtained title to the lands between the Atlantic and the Pacific. If you read the annual reports from the Bureau of Land Management, you might think we bought most of it in arms-length transactions, when many of the cessions from other countries followed armed conflicts or negotiations backed by threats. A gift for aggressive, obsessive real estate acquisition by whatever means available is the real engine of the American experiment, from which everything else involving the use of that land follows. And the real secret to how that works is evidenced in the law.

The case of *Johnson & Graham's Lessee v. McIntosh* was decided in 1823 by the US Supreme Court, in an opinion authored by Chief Justice Marshall, one of the vaunted founders of American jurisprudence all law students learn about, creator of the doctrine of judicial review that is at the heart of our constitutional system. In *Johnson v. McIntosh*, the court was faced with the question of who owned much of the land that became Illinois and Indiana: the developers who had bought it from the tribes who once occupied that land, or the other developers who later bought it from the US government. After a lengthy and elegiac discussion of the self-evident sovereignty of the Indigenous nations and their freedom to contract regarding the property they clearly owned by the standards of Anglo-American property law, Marshall acknowledges the pragmatic reality that must trump the result that legal reason would otherwise compel: "Conquest gives a title which the courts of the conqueror cannot deny." All property, in other words, is really grounded in theft. And the legal system, behind the black robes and statues of blind justice, is really a mechanism for the legitimization and perpetuation of that theft, ordering the allocation of its bounty among the lords of the conqueror. When you learn our system of property law is, at its essence, little changed from what William of Normandy and his heirs implemented to allocate control over the conquered lands of England among their military officers, it makes perfect sense. *Johnson v. McIntosh* is the *Dred Scott* of American property law. But unlike *Dred Scott*, its ugly

- - - -

admission of the victory of raw power over justice and reason remains good law, still cited on occasion to justify the way things really work here.

No wonder the idea of the right of revolution made such intuitive sense to the founders of the American republic. It's like the Gonzalez battle flag Texans like to repurpose, a relic of the uprising against Mexico that features the image of a cannon used to assert their control of the land, and a dare: "COME AND TAKE IT." Behind the elaborate systems of right articulated in the almost endless volumes of casebooks and treatises you can pull from the shelves at any law library is the truth of the old saw: Possession is nine-tenths of the law, and the way you gain it and keep it is the same way other predators do in the wild.

You can go to your county clerk's office and look up the long history of the deeds recorded by prior owners of the land on which you live. But if you go all the way back to the beginning, you might ask yourself: What came before that?

Native Texans and Other Neighbors

In the summer of 2013, in the warehouses that used to block the view of the heron rookery, some guys who had set up a kayak rental place got the genius idea to open a river tubing business. It was an immediate hit, and within weeks the normally tranquil river was a parade of young people with coolers, beer, and boom boxes floating by. Even Frodo floated—fellow Iowa boy Elijah Wood, in town working on a movie, a big smile on his face in the pictures that appeared on social media of him getting off the river under the bridge. My initial reaction was laissez-faire: The river is the public commons, a federally protected navigable waterway, free for all to enjoy. My neighbors asked me to get involved, I guess thinking my being a lawyer could prove helpful. Most of them were "native" Texans and avid naturalists who had moved to our little street for the same reason as me, because they loved the river. They told me how commercial tubing had trashed the Comal and San Marcos rivers just south of us, and their arguments were persuasive, especially when you considered that the real issue was whether and under what terms a private business should have the freedom to profit off selling access to the public commons and parklands. That we would walk out on Saturday afternoons to find people blocking our driveways and peeing in our front yards was an additional inducement. But I was still wary, having seen in older, whiter

neighborhoods how neighborhood associations can accrete power in a small group of people who invent rules designed to protect a status quo that benefits them. But the idea of trying to protect that wild slice of urban river from capitalist commercialization was one I could get behind.

The leader of our fight was our neighbor Daniel Llanes, a long-haired musician, dancer, and healer who lives in a house he made from an old auto body shop. I had introduced myself to him once, when we were both pumping gas down the street, and he was polite but wary. Working on the tubing fight, we got to know each other. He was an unlikely fighter—an exceptionally groovy person whose love of the beautiful things in the world made him so emotionally invested he had to take action. Daniel was complemented by his next-door neighbor Dave Moriaty, a seventy-something Austin hippie who went to high school in Port Arthur with Janis Joplin, fought as a Marine in Vietnam, cofounded San Francisco's Rip Off Press and then Austin's first independent weekly. He found his way to this weird little street in the 1970s and built a two-story octagon house with his own hands. Dave's late wife had been one of the main advocates for the protection of the undeveloped land across the river, and when he suited up to speak for the wild, her legacy and love of this place charged his words.

Daniel introduced me to Susana Almanza from across the river, who was the real leader of East Austin's wider neighborhood struggles for environmental justice, as the founder of PODER: People Organized in Defense of Earth and her Resources. I learned from them where the pipeline that ran through my yard had come from—a giant petrochemical tank farm that had been operated up the road for decades, leaking and poisoning the families who lived around it until Susana—then the twenty-something daughter of migrants who had matured into a committed activist for her community—led a fight that took on five major oil companies and won.

Our coalition of river advocates won the fight with the tubers, when our neighbor Mike Bayer—an art director and champion fisherman who grew up downriver in the town made famous by a ZZ Top song—was able to show river-flow data that convinced the city that tubes were not safe in the spillway of the dam. A local judge concluded that the land the outfitters were crossing to access the river was accreted public land—an area that had been an older path of the river and was now owned by no one. The experience made us see that the riparian corridor below the dam and the wildlife that lived in it lacked human advocates who would help protect them from the corporate development we could all see coming, and that the alliance of neighborhood, environmental, and outdoors groups we had improvised could have an impact. I learned to see how my neighbors' fights against the displacement of families from the neighborhood they had grown up in and their fights to protect the river and green spaces were part of the same struggle, a struggle that had been going on for centuries. You didn't need to be a lawyer to see which side was the side of justice.

We had a lot of early successes in community conservation activism. We were able to use existing rules to persuade developers to sit down at the table with us and work out deals that would enable redevelopment of legacy industrial sites while maintaining balanced protections for the river corridor. My experience as a business lawyer proved helpful: being able to get better information about the inside deals that were being brokered, and being able to navigate the labyrinth of rules that seemed designed to prevent people from understanding them. We built alliances with the local parks and watershed authorities, conferring on opportunities to better protect our wild urban spaces. When Tesla announced its new plant downriver, just outside the city limits, we were able—after a lot of work—to get the company to the table and lay out plans to restore the riparian portion of their land, as the company's CEO had declared he would do, only to show no follow-through. Our coalition around the community impacts of Tesla widened to include labor and social justice groups, as well as environmental stakeholders, culminating in a big summit in the summer of 2022.

The more we achieved, the more you could see how small the victories were and how rigged the game is. You can rarely stop a bad project—usually the best you can do is influence it, by persuading the approving authorities to mitigate its harm and negotiating directly with the developers to get the best deal you can. The members of the City Council and all their appointed boards were, and are, dominated by people funded by real estate interests—even the seemingly radical crusaders who would be on the front lines with the protesters when the issue was immigrant detention or police violence, but who always sided with the developers, even when the "product" was housing for the affluent. The river had some protections put in place in the '80s, when the town was more authentically liberal and as

interested in preserving the natural assets it had as in propel-
ling new growth, but they ended not far from our homesite at
what had been the edge of town. When I learned from a visiting
German journalist that to build its almost identical factory outside of Berlin, Tesla had to negotiate a 500-page agreement of
elaborate environmental protections—compared with the short
list of jobs and school-board spiffs the company had to promise here to get multimillion-dollar tax breaks, accelerated per-
mitting, and direct access to city utilities in a poor part of the
county where all the neighbors have to get their (often unclean)
water from predatory corporate utilities—I better understood
what systemic challenges we had. And that we are not alone.

"Think globally, act locally." You don't see that dorky
bumper sticker slogan as much as you used to, maybe because
the generation that thought it was going to have a revolution
and then settled for smaller, community-focused changes is
retired or gone to the other side. Through my work, I've gotten to know people fighting for climate justice on the global
stage, working on multinational agreements to reduce carbon
emissions, protect the last great rainforests, and deploy greener
energy solutions. But there's another front line of the climate
and biodiversity struggle, where what's left of the wildlife on
this planet is being slaughtered. It is a front line where each of
us can have a real impact—at local zoning boards and city councils, where hundreds of decisions are made every week about
what humans are allowed to do with the land. They are small
decisions, when considered individually—an acre here, a few
hundred feet there—but they add up to our encroaching sprawl

----

across the continent, and the planet. And those decisions are made in places where the activist engagement is sparse, but the potential for real change is closer.

IN THE SUMMER OF 2023, the largest turnout ever for an Atlanta City Council meeting gathered to speak up against the destruction of an ancient forest to build a fake city designed to train police officers to fight citizen riots—maybe the climate justice riots they can see are coming as multinational treaty negotiations produce little change. There were locals of diverse politics, from social democrats to libertarians, ecology activists to racial justice activists, neighbors and EMTs. Members of the Muskogee Nation, whose ancestors fertilized the trees of that forest, traveled from the reservation in Oklahoma they were relocated to by force shortly before Atlanta's founding. Activists from other cities facing similar battles back home came to ally with that shared cause. All of this after one activist trying to protect the forest, known as Tortuguita, was killed. And after they were all done, the Council cleared the project to proceed, mostly deaf to the passionate dissent.

Municipal governments—as you learn if you try to influence their decisions—do not function like democracies. They function like quasi-public companies, because that's really what they are in the law: municipal corporations chartered by the state to govern local land use, infrastructure, and public safety. The city councils are the boards of directors, and the staff are the executives and employees. The shareholders are the developers and other business interests who fund the campaigns and provide the largest amounts of capital underlying the tax base. The customers are us, the voters. And the only real choice we have if we don't like the product is to move to another town. Not that different from the animals who get displaced by new development as the city sprawls.

As corrupt as our local governments can be, serving as the primary enablers of small-scale environmental destruction, we have the power to influence them, by electing leaders invested in building a greener world and by holding those leaders accountable for the future. At the PODER offices, Susana has a picture of Cesar Chavez with one of his best-known quotes: "We don't need perfect political systems; we need perfect participation." It's true. But we also need better information. We need people to see that the decisions made by local land-use authorities are where we can often have the biggest and most immediate impact on the environment in which we live. And that engaging in that activity can be rewarding, achieving positive outcomes and experiencing the wonders of the urban nature we can nurture. It can also be fun, a way to get to know your neighbors and experience real life and real community instead of the algorithmically mind-controlled simulation we pass our days living in inside our digital screens.

In the mornings when I head out to work, I see the young new residents of our neighborhood walking their dogs outside the apartments freshly tilted up on the old industrial sites—not far from the elementary school they just closed because the neighborhood now has more dogs than children—and you can pretty safely assume they have no idea what was here before. Most of them probably just moved here from some other town for a new job, like I did twenty-five years ago. I wonder if they ever look up from their phones and notice the sad yet hopeful remnants

- - - -

of the ancient prairie coming up out of the drainage ditch where their dog is about to defecate. The native flowers that have not yet given up. I wonder, if I went up to them and pointed out the tiny pink powder puffs growing along the edge of the industrial drive-way across the street, if they would be able to see it. If they might learn to see it themselves, and connect with it, before it's too late, and find their own true selves in the process.

10

Breaking the Haze

Cities and Sacrifices

On October 30, 1520, not long after the death of Moctezuma, as the first smallpox epidemic raged through the population of Mexico, conquistador Hernan Cortés wrote a letter to the emperor of Spain, Carlos V, describing the wonders of the place we now call Mexico City. His relation of what he witnessed is suffused with awe, for the place and its rulers, suggesting its author saw the people he had found there as peers, not primitives—though one has to filter for the puffery of an adventurer reporting back to his patron, like an entrepreneur pitching their investor.

Cortés situates the location: a region of lakes surrounded by mountains, with the principal seat of imperial power on an island in the middle of one of those lakes, connected to the surrounding cities by grand causeways. He compares the city to Córdoba and Seville, traversed with grand boulevards and canals. He describes marvelous markets and public squares in which all manner of commerce is conducted. Jewels, gold, silver, brass, copper, tin, stones, bones, snails, and feathers. Bricks burnt and unburnt, timber hewn and unhewn, blocks of cut rock. A street devoted to wild game—fowl, partridge, quail, duck, flycatchers, widgeons, turtle doves, pigeons, reed birds, parrots, sparrows, eagles, hawks, owls, and kestrels. Rabbits, deer, and little dogs. Skins, feathers, furs, and claws. Onions, leeks, garlic, watercress, nasturtium, borage, sorrel, artichokes, thistle; cherries and plums; bee honey and wax; corn and honey from maguey. All manner of paints and cotton textiles, woodworks and clayworks, and things made from corn. Things to eat, things to use, and people to serve you.

He describes the grand residences of the wealthy elite, who reside in the capital city part of the year, each of them enriched with conservatories of flowers. In one of the palaces he describes an even grander garden, with ten pools of water, some fresh and some saltwater, in which were kept living exemplars of all the different species of waterbirds found in the country. Next to them, a series of galleries of cages containing all the great predators of the nation—lions, tigers, wolves, foxes, and others Cortés could not name. All of them tended by specialized keepers, who were just a

small part of the armies, servants, and laborers who spent their lives in service to the ruling elite.

Cortés paints a picture of the places of worship of the Aztecs, the chambers he was admitted to in the great pyramids. Only there does Cortés express negative judgment, at the images of gods he saw as demons and monsters, and at the practices he saw as against the commandments of his God. He describes one type of gigantic idol that particularly fascinates: humanoid figures sculpted from masses of seeds and leguminous plants ground up, mixed together, and kneaded with the blood of human hearts taken from living persons in sufficient quantities to create an abundant material for artisanal use. The image is genuinely horrific, even as it seems to reveal a truth about all great cities—the way the abundant wealth they embody is tied up with agricultural production, the possibility of surplus, and how, no matter how far we may advance in our arts and sciences, we ultimately live at the mercy of nature. And it always has the capacity to reduce us to primitive efforts at mediating its temper through sympathetic magic.

It is said that the popular children's rhyme *eeny meeny miny mo*, the ubiquitous sorting game, was passed down to us from ancient Wales, where it was used to choose which child would be pulled from the group for the druidic sacrifices designed to appease nature and keep the rest of us alive. We like to think the savagery of such practices is long behind us. But when I watch the news, with never-ending headlines about school shootings, child victims of territorial wars, border violence, and the dying off of much of the wildlife of the planet, I can't help but wonder what it is they

----

are all being sacrificed for, and whether a radical reset of our relationship with the natural world might be the real remedy.

Loafers and Laborers

My favorite cap to wear on my walks in the urban woods is also my ugliest item of headgear. Most of the clothes I wear on such walks meet that standard. You quickly learn that what you want to wear when you are likely to get dirty and wet is not fancy gear from some high-end outfitter, but the same kind of already-dirty clothes you would wear to work in the yard. And part of the reason the hat is so ugly is because it is designed for safety, dominantly colored the fluorescent orange that is meant to keep other hunters from mistaking you for a deer or, as might be more likely in my case, a turkey.

I bought the hat for $5.99 at a gas station in Johnson City, on the old highway through the Texas Hill Country. The hat is garish and cheap, the orange blended in with a brown and black camo pattern, emblazoned with the head of a stag above a pair of crossed rifles and embroidered with a redneck aphorism that is also a deep evolutionary truth:

BORN TO HUNT

FORCED TO WORK

I am not really a hunter. While I loved to mess around with guns as a boy and young adult, and I did a bit of bird hunting here and there, it wasn't something my dad did. He told us plenty of stories of hunting when he was young. We had a picture of him,

----

his dad, and a family friend standing in front of a trailer hung with two strings of pheasants they had killed somewhere in South Dakota. He never bought any guns until he and mom retired to the country. When he died, I found a small-gauge shotgun, loaded with a shell, next to his bedside table, on which laid a collection of the country stories of Turgenev he had been reading. Mom said he used the gun to deter the raccoons from crapping on the porch. There are a lot of wild turkeys at their place, and amazing deer, but no pheasants that I have seen. The last time I saw a pheasant in Iowa was probably in the late 1980s, running into a ditch along a gravel road. Once abundant across the prairies, their population has declined so precipitously over the long century of our agricultural dominion, first with the erasure of the prairie to bring it under the plow, then with the poisoning of what life was left with pesticides and herbicides that obliterated much of the food chain. Maybe that's why dad didn't hunt—because he knew there wasn't anything left alive in the few remnants of prairie you could still find. Or maybe it's just because the mantra on that hat didn't apply to him. He was born to work, so much so that he was almost incapable of leisure. I learned how to work from him and my mom, as many of us did, with childhood chores and the mandate to get summer jobs as a teen. I was pretty good at it, but I also resisted the program, sometimes baiting Dad to call me a loafer.

The word "loafer" is an American invention. Its first recorded appearance was in 1830, right at the dawn of the industrial revolution. Richard Henry Dana Jr. happily uses that "newly minted Yankee word" in his 1840 memoir about his time as a Harvard dropout turned merchant seaman, *Two Years Before the Mast*, to deride the perceived indolence of cultures he encounters in warmer climes. Over the following century, the word proliferated as a pejorative, parallel with the accelerating mechanization and urbanization of life and labor. It describes someone who doesn't do their part to keep the machine running, whether in the factory, field, or office. That it comes from the German word for "vagabond" tells another part of the story, as does the comparable French word *flâneur*, denominating the idle urban strollers who inspired the psycho-geographers, thought to be derived from an ancient Scandinavian word for wandering. Or consider the British term "slacker," which appeared in England in the late nineteenth century as a way to deride sailors and soldiers who didn't do their part. A century later it was appropriated by Austin filmmaker Richard Linklater as the title of his film that follows Gen X kids getting happily lost on the streets of Austin in the days after the 1980s real estate crash, when rent was so cheap twenty-somethings could afford to do nothing for a few seasons. The romance latent in our lexicon of laziness reveals that the aimless wanderers tagged with these terms may be living closer to our true nature than the bosses and busybodies would have you think.

I can vividly remember the first time I began to notice my own true nature as a stalker, walking early morning in the fields behind the factories when the deer were out browsing. I was with our dogs, both of lineages bred to help humans hunt. Bushwhacking through the waist-high wild grass, I noticed how the hounds could no longer see any further than the front of their noses, which they put to work energetically tracking the scents of bigger animals that may have moved through that spot a moment before, or

----

many hours. They would be able to follow the scent to the source, eventually. But I could immediately scan across the horizon line of that weird Anthropocene savanna and see the deer long before the dogs, usually at just the distance from which I could have reached that potential family meal for a month with a spear, slingshot, arrow, or gun. I only had a camera, but it got me part of the way to that feeling—the feeling of exercising what we are all designed by evolution to do.

The stalker is also the forager, who finds wild food without the need for violent predation. Our way of walking, seeing, and handling is also well adapted to finding edibles in the field, and our mastery of language enables us to share our species' accumulated knowledge of what's out there. We have gotten pretty bad at learning such knowledge, in a world of supermarkets and home delivery, but when you make what are (to you) fresh discoveries of wild flavors in the margins of the city—the deliciousness of wild primrose leaves when they first appear in the drainage ditch before the bloom, the tang of the purple mustang grapes that hang from chain-link fences around industrial parks, or the spice of the wild chiles that appear in unmowed fields—it makes life feel a little more real.

It can also help you survive in times when the machine fails, as writers like Frances Hamerstrom and Euell Gibbons learned from elders who had lived off the land during the Great Depression. Shortly after we moved into the cottage, I read a remarkable story about a staffer at the Carter Foundation in Atlanta named Kelly Callahan who, in the aftermath of the Financial Crisis, became a forager of the gardens and yards of homes that had

----

been foreclosed and allowed to go wild by the banks that owned them. On one long trespass into the economic dead zone with a reporter, she collected a load of figs to make jam for the homeless, five pounds of tomatoes, two kinds of squash, and a Sugar Baby watermelon for herself. Even before I had learned to make similar finds myself, I intuitively sensed how the rewards of such excursions were more than nutritional. Not a replacement for the way we live, but a practice to integrate into it, to better experience nature—our own and the world's—even if we go no further than the vacant lot down the street.

It is not human nature to sit in front of screens and manipulate pixels, or work an assembly line putting machine parts together. But those tasks mimic some of the instinctual tasks for which we are wired, like scanning our field of vision for predators or prey, handling a weapon, or spotting edibles in the wild field. We are evolved to hunt and forage every day to live, not to farm crops to fill silos, nor to farm data to fill up investment accounts. The more I have learned to find ways to integrate daily rambles through the urban outdoors into the routine of my life, the more balanced I have felt, more in tune with my real self and more capable of devoting myself to conventional contemporary work without that feeling you are on a mental and emotional treadmill whose speed you do not control. Learning to see the wild nature around you, in the heart of the city, can also help you reawaken your own true nature.

Cozy Catastrophes

In the middle of the hours before sunup Monday morning on February 15, 2021, I was awakened by silence. I have a hazy memory of an abrupt knock, like a breaker trip, but what intruded upon my sleeping mind was the absolute quiet in our room, as all the white noise of the machines that keep our little house cozy and habitable had stopped. I opened my eyes, and quickly realized the power was out. The room, which also contained my wife, our eighteen-month-old daughter, and our two dogs, was cold. I looked at my phone on the bedside table, intending to check the time, and found a push notification from an entity that had never messaged me before: the electrical utility, advising us that rotating outages had been implemented and should not last more than forty minutes.

It was a little after 3 a.m. I checked on Agustina and Octavia, made sure they were warm enough, then pulled on my pants and

boots and stepped outside to better assess the situation. I thought about getting back into bed myself, but decided I should at least check our breakers and get some more information. When we headed to bed around 10 p.m. the night before, a light dusting of snow had begun to fall, something that used to happen only every five or so years in Austin. It had already gotten colder than it ever used to get here. That Saturday, after a patch of freezing rain, I had busted the padlock on our back gate by defrosting it with a hammer. When I jogged to the feed store later in the day to get a replacement, I saw a guy at one of the frontage road tire shops working by a fire he had made in an old truck wheel, an image that would later seem like a premonition.

On the bulletin board outside the store, someone had posted a flyer that would soon feel like a memory from the other side:

LOST PEACOCKS
PAVOS REALES PERDIDOS
MISSING 4 PEACOCKS,
3 MALES AND 1 FEMALE
PLEASE CALL
$$REWARD$$

There were no peacocks when I opened the bedroom door, which opens directly to the outside. There was cold air—colder than I had ever felt here—and snow. Real snow, drifted up against the glass. Real winter, the kind I thought I had left behind when I moved to Texas. My son had just one snow day in an entire childhood here, which was really an ice day, and the few light dustings

- - - -

of snow we'd had in our years on the urban river were always the kind that melted by midmorning. It never really snowed because it never really got cold; any hard freeze was a major news event, and the houses showed it. I noticed it immediately as a transplanted Midwesterner—all these drafty little wooden bungalows that don't contemplate the occupants having to spend a lot of time inside. Or that they could need the house to protect them from the cold for an extended period of time. The only place anyone would ever make a fire is in the backyard, where the real Texas hearth is, a memory of campfires in the land Hestia was afraid to visit.

It must have just stopped snowing when I stepped out into the drift between our rooms, accompanied by our dogs. The eerie sky was clear but for a few cotton-ball clouds cruising low in the cold wind, and the world was aglow, brighter than any full moon, even though all the lights were out in every direction. Even more breathtaking was the silence. The ambient rumbles and hums of the nearby factories were gone, and the forest behind them was equally quiet, all the animals hunkered down. Even the wind seemed noiseless, but you could feel it. Nine degrees Fahrenheit, according to the weather app, but colder in person.

The tranquility of the city brought to a stop by a heavy snow-fall is one of the things I had missed the most since moving here from colder climes. But we never had winter blackouts, and if we did, we could start a fire in the fireplace and huddle around it. The feeling that comes over you when the heat and power are out, the outside temperature is dangerously cold, and you have a young child to protect is a bit more bracing. At least we had gas and water, our cars, plenty of matches, and a cell signal—though

----

our phones had not fully charged in the night. Agustina had presciently gone to the store the day before to stock up for the week. We had a prepper-grade water filter and a cooler that had been sitting outside full of melted ice, now refrozen and ready to preserve our baby's milk and other essential perishables. I found our flashlights and two little candles, began to charge my phone from my half-charged laptop, and researched what was going on while I waited for the promised restoration of power that would come any minute.

It came back on at 4:50 a.m., to my great relief. And then it went back off ten minutes later—and stayed out. As I read the early reports there, under the eerie glow of an LED flashlight aimed at the ceiling, the only sound the cross vine scratching at the high windows, I registered the concerns from the authorities that the whole statewide grid could catastrophically fail in that unforeseen event. I started looking at the outage maps and found myself wondering what we would do if the power never came back on. And thinking about how much of our lives are devoted to keeping the power running and feeding the machines.

Over the course of the days that followed, we got to learn what it feels like to find that your bargain with the sovereign is not what you thought—when, on the coldest night in sixty years, the electrical utilities elected to turn our power off and leave us to find out whether our house would retain enough heat in the night for us to survive. I have camped outside in winter, and lived in northern dorm rooms where the glass of water on the windowsill would be frozen in the morning. But in those situations you already know what to expect and are generally prepared for it. Add in the responsibility for the safety and well-being of a young child, and you get out of your own head in a hurry.

The winter storm of 2021, which left much of Texas in the cold and dark that week, is just one of the climate-related crises we've experienced here in the past decade. We've seen floods that came over our back fence, a hurricane that submerged Houston, wildfires that come dangerously close to town, and summer heat waves that break the power grid from the other direction. Some of our hottest days now give you a sampling, if you are brave enough to go outside in the afternoon, of the unlivable "wet bulb" temperatures that the climate doomsayers have been warning us of for years, in which the combination of high temperature and high humidity leaves your body unable to cool itself.

I grew up in a popular culture flush with narratives about mass catastrophes that test civilization's very ability to endure. Disaster movies and warriors of the wasteland apocalypses that took evident pleasure envisioning great cities leveled by tidal waves, earthquakes, and nuclear fallout. Most of them were fantasies—the sorts of stories science fiction writer Brian Aldiss dubbed "cozy catastrophes," in a which a small band of survivors finds itself holed up in a nice hotel, secretly enjoying their unexpected liberation from the workaday monotony of everyday life, the rediscovery of their primitive natures, and a world of abandoned property for the taking. Conventional wisdom would tell you those types of stories are meant as warnings, and in some ways they are, but they also express our repressed yearnings—the existential yearning for the kind of crisis that can shatter the malaise, and the unspoken desire that comes with the last wave, or the jungle that overtakes the abandoned city, for nature's correction of our hubris and restoration of balance. The disaster movie is no longer a fiction. It's real life, getting realer by the day.

The fear we all feel of what's coming somehow makes us also feel deprived of agency, when it should do the opposite. Crisis is the most powerful force to break us out of the haze of alienation that characterizes our lives. Taking action—to help your family, help your neighbors, help the animals living around you—is the thing most certain to make you feel authentically alive. It doesn't have to come at the expense of your creature comforts. Indeed, it is necessary to protect them, or whatever remnants we are going to be able to have on the other side of what's coming. And it starts with the simple act of learning to see what's really going on around you. Remembering that, contrary to the Hobbesian cynicism we are prone to, in a crisis, most people's first instinct is to help each other. It starts at the hyperlocal level, where it's easier to do, tying into the leaderless communal bands that are our human roots. And on the other side is the possibility of a better future, instead of a scarier one.

11

Wild in the Streets

The Big Molt

On a Tuesday night in May 2022, I found an empty can of Freedom in the parking lot of the strip mall where I stopped to buy avocados on my way home. They had renovated the grocery store that anchors the shopping center the year before, and took a stab at upgrading the tenants of the other spaces, but were only half successful, and it remains one of those centers of American commerce where you can feel the collective desperation sweat out of the asphalt at the end of a long hot day.

"Freedom" is another name for Budweiser. The European-owned beer had a similar patriotic rebranding in May 2016, as "America," citing at the time the sense in the air, with elections, Olympics, and Copa América, that it would be "probably the most American summer of our generation." They replaced their usual slogan "The King of Beers" with "E Pluribus Unum," and replaced the description of the brewing process with the lyrics to "The Star-Spangled Banner." Just how resurgently nationalistic that long summer would be only became evident on election night that November, proving Madison Avenue's gifts of demographic insight and zeitgeist forecasting—and maybe even their powers for influencing the outcomes of things far beyond the unit sales of products that numb our sensitivities to the pains of contemporary life. In the seasons that followed, I would often find empty cans of

----

America in the landscape, sometimes in the dappled light of the river shallows or the grass of the hidden prairies, slowly working their way back into the soil.

This particular can had the subtitle "LET IT RING" below the name, and a toast to freedom inscribed across the top. It was right by the curb, at the edge of the little median along the covered walkway behind the budget dentist. There were two more empties nearby, one a tall boy of Modelo and the other some high gravity lager. In the shade next to the back wall a bearded old white dude in tank top and shorts was sitting in a camp chair drinking another beer and watching the early summer sun work its way down. We looked at each other, and I noticed he was framed by a diptych the landlords had commissioned from some upbeat muralist during the renovation, with two words in airbrushed rainbow colors: **DREAM** and **BIG**.

When Agustina and I were dating, she briefly worked for a local landscape architect tasked with redesigning the urban streetscape along the major east-west road that strip mall anchors at its eastern end. The plan was an earnest effort at dialing up the urbanist utopian, with walkways, bike lanes, and cobblestone intersections lined with century plants that blossom like floral fountains dripping ivory petals. The road is the main route that connects the airport with downtown, and the idea was to pretty it up to greet visitors. Like most such undertakings, it was no match for the entropic power of the late capitalist city.

The bike lanes and walkways are still there, more or less, but half the old businesses are shuttered, and the other ones are more endangered than the jaguarundi neighbors had reported seeing a little further east that same spring. Anonymous apartment blocks are mostly what replaces older buildings that once housed neighborhood restaurants, pharmacies, dry cleaners, and the like, bringing new people from faraway who have no thought that there was ever anything else. But the postapocalyptic Sonic still stands, the shelter of its drive-up lanes turned into shanties, and in the evenings the guys who camp along the concrete creek behind the rec center come out to party. You might reasonably wonder why they don't build a new apartment block for those folks who already live there, if you were a visitor from the future who did not understand the Darwinian political economy that is this society's operating system. You can see the tenuous grip most folks have on the roofs over their heads and the foods on their tables when you enter the

grocery store, people lined up at the bill-pay counter and checkouts, where household budgets are expressed through the things that fill the carts, at the end of the supply chain that is also a food chain.

Out back, in the secret alley along the rail tracks, the rodents come out at night to feed around the dumpsters. Sometimes people are foraging the dumpsters, too. When the humans are gone, the foxes that den in the slivers of green cover behind the fences come out to hunt the rats and mice. All of them getting their calories, directly or indirectly, from the meat we make from animals raised in giant confinement facilities, killed with air guns to the head at the end of the chute, and cut up into pieces and wrapped in Styrofoam and plastic, only to go unsold before the expiration date.

The morning after, a few blocks further east, I came upon a group of seven black vultures scavenging some roadkill behind the abandoned lighting factory. They were having quite the jostling over who got the choicest morsels of still-moist innards, roostering without audible sound in the way vultures do, arguing among themselves while ignoring their arriving audience like some kind of demonic mime troop. One of those scenes where the more you look, the more vultures you see—over there on the fence, up on the telephone poles, flying in from farther away. You wonder how they know, those birds that do not sing. The answer is they are always watching, and waiting.

In recent years observers have started to see black vultures over Manhattan, miles and miles above their historic range. The stories appear in the headlines, with omens so obvious you could not credibly use them in a work of fiction. And on we go, popping the top on another can of America.

The vultures that Wednesday morning were so intent on their prize that they didn't even move until my dog and I got close enough to smell them, close enough that you could almost feel the air rush from their lazy, reluctant wingbeats. Even the canine energy didn't deter them. Maybe because that was what they were eating. Not just any dog, but a wild one that had emerged from the woods behind the industrial park to hunt the night city, only to get hit by a car. A big fox, flattened like Wile E. Coyote after the Road Runner drops an anvil on him, but still recognizable from the trademark banding of its tail, even if it had been sullied by the filth of the street. On the wall of the lighting factory behind them, a tagger had painted a new message the night before: **THE GOLDEN YEARS ARE OVER.**

As we worked our way back, I noticed that our neighbor who lives in a trailer behind the wind-chime workshop had set up an archery target made out of a cardboard box. He had been practicing, grouping his arrows pretty tightly in the bullseye at the center of five rough circles he had drawn on the bottom of the box. Practicing for what, I wondered, only to suspect I already knew. It was the season when the bugs of summer start to make their appearances, their coming heralded by the big butterflies who start fluttering around the yard when the first flowers bloom, leaving their empty carapaces on chain link and the steel exoskeletons of shipping containers. Aphids, assassins, scarabs, stink bugs, wheel bugs, walkingsticks, and hundreds of grasshoppers, finding abundant food as the green roof gets actually green.

That Wednesday afternoon I was chatting with Agustina through the door to her office when I noticed the freaky scene of

----

a grasshopper molting, three extra legs emerging from its ass end. I couldn't even tell at first which parts were the new and which the old, confounded by the patterns of pigmentation and the absence of motion. After I looked away for a moment I saw the new body had stepped out of the shell of the old. One of the Aztec spur-throats, whose brightly colored juvenile forms appear so often on our windows and whose Pokemon-like life cycles I only know fragments of.

When I found that empty can of Freedom in the grocery store parking lot the evening before, I had been listening to the everyday dark backgrounding of the radio news—forebodings of economic crisis, political extremism, democracy's demise, and horrific violence on both the other side of the world and the other side of town. They usually save the climate forecasts for the mornings, maybe to avoid ruining our sleep.

The idea that a better tomorrow is possible seems to have burned out with the new century, overtaken by a resigned nihilism that now seems to run through all our politics, against the background of even grimmer climatic outlooks. When I wonder what new vision could emerge from this darkness, I find clues in the wild world that persists in the margins of the city, reminding us that nature's resilience is greater than we might think. And that hope for us lies in opening ourselves up to its lessons.

Fighting City Hall
Few things are as depressing as going down to city hall for the first time to fight for something you believe in, something you care about, something you feel responsible to protect. You only

have to do it a couple times to realize how rigged the game is, especially if the fight is about turning land into money. And yet sometimes you can have a real impact on the outcome.

It makes me think of that Norman Rockwell painting, the one with the guy nervously standing up at his town meeting, speaking in public for the first time. He's not dressed as well as the folks around him, wearing a casual shirt and a beat-up bomber jacket while men in ties turn to listen to him. Wartime propaganda about the virtues of democracy, the image reveals a lot about how freedom of speech exists in tension with class and systems of power—and about how white our idea of the polity was and is. That image was everywhere when I was a kid, presented as truth. And it kind of was. It just didn't tell us how unlikely it would be that anything we said when we stood up to speak would make any difference in what happens. Real change comes through collective action—through the chorus of the community, however dissonant it may be—not through the voice of a single speaker, however well-spoken or persuasive they may be. In a society where everyone is so busy hustling to get by and live their lives, it takes extreme circumstances to motivate people to make time to organize and advocate. Like when my wife, with my encouragement, left baby and me at home on a Saturday afternoon to go downtown and help take over the streets, and even shut down the interstate highway, in the aftermath of the murder of George Floyd. Or when my East Austin neighbors, before I even moved here, organized to fight the oil companies whose petroleum storage tanks were killing families in the homes on the other side of the fence, which the seeping benzene did not pay any attention to.

The neighbors I met at city hall that afternoon were in those fights. The first time I appeared at a public hearing with Susana and Daniel, ten years earlier, I got a call the next day from one of the board members, a man whose day job was as an executive at a major land-conservation nonprofit, saying how glad he was that I had come to the meeting. He didn't like how my two friends "always play the race card." It wasn't the first reveal I'd experienced of how things really work in supposedly liberal Austin. But it helped me understand that, beneath the surface, things hadn't changed that much here since the Jim Crow days, in a one-party town that still bore the imprints of LBJ's long reign over Austin and the surrounding counties. The evidence was there before your eyes, in how the neighborhoods were structured and how the decisions were made. Machine politics, in which the dispensations of the sovereign are available to diverse constituencies as long as they kiss the ring, pony up when the collection plate or request for endorsements comes around, and don't call attention to the racist nature of the power structure.

When I go to city hall, it is usually about a fight to protect some pocket of vacant urban land from redevelopment. The fight to protect what open space we can for nonhuman life, especially in areas like the urban river corridor that provide vital habitat. Nature, in such situations, often stands in direct opposition to the desire for more human housing. Not always—often the project is some kind of commercial establishment hoping to profit from proximity to green space or open water.

One Tuesday in the summer of 2023, we learned the kinds of dirty tricks you can still get away with here, in a town with little in the way of functioning media—a local daily that has been cannibalized by corporate consolidation and a free weekly that acts like it's radical but has been co-opted by its financial stake in the big-money festival culture that it originated. We were trying to influence a proposal by a major developer to build a gigantic high-rise, mixed-use development on the site of an old milk plant that sits adjacent to a riparian wildlife sanctuary—to turn the natural edgeland into a corporate colony. We didn't oppose the redevelopment, because we knew we would lose. We just fought the density, which would almost double the impervious cover from 50 percent to up to 95 percent, erect tall buildings visible from the river and in the flight path of birds that migrate along its corridor, increase vehicular traffic from 500 to 20,000 trips a day, and have a major adverse impact on the wildlife of the preserve, which for forty years has benefitted from a twenty-acre buffer of empty land between its woodland and the plant.

We worked hard to negotiate a compromise with the developer, knowing the odds are always against us in such cases, and got close, but not close enough. So when the developer pressed forward without our support, we went to our district council member, a newly elected young guy from the neighborhood. He said he would oppose anything going forward without the support of our coalition. But when we got to the hearing, after all the people who had missed work to come down to testify were done with their speeches, we found out our representative had been silenced. The developer had managed that by entering into an agreement to provide certain community benefits with a housing nonprofit the council member had worked for before his election, thereby creating a conflict of interest that precluded him from voting on the matter. A clever and ethically astonishing maneuver that succeeded in disenfranchising all the residents of a district designed to represent the oldest Hispanic neighborhoods in town. No one on the council blinked, even after passionate remarks that brought the social injustice into stark relief, and the item was approved without discussion. The council member was later sanctioned for his ethical breach, but that did not change the outcome for his constituents.

We did not give up hope, especially since the process injustice gave us something to work with that the love of nature did not. The law is not without tools you can work with, even if they are designed to perpetuate the system that got us here.

The people on our council are not villains. They just care about housing for people more than space for wild animals, and are resigned to the idea that the only way to get more housing is with the kind of "products" big developers are attracted to. They're stuck with the binary conception that the trade-off between their voters and nature is a zero-sum game. Just like the institution they serve, they don't see, and therefore don't value, the slivers of wilderness the city hides.

My friend Susana speaks about the ways in which, as a person of Indigenous heritage, she was taught to think of other life in nature not as something separate from us, but as part of a connected community—other species as something like extended family, meriting equal protection as our human neighbors. My colleague Chiara Sunshine Beaumont, with whom I serve on the board of the nonprofit that manages the Circle Acres preserve, grew up knowing that she was a member of the Karankawa, an

Indigenous community long declared extinct. She now divides her time between fighting the desecration of Karankawa lands around Corpus Christi by oil and gas production and teaching the descendants of colonizers Indigenous ways of experiencing nature at a luxury resort. Reprogramming the way we think about the natural world is hard, when our alienation from nature is embedded in our very language. Adam and Eve walked into a world that had been made for them and their children to reap. They were charged with stewardship, but in the way of taking care of your property so it doesn't lose its value. We are failing miserably at even that low standard, but we still haven't begun to really hold ourselves to account.

The current crisis is producing some fresh thinking about how to find a new path, mostly in the margins. We have green parties, but we don't have a coherent theory of the greener world that could be. We can see the damaged future we have made as clearly as we can see the sky turning a dystopian shade of orange, but our capacity for meaningful action is paralyzed by our inability to imagine how else it could be.

IN QUINCY, MASSACHUSETTS, IN a neighborhood a few blocks from the shore, there's a little green hill called Maypole Park. On that hill on May Day in 1625, a mixed group of colonists and Natives gathered around an eighty-foot maypole topped with antlers and celebrated a joyous bacchanal that blended English and Indigenous traditions of welcoming the season of flowers and fertility. The event had been facilitated by Thomas Morton, a lawyer and trader who had taken over his company of early American entrepreneurs after encouraging the indentured servants to rise up against their boss. Morton advocated a different approach to intercourse with the American continent—a hunter who loved the wilderness more than feared it, built relationships with the Indians more like the French trappers, and, most heretically, armed them with guns, in part to secure superior trade. He managed, through his success at cultivating his vision, to piss off the Pilgrims so badly that they dispatched Myles Standish to cut down the maypole, disband the colony, and arrest Morton and ship him back to England. As retribution, Morton got the Plymouth colony's charter revoked and wrote a popular book ridiculing the Puritans—including the diminutive Standish, who he nicknamed "Captain Shrimp." His experiment's traces are still evident in some of the place-names around Quincy, but his efforts to get back to the place were not really successful. The America we got is from the mold the Pilgrims made.

As the climate and biodiversity crisis comes home to roost, there's been a resurgence of popular fictions that mine the folk horror potential of May Day celebrations, and the memories of European traditions of ritual sacrifice meant to secure our not-so-reciprocal exchange with nature, the other life we manipulate to sustain our own. These stories layer on top of our popular visions of apocalyptic futures, sometimes blending them in unexpected ways, painting visions of a rewilded Earth achieved through massive depopulation by plague, war, or other disaster. The waking collective dreams and anxieties those narratives express are not hard to divine, even as they are genuinely horrifying to confront, in a society where the political systems that have mostly maintained peace and prevented genocide since 1945 seem to be fraying before our eyes.

It's possible to take steps toward a philosophy of rewilding that is not polluted with eco-fascist fantasies of compulsory depopulation. It requires some simple first elements. Like protecting every slice of wild space that still exists, including the interstitial kind I have documented in this book. Working to rebalance and blur, if not obliterate, the boundaries between human space and wild space, bringing real life into the realm we occupy, building detente with our animal and arboreal neighbors. And making sacrifices, not of life, but of some of our bloated so-called affluence—some of that surplus we have been piling up and fighting over the last 10,000 years, since we figured out how to control the reproduction of other species. Maybe we can trade it for some of the other surplus we are so blindly squandering, like the three-quarters of the Earth's fresh water stored in our rapidly melting glaciers and the groundwater we have sucked up so fast it has changed the tilt of the Earth. We probably can't undo the design flaws of the agricultural revolution—not without giving up the cultural riches it gave us. But by learning to see them, and learning to see the real world around us, we can liberate ourselves from the prison of our alienation, start to really live in the world, and begin to bring back the balance it needs—and that we need as well.

"Nature is Healing"
That was the meme, usually expressed as a hashtag. It accompanied all manner of photos and videos and links to news stories about wild animals coming out into the open, in the heart of the

cities of the world. Dolphins swimming in the canals of Venice, civet cats foraging in the center of Kerala, foxes, like sentimental familiars, hunting in redbrick London. Images shared and reshared in the earliest days of lockdown, reflecting the sense of possibility that the sudden pause of the global capitalist machine sparked in people's minds, and the emotional volatility people experienced with the fear and abrupt change of the global plague. The meme quickly shifted into ironic parody—with images of Crocs and Lime scooters returning to the rivers, dinosaurs in Times Square—but the yearning it expressed was real. And you could see it in the way people began to flee the urban centers, giving witness to the truth of the earliest permanent human settlements: that cities are incubators of disease.

In the aftermath, there were numerous ecological studies to assess what truth may have lain behind the meme. The initial research was mostly inconclusive, confirming the explosion in observations of wild animals—mostly mammals—in developed human space, but unable to determine how much was due to an actual increased presence of animals and how much was due to people having more time and freedom to see what's going on outside. Atmospheric observations were more conclusive, showing how abruptly carbon emissions had plummeted as people stopped driving, planes stopped flying, and manufacturing operations were pulled way back. Anyone could feel that change in the air. And in my own daily roamings around the place where we live, I could see signs of wildlife coming out less warily, including in the tracks on the freshly terraformed berm where they would soon build an on-ramp for the new tollway. Experience had already shown how wildlife knows when it's safe to come around. The most recent study, as I write this, synthesizing data from across Europe and North America, showed more definitively how animals had become less wary of humans, at least in the early days of extreme lockdown. Mountain lions became more comfortable penetrating the urban edges, porcupines became more abundant inside cities, brown bears explored new corridors to travel. Based on my own field observations around here, I worry the ultimate impact of the pandemic was to push wildlife further into marginal spaces by bringing more human explorers out into the green spaces, a paradox that may also be attributable to the extraordinary population growth Austin experienced during the years of quarantine.

- - - -

Somehow lost in the generally acknowledged learnings of the pandemic was the evidence that its ultimate origins lay in the expansion of real estate development into zones of wildlife habitat around the Chinese city of Wuhan. This is true of a majority of zoonotic diseases that have emerged in recent decades, including disaster-movie scary diseases like Ebola and MERS, and others like Lassa, whose impacts have been more regionally confined. Strong evidence exists that such outbreaks are triggered by habitat destruction, urban expansion, roadbuilding, and our unstoppable appetite for consuming the Earth's natural resources, especially through logging of forests. Bats are among the planet's most effective carriers of coronaviruses, and much of the reason for their increasing identification as vectors of the diseases that pose the greatest threats to the human population is the way they have been forced to adapt to living in an anthropogenic environment.

Consider the bats of Austin. In the very heart of downtown, the main bridge that crosses the river was designed with seams in its concrete underside that happen to be the perfect size for broods of Mexican free-tailed bats to hang from during the long, hot days. This region has long been one of the bats' major breeding areas, and shortly after the bridge was built in the 1980s, they discovered it. They come for the summers, dropping down and taking flight in beautiful black clouds that partially eclipse the setting sun, doing their part to devour our population of mosquitoes. And every night the crowds gather on the bridge and the riverbanks to watch their emergence, a live entertainment that requires no festival pass. On good nights you can see the wonder, adults agape with the eyes of children.

It's a beautiful scene, and at the same time a sad one. The rarity of seeing wild animals in those kinds of numbers, swarms of more than a million taking to the sky, when a century ago that was still a common experience. The astonishing capacity of those animals to adapt to our transformation of their world into a horrific cyborg version of what it once was. The capacity of people to appreciate their presence, even building post-pagan totems of sympathetic homage on a traffic island by their roost. But then you consider what the bats' presence here reveals about the disappearance of their natural habitat. And realize how ephemeral their current presence is, as photographers and conservationists who have been watching them since the beginning report that their emergences get shorter every year—a fifth now of what they once were. Downriver, the riparian refuge below the dam seems likely to disappear soon, with the Tesla factory on its banks at the county line and all the other vacant private lands between there and downtown about to be redeveloped as fancy new corporate colonies that will probably make the green river part of their brand, even as they extinguish its wildness. Similar stories are going on in every city, as growth envelops the edgelands.

Once I started paying attention to the ways wild animals adapt to the human city, I realized that a big part of the reason they do so is because humans are so relentless in destroying wild nature that they have no other place to go. It helped me see what a critical juncture we are at in our relationship with the natural world. A moment when we can take the lessons urban wildlife teaches us, about how we and our wild neighbors share the same habitat and ecology, and learn to do so by design, in a way that will help us

- - - -

ensure our own future and theirs and enrich our lives in the process. Or else we will continue on our apocalyptic trajectory. The question is not whether nature will survive—it always does. It's whether we will. And if you can learn how to get lost in the hidden wild margins of the city where you live, you can glimpse what both futures look like.

IN THE FALL OF 1969, a UCLA law professor named Christopher Stone improvised a blackboard hypothetical for his students to consider: "If corporations have rights, why can't trees?" It was far out, even transgressive, but also intrinsically compelling. It led to a law review article so persuasive it ended up in important dicta in a US Supreme Court opinion, and a book by the same title, *Should Trees Have Standing?*, referring to the legal doctrine that determines which persons can initiate legal action to protect their rights. Stone wasn't the only one thinking along such lines, as others developed theories of the rights of nature extrapolated from their own civil law traditions or from the customary laws of Indigenous and other cultural groups. In the past decade, the idea that ecosystems can be endowed with personhood in the eyes of the law has gained significant traction, from a Cleveland ordinance recognizing the rights of Lake Erie to the Ecuadorian constitution and decisions in New Zealand and India to recognize the rights of major rivers. The courts of the conquerors still have trouble getting their heads around the idea, as evidenced by the decision of the New York Court of Appeals in 2022 to deny access to habeas corpus by Happy the elephant over its confinement in the Bronx Zoo. But the well-argued dissents in those cases give one a clear sense of where things are going. The law protects many categories of persons who don't have the capacity to state their own case—including children, corporations, and, most controversially, fetuses—and has well-established procedures to provide them legal guardians and counsel. It feels like it's just a matter of time. And when the rights of nature versions of *Brown v. Board of Education* decisions start coming down in favor of rivers, soils, forests, and species, it's easy to imagine how much human dominion will be rebalanced. We will see whether such changes will come in time to help stall the mass extinctions currently underway.

Activists, environmental advocates, and tribal groups are looking to courts for such remedies because they have mostly given up on governments and NGOs. Our post-Westphalian order of sovereign and competitive nation-states is not really capable of tackling global problems—not yet. The greatest hope in the short-term lies in grassroots rewilding—individual, household, neighborhood, and community action to achieve the rebalance our systems of law and government cannot. This kind of change happens on a local, and sometimes hyperlocal, scale: guerrilla gardening and urban foraging, green roof building and pocket prairie planting, conservation easements and industrial infrastructure allowed to go wild.

It's about dreaming the feral city, and making it real, where you can.

12

Black Witches and Other Omens—A Coda

The week I signed the contract for this book, my dad died. He had lived a long and mostly happy life, was ready to go, and my mom and I were able to be there with him as he passed. When he was gone, we drove back to their place in the country, down Interstate 35, a landscape of boring postcards in which I have spent most of my life. When I got back to Austin, I finally opened the weather radio my dad had sent me the year before, which had sat in my office in its packaging. It took me a while to figure it out, but after some fiddling I had it running, set to the correct local date and time, the red light indicating it was set to preempt any other programming with urgent weather alerts as they came in.

Dad was one of those guys who loved nothing better in his golden years than to watch the Weather Channel and wait for the crisis that would make life seem more alive. I never thought of him as much of a nature lover, but the radio reminded me of a connection we always had that I had never really appreciated, and that I now saw could last the rest of my lifetime and maybe even get passed on to his grandchildren.

In his book *The Spell of the Sensuous*, ecologist, philosopher, and sleight-of-hand magician David Abram helps the reader understand where real magic exists in the world. He relates how, as a young scholar living among Indigenous peoples in Bali and the Himalayas, he came to understand that their idea of a magician was not, as we think of it, a person who had acquired supernatural

----

powers to exercise their will over others. It was, in the figure of the shaman, a person who had developed their intuitive gifts for connecting with the nonhuman world, and taken on the role of living at the outskirts of the village and mediating the village's relationship with its environment. Giving and taking, in an effort to maintain the balance of exchange, to achieve what harmony can be. Abrams then describes what it was like to return to the United States after those trips, and see how deeply out of balance the way we live was, even amid—and maybe because of—the supposed riches we had accumulated in our technological mastery.

I never thought of my dad as any kind of a shaman. He was a dentist from Des Moines who liked to play golf, loved Christmas, and was eager to teach you about dental health and how it tied to mental health. He was the sort of dentist whose patients got other kinds of therapy in his chair. In a way, I see now, he was also a mediator of their relationship to nature, through his attention to that way in which we interact most directly with the natural world: by eating it. Maybe we all are some variation of such mediators, if we think about it right. Or choose to be, in the quotidian fabric of our everyday lives, where the impact can be far more real and profound than you might imagine.

One afternoon the week after Dad died, I was startled as I opened our front door by a shadow so vivid I could feel it rustling my hair. I reached for it and turned, only to realize it was a butterfly, bigger than my hand. The creature tried to fly in, and I shooed it back and pulled the door shut from the outside as it alighted atop the doorjamb. It was dark—the dark browns, mottled blacks and chalky whites of the woods at night, with an owl eye on each

- - - -

wing. It had a big chip out of its right forewing. I admired its fragile majesty for a long moment, then entered the house through a different door.

That night, I saw it again, on the seam of the back door. I recognized the rip in its wing. It was dark out, and I had put our daughter to bed. Again, I felt compelled to try to keep it from entering the house, for fear it would end up trapped where we could not catch and release it. It was still there in the middle of the night when I had to get up, as the dogs were going nuts over the sound of raccoons screaming in the trees.

In the morning, it was gone.

During the week, I tried to identify the butterfly, but found myself stumped. Saturday afternoon, I texted a picture to my mom, and she replied with uncharacteristic immediacy: "That's a black witch." She also added the scientific name, *Ascalapha odorata*. Which is not a butterfly, as I should have already figured out, but a moth.

The black witch moth—*mariposa de la muerte* to the Mexicans, *pirpinto de la yeta* to the Argentines, duppy bat to the Jamaicans, *sorcière noire* in the former French colonies—is, as I quickly learned upon looking it up, found across the tropical regions of the hemisphere, and associated with death in the folklore of every one of those regions. The stories vary from country to country. In Mexico it is a harbinger of death if it enters the house of a sick person—perhaps provoking my instinct to keep it out. In the Rio Grande Valley, that myth has a more specific requirement that the moth travel to all four corners of the house—there's also an alternate Texas version where it means you are going to win the lottery. In Jamaica, they believe it to be a soul not yet at rest. I gravitated to the Hawaiian version: that it is the soul of a recently departed loved one coming to say goodbye.

A week later, after Dad's memorial service, we took my mom home and enjoyed some family time in the days before Hallow-een. That Sunday, we headed out for the hourlong drive to the airport a little before noon. And just as we pulled out on the gravel road that connects the farm to the old highway, across the little bridge that traverses the creek, we saw another strange flyer. It was big, with wide, lazy wings, coasting low in the thermals over a dried-out cornfield, very close to our vehicle. Backlit by the late morning sun, gliding without moving, it looked almost like a shadow. Until the underwings finally caught the light and you

could see the mottled splotches of dark and white in its feathers, like a Jackson Pollock variant of herringbone tweed. It was a juvenile bald eagle, checking us out in the unwary way of young birds, as we stopped and opened the windows to do the same.

IN A WORLD GOVERNED by human reason, we experience an abundance of surplus and a poverty of meaning. We believe ourselves to have banished magic and superstition from the world. But the magic is still there, all around us. The trick is learning to see it, for what it is: the seemingly supernatural wonders produced by everyday interactions among different elements of the natural world. Things that can all be explained by science, but also understood by poets. Even in the most urbanized human terrains, those wonders can still be found—most often at the edges where the pavement ends and the wild is allowed to express.